£35

CENTRAL ASIA IN WORLD HISTORY

Central Asia in World History

S. A. M. Adshead

Reader in History
University of Canterbury
Christchurch, New Zealand

MACMILLAN

First published 1993 by
THE MACMILLAN PRESS LTD
Houndmills, Basingstoke, Hampshire RG21 2XS
and London
Companies and representatives
throughout the world

ISBN 0–333–57827–9

A catalogue record for this book is available
from the British Library.

Printed in Hong Kong

For Mark and Debbie

Contents

Part I
Before the Explosion

1 World History and Central Asia – Time, Place and People

This chapter is concerned with definitions. It sets out to indicate the meaning of the terms World History and Central Asia and to designate the plot, the stage and the characters. Neither World History nor Central Asia is unproblematical. World History can be as broad as an ideal of knowing every-thing about everything, a total history. It can be as narrow as the diplomatic relations between states, an international politi-cal history. It can take a middle course and study patterns, whether Hegelian, Marxist, Toynbean or Teilhardian, suppos-edly common to all histories: not the whole of history, but the whole in history. None of these senses is exactly what will be meant in this study. Similarly, Central Asia can be as broad as Inner Asia or even as Central Eurasia, and there are reasons in physical geography for so regarding it. It can be as narrow as the oases of the three Turkestans, Russian, Chinese and Af-ghan, and this has good foundations in ecology, linguistics and ethnology. It can take a middle course and become synony-mous with Middle Asia: Mongolia, Sinkiang, Tibet and the five Soviet Central Asian republics plus Afghanistan, and this too has advantages in terms of sources and frontiers. Again, none of these senses is exactly what will be meant in this study. This study seeks to present the history of Central Asia as a factor in World History. In this conjunction, it is World History which is the defining term and this is less a question of space than of time. For world history, in the sense in which it will be used here, has not always existed, and having come into existence, may one day cease to exist, though this seems improbable. Once the Time is defined, the Place will follow naturally, as will the People, not so much logically as by the historian's need to seek further explanations and to find a unity of plot, stage and characters. We must start with Time, therefore, the time of what Joseph Fletcher (1934–1984), the greatest modern Central

Asianist, called 'the interlocking of histories' and dated 1200 to the present.[1]

TIME

A striking feature of the modern as opposed to the traditional ancient or medieval worlds is the increasing interconnection and interdependence of all states, societies and cultures. More and more, people think the same thoughts, eat the same food, wear similar clothes, live in similar houses, suffer the same germs, and act as part of one world, citizens of Planet Earth and denizens of a Global Village. Challenges and responses, problems and solutions are increasingly world wide. None of this was true in Antiquity or the Early Middle Ages. Then there were separate civilizations, separate barbarisms, both generally based on religion, separate ecologies, separate diseases. In particular, the four primary civilizations of Western Eurasia, East Asia, Black Africa, and Meso-America, were, despite their common palaeolithic foundations, only in tangential and irregular contact. In ecology, maize was confined to America, the soya bean to East Asia. There were few horses outside northern Eurasia, few camels outside southern Eurasia and northern Africa, few elephants outside Africa or India. Among diseases, plague was confined to High Asia except for sporadic invasions, cholera was confined to India, syphilis, probably, was confined to America. Commodities familiar in one place, were unknown in another. Tea was unknown outside China, coffee was unknown outside Arabia, tobacco was unknown outside America. What was to end the ages of isolation was the development of a global overlay, an interlocking set of institutions, which made the world less many and more one. It is these institutions, or world networks as they may be called, which form the subject matter of world history, as it will be understood in this study. World history, in this sense, is not super-history. Indeed, especially in its earlier stages, it is somewhat marginal history. It is simply the history of rather pervasive institutions or networks which operate, if not in all four primary civilizations, at least in more than one of them. At the present time, eight such agencies may be recognized and given names: the basic information circuit, the microbian common market, religious internationals, the republic of letters, the global armoury, the world commodity market, the world technological bank, and the common co-consciousness, particularly as expressed by the increasing use of English as a high-level international language. The neologisms are barbarous, but terms are needed to distinguish realities which have not always existed or been recognized.

For the global overlay has a history. When, where and how did the interlocking of histories via the rise of world networks start? Possible candidates would be the discovery of America by the West, the Industrial Revolution, or the changes of the mid-twentieth century, decolonization in particular leading paradoxically to a more unified world. Joseph Fletcher argued, however, that the interlocking of histories, really began much earlier, at the beginning of the thirteenth century with the conquest of Central Asia by the Mongols of Chinggis Khan. This is the standpoint which will be adopted in this study. The Mongolian explosion was the first real global event. It deeply affected China, Persia, Russia and eastern Europe. Indirectly, and at one remove, it affected India and Southeast Asia. Negatively, it affected Japan, Egypt and Western Europe, by not conquering them, and giving them their chance, so to speak, in their respective cultural areas. More remotely, it entered the causal network which led to Christian expansion in America, Moslem expansion in Africa and Southeast Asia. Indeed, the Mongolian explosion can be seen in the head waters of all the eight components of the global overlay, though obviously many powerful tributaries, perhaps carrying more water, have entered the streams lower down. There is a real sense, however, in which the Mongolian explosion was the beginning of continuous world history. Before that time, world institutions or networks had occasionally existed, and they and Central Asia's part in them will form the subject of Chapter 2, but in the main they were evanescent, at least in their original forms, and did not co-inhere with one another. Since that time, successive world institutions or networks have not only en-dured, under a variety of forms, but have also co-inhered to constitute an embryonic world order coextensive with particu-lar regional orders and, currently, increasingly predominant over them.

The global overlay began with the initial singularity of the Mongolian explosion. Since the Mongolian explosion took place in and through Central Asia, it also defined Central Asia, at least in its relation to world history. So from the time, one moves naturally to consideration of the place.

PLACE

Chinggis Khan was not initially a universal conqueror. His first campaigns outside Mongolia proper, against the Turco-Tibetan state of Hsi-Hsia in northwest China and northeast Tibet and against the Jurched Chin dynasty of Manchuria and northeast China, were not completely successful and did not result in the destruction of the states against whom they were directed. Chinggis only became a potential world conqueror when he conquered and destroyed first the Khitan, later Liao state of Kara-Khitai in eastern Turkestan, then the Khivan state of the Turkish Khwarazmshah in western Turkestan, and devastated the Persian cities of the shah's empire in Khorasan and Afghan Turkestan. Without these conquests in the west, which shattered the bulwarks of the Islamic world and made him a scourge of God, Chinggis would have been a purely local, East Asian, figure whose political machine would probably not have outlasted his death. Moreover, it was Central Asia which made Chinggis more than simply a Mongol conqueror. The invasion routes to Kara-Khitai and the domains of the Khwarazmshah led the Mongol army through the steppes of Zungharia and Semirechie to the north of the oases of eastern Turkestan and out into central Kazakhstan. As the army expanded, took prisoners, replaced casualties, enlisted auxiliaries, it recruited other nomadic people along the way, especially ex-enemies, the Turks of the Khwarazmshah, i.e. nomads of the Kazakh steppe. In this way, the Mongol armies became first Turco-Mongol and then Turkish, with only a conservative elite preserving the Mongolian language for a couple of generations. The armies which played a part in world history: in Persia, Russia, the Middle East, even China; were as much Turkish as Mongol. That Turcification the Mongols owed to their passage through and residence in Central Asia. So the Central Asia which has to be considered in relation to world history is not just the three oasis areas of eastern, western and Afghan Turkestan, but also the associated steppe areas to the north: central Kazakhstan, Semirechie and

Zungharia. It is these six areas which constitute the Central Asia of this study.

Apart from its relationship to the conquests of Chinggis and hence to the onset of the interlocking of histories, Central Asia in this sense should also be seen in its historical geography as part of the much wider region which may be called Inner Asia or Central Eurasia. For, stretching at its greatest extent from the Carpathians to Korea on a west–east axis, from the Arctic ocean to the Himalayas, is a region unified by distance from the sea, continentality of climate, and shortage of rainfall, but diversified by distance from the pole and orography. Inner Asia is the land which the monsoons never reach, which the westerlies hardly reach. Its water resources, which in themselves are not inconsiderable, therefore take the concentrated form of snow, rivers and lakes rather than the dispersed form of rainfall, which is more convenient for human agriculture. Inner Asia lacks not so much water as utilizable water and to use what is readily available human beings there have had to develop a special type of arable farming in oasis agriculture, a special type of stock raising in nomadic pastoralism. Water, or the lack of it, unifies Inner Asia: temperature and height diversify it in a series of five immense latitudinal layers along the west–east axis.

Starting from the north, there is first the tundra, the frozen marshes of the Arctic lowlands, which finally immobilized in ice the waters painfully carried by the great rivers from the Himalayan system. For pre-modern man, the tundra offered little except reindeer, some fisheries and a few fur-bearing animals, such as the ermine. Next, there was the taiga, the vast coniferous Siberian forest of spruce and fir in the west, pine and larch in the east. Impermeable, except on its margins, to pre-modern farming, the taiga offered river and lake fisheries and a wide range of fur-bearing animals: squirrel, marten, lynx, sable and mink.[2] Third, there was the steppe, the region of grassland touched by the westerlies and their rainfall and endowed with mighty lakes such as Aral, Issykkul, Balkash, Zaisan and Baikal. This was the home of nomadic pastoralism, the ecological system, on which the conquests of Chinggis were based. Fourth, there was the desert, the region of no moisture, useless in itself except as a source of salt, but modifiable along its southern rim by oases, natural or artificial, which exploited shortlived water sources by wells, dams and drains. Finally, behind the rim of oases, there was the mountain which shut the monsoons out, immobilized their water in snow, as the tundra did in ice. Here on the uplands of Afghanistan, the plateau and valleys of Tibet, was another kind of nomadic pastoralism, another kind of oasis agriculture. These areas, however, though part of Middle Asia, were only occasionally, irregularly and tangentially parts of Central Asia.

The Central Asia of world history was a portion of Inner Asia. It comprised the central part of the steppe, a segment of the southern oasis rim of the desert, with margins in the mountain spokes coming out from the Pamir knot: the Tien-shan, the Karakoram and the Hindu Kush. The intervening deserts of the Kara Kum, Kizil Kum and Taklamakan were of lesser historical significance except as barriers. Within the major components of steppe and oases in Central Asia, there were, however, considerable differentiations of terrain, resources and spatial organization. The characteristics in these respects of each of the six elements of Central Asia need to be taken into consideration as background to the history.

The centrepiece of Central Asia was western Turkestan, otherwise Russian Turkestan, Transoxania, Mawara-an-nahr, the land within the rivers, 'Mesopotamia'. Here was Samarkand, the metropolis of Central Asia's only period of political unity, at most times its largest agriculture settlement and chief international trading centre. In terms of terrain, western Turkestan was dominated by its two great rivers, the Oxus or Amu-darya and the Jaxartes or Syr-darya. Both of these flowed normally into the Aral Sea, though in the past the Oxus has flowed into the Caspian, while in the future it is possible that neither river will reach the Aral because of the amount of water taken out of them upstream. In terms of resources, in traditional times, most of the water used was provided by tributaries: in the case of the Oxus, by the Zerafshan which was so depleted by first Samarkand and then Bokhara that it never reached its outlet; in the case of the Jaxartes by the numerous parallel streams which flow into it from the north in the part of its upper valley known as Ferghana.

In terms of spatial organization, western Turkestan fell into three parts. These parts were groups of fairly permanent, natural oases, though the site of the chief centre might change because of local desiccation, military destruction, or shift in commercial or cultural advantage. In Central Asia even towns had a long term nomadic character. First in the south, there was a group of oases associated with the Zerafshan, of which Samarkand and Bokhara were the principal.[3] These were the secular and spiritual capitals of Central Asia in the period of world history and its area of greatest sedentarization. Second, in the north, there was a single oasis associated with the delta of the Oxus in the Aral, whose chief centre has been variously located and named as Urgench, Khiva and Khwarazm. In contrast to Samarkand and Bokhara, Khiva (as it will generally be called) was closely enclosed by the surrounding desert and steppe.[4] Third, in the east, there was a group of oases in the Ferghana valley, of which the principal was Kokand. In contrast to the other oasis groups, Kokand was associated with the mountain, especially the territory of the Kirghiz, both as a source of camels and a means of access to eastern Turkestan. Samarkand and Bokhara looked both east and west, Kokand looked mainly east.

Next in importance, though always slightly provincial, country-cousinish, and old-fashioned (Babur in his memoirs has a famous description of the khans of Moghulistan, the rulers of this area, in these terms), was eastern Turkestan, the southern part of the Chinese province of Sinkiang. In terms of terrain, eastern Turkestan was dominated by the encircling mountains of the Karakoram and T'ien-shan, by a single river system, the Tarim basin, and, at its heart, by the Taklamakan desert which, in combination with the water withdrawals of the oases, desiccated the river before it reached its terminal lake of Lob nor, not far from the meeting point of Sinkiang, Chinghai and Kansu. In terms of resources, most water was again provided, not by the main river, but by its tributaries, of which there were a considerable number descending from the encircling mountains.

In terms of spatial organization, this water pattern produced a chaplet of oases, more numerous but smaller than in western Turkestan. These oases fell into two groups. First, in the southwest there was the Altishahr ('six cities', variously listed). Here the principal centres were Kashgar in the far west, Yarkand and Khotan to the southeast, Aksu and Kucha to the northeast. At various times, each of these centres competed to be regarded as the capital of eastern Turkestan, Kashgar having perhaps the best long-term claim because of its access to routes both north–south and east–west. Second, in the northeast, there were the oases of Uighuristan, notably Turfan and Hami. These were distinct from the Altishahr because relatively independent of the Tarim system. Turfan had its own sources of underground water, Hami had its own brief river. Turfan was also distinct because it lay at the bottom of a deep depression with its own microclimate which was especially suitable for grapes, as Hami's was for melons. Hami was further different in that, like Khiva in western Turkestan, it was more closely associated with the steppe and the desert than the other oases of eastern Turkestan. Its satellite oasis of Barkol was well-known for the raising of high-grade cavalry ponies, as Kokand was for the raising of camels, and like Kokand, Hami looked east, to China, as much as to its colleagues in the west.

Third, smallest of the oasis areas of Central Asia, sometimes metropolitan, sometimes provincial, was Afghan Turkestan. This was a misnomer really, though a convenient one, because throughout historical times, most of the inhabitants have been Iranian speakers, Persian or Pashto, though considerably infiltrated by Turkish-speaking Uzbeks from the north.[5] In terms of terrain, Afghan Turkestan was dominated by its mountain backdrop, the Hindu Kush and its westward extension in the Kopet Dagh along the border between Turkmenistan and Persia. Afghan Turkestan was essentially a piedmont. In terms of resources, its water was drawn from three relatively short rivers which descended from the Hindu Kush: the Balkh river which joined the Oxus, the Murghab and the Hari Rud which died of desiccation in the Kara Kum desert to the west of the Oxus. In terms of spatial organization, there were three groups of oases, though, historically, seldom was more than one important at a time. The Balkh river supplied a city, destroyed by the Mongols, which was possibly the site of the ancient Bactria, mother of cities and a capital of Zoroastrianism. The Murghab, near to its terminus, supplied the oases of Merv, which was always debateable land between Central Asia and Persia, and a touchstone of a greater or lesser Iranian state. The Hari Rud, longest of these rivers supplied Herat, cultural capital of one of the greatest periods of Central Asian history, while on one of its tributaries lay Tus and Meshed, cultural cities again, more Persian than

Central Asian, but, on occasion, arguably part of Central Asia, unlike Khorasan as a whole. In Afghan Turkestan, the Central Asian oasis world reached its southern frontier, just as in the north it reached another frontier in the steppes of central Kazakhstan, Semirechie and Zungharia.

The centrepiece of the steppe component of Central Asia was the Semirechie, the land of the seven rivers, mostly finding their terminus in Lake Balkash, the shallow crescent lying at the bottom of a system of interior drainage. Here were the head-quarters of some of the greatest Central Asian political constructions: Kara-Khitai, the khanate of Chaghatai, the Kazakh confederation, the Zunghar empire. In terms of terrain, Semirechie was dominated by its northward location, the mountain behind, the lowland in front, and the rivers linking these. In terms of resources, Semirechie had the best availability of water of any area in Central Asia. On the one hand, there were the readily abundant rivers descending from the mountains behind to the lowlands in front. On the other hand, the wester-lies as they struck the mountain rim deposited more rainfall than in other parts of Kazakhstan: ten to twenty inches compared to under ten elsewhere. Semirechie therefore had both concentrated and dispersed water, and enough was available to make sedentary agriculture and non-nomadic, ranch-type pastoralism in principle possible. That Semirechie was generally nomadic steppe was a fact of culture and history rather than nature and geography. In terms of spatial organization, Semirechie, despite the diversity of its terrain, formed a remarkable unity, since there was no barrier between its uplands and lowlands and no obvious divisions within them. Thus the Kazakh Great Horde, *Ulu Zhuz*, wintered on the plain and summered in the hills, practising transhumance rather than true nomadism, with a migration cycle of only two hundred miles.[6] This spatial unity, plus the capacity for limited sedentary agriculture, made Semirechie advantageous for political organizations. Another advantage it enjoyed was openness: to the west, across the steppe to the Volga, to the east, via the rich Ili valley, to the *T'ien-shan pei-lu*, the route north of the Heavenly Mountains, and to China. Semirechie was the most favoured steppe region of Central Asia.

Next in importance, but definitely in second place, was Zungharia, the original home of the Zunghars, but not the main seat of their empire. Zungharia may be defined as the pastureland within the triangle of the T'ien-shan, the Tarbagatai range, and the line of the Altai running southeast, plus an extension south of the T'ien-shan in the region of the Bagrach Kol.[7] In terms of terrain, Zungharia was dominated by its perimeter mountains and their piedmonts, and by the fact that its centre was a region of near desert and quicksand. In terms of resources, Zungharia, on the inner side of the mountains from the westerlies, received less dispersed moisture than Semirechie: under ten inches a year, and its winter cold was extreme. On the other hand, it possessed a major river, the Irtysh which ran through and out of Lake Zaisan, finding its way to the Ob and eventually to the sea. Unlike Semirechie, therefore, Zungharia was not a region of purely interior drainage, and Chuguchak or Tarbagatai was known locally as the 'city of seagulls' because of these winter visitors from the Arctic ocean. In terms of spatial organization, Zungharia, because of its dead heart, was less of a unity than Semirechie. The pastoral populations along its perimeters were not in close touch with each other, and they were not always a political or administrative unit. Under Chinggis' successors, Zungharia was divided between the *ulus* of Chaghadai and Ögödei; under the Ch'ing, while the southern part was under the jurisdiction of the military governor of Ili, the northern part was under that of the Uliasutai military governor or the Kobdo amban, and it was not until after 1912 that the Altai region separated from outer Mongolia and made the whole of Zungharia part of Sinkiang. Within the area, the Buddhist Torghud Mongols of the north were separated from those of Karashahr in the south by Moslem Kazakhs and Kirghiz, as well as by the half-Moslem, half-Chinese oasis of Urumchi. Consequently, like eastern Turkestan to the south, Zungharia seldom acted as a single, coherent entity. Another disadvantage it suffered was that, while it had a number of lines of access to the outside world via the Zungharian gap, Tarbagatai and Hami, the best of them, the Irtysh valley, was eccentric to the main centres of population and led only to southern Siberia.

Third, largest of the steppe areas, but of low population density and fluctuating political importance, was central Kazakhstan: the pasturelands north and east of the Aral sea and the Syr-darya as far as Semirechie in one direction, Tobolsk in another. This area had its periods of leadership: under Urus

Khan, in the days of the first, nomadic, Uzbek empire, and, after the defeat of the Zunghars, under Ablai Khan of the Middle Horde. Generally, however, it was subordinate to Semirechie in the east or to successive powers outside Central Asia on the Kipchak steppe to the west: the Khazars, the Golden Horde, the khanate of Astrakhan, the Kalmuks, the Cossacks of Orenburg. In terms of terrain, central Kazakhstan, unlike Zungharia, was relatively featureless and uncompartmentalized, a series of plains with only low differences of elevation. In terms of resources, it was not dissimilar from Zungharia: little dispersed moisture, under ten inches a year; in the north a region of exterior drainage, the Ishin and the Tobol going to meet the Irtysh-Ob; in the south, a region of interior drainage, the Chu and the Sari su failing to meet the Syr, which adjoined another in the middle centering on Lake Tengiz. Central Kazakhstan was not well-provided with water, as Khrushchev's virgin lands program was to find out to its cost. In terms of spatial organization, it was relatively united, more like Semirechie than Zungharia, but because moisture was less, migration cycles had to be longer. Thus the Kazakh Middle Horde, the *Orta Zhuz*, wintered on the lower Syr, but summered in the valleys of the Sari su, Tobol and Ishin, a true nomadism with a migration cycle of seven hundred miles and more. Considerable dispersal of a scanty population over wide areas of poor grassland, to which local initiative was required to adapt, weakened the authority of the khan and the *zhuz* at the expense of the elders, *aksakal* and the family encampment, *aul.* Lacking clear definition, central Kazakhstan was exposed in all directions and lacked means of defence except its size and relative poverty.

These, then, were the places: the stage whereon Central Asia acted its role in the play of world history. Beyond lay the margins: to the south Afghanistan and Tibet, to the east Mongolia, to the west the Kipchak steppe, to the north Siberia. These adjoined Central Asia and influenced it, in the case of the Mongolian explosion decisively, but essentially they beat to their own rhythms. Beyond again were the homelands, the independent centres of civilization, China, Russia, Persia and India, to which Central Asia transmitted the impulsions of World History. Within this ambience, whatever its diversity of terrain, resources and spatial organization, Central Asia possessed a distinctive human unity. This unity consisted of three constants and a variable. The constants were shortage of water and the alternatives of nomadic pastoralism and oasis agriculture as a means of combating it. The variable was the relationship between nomads and sedentarists. It was this which was to be radically changed by the Mongolian explosion.

PEOPLE

In the absence of true sub-species or ethnicities, human groups may be characterized most concretely with respect to ecology, language, script and high culture. Central Asia was characterized by the co-presence of two sharply contrasting ecologies: nomadic pastoralism and oasis agriculture, each an extreme of development. Each too may be further analysed with respect to basic technology, social structure and political institutions. It is best to begin with nomadic pastoralism. It was the more recent, the more original of the two and the basis for the Mongolian explosion which precipitated the interlocking of histories and the role of Central Asia in world history.

(1) Nomadic Pastoralism

Basic Technology

Water, we know, is essential to life, whether human, animal or vegetable, and all Central Asia was short of water, especially the dispersed moisture of rain. The mountains kept out the summer monsoons of Coastal Asia. High pressure and winds kept out Mediterranean winter rain. The summer westerly airflow from the Atlantic only just reached Central Asia and was subject to variations. The winds followed a low pressure 'gully' between polar high pressure to the north and Saharan high pressure to the south.[8] The size of the Saharan pressure zone fluctuated according to solar activity, so the position of the gully varied. When solar activity was stronger, the gully would lie further north, through Central Europe or Scandinavia, and the steppe would receive little moisture. The taiga would benefit, some of the tundra might melt, so the Caspian, fed from the north via the Volga, would rise, while the Aral, fed from the south via the Oxus and Jaxartes, and subject to increased desiccation, would fall. When solar activity was weaker, the gully would lie further south through the Mediterranean, Black Sea and North Caucasus, and the steppe would receive a measure of rainfall. The taiga would be colder, the tundra would remain frozen, so the Caspian would be low, the Aral full, like the opposite figures in a Victorian child's barometer. In either position of the gully, however, rainfall in Central Asia was limited and, perhaps worse for arable farming, unreliable. In this situation, there were only two alternatives for human ecology: stay with water where it was or follow water wherever it could be found.

The second choice was nomadic pastoralism.[9] It meant complete abandonment of arable farming, even where this was meteorologically possible, and concentration on stockraising in a particular way: not just sedentary runholding moving herds from pasture to pasture round a fixed point, but moving the point itself, generally in a fixed cycle. The basics of nomadic pastoralism were grass, animals and mobility. Together these could supply the fundamental human material needs of food, clothing and shelter. Food came from milk products and meat, though meat was a luxury for the poorer nomad. Clothes were sheepskin, spun and woven woollen goods, leather or felt boots, fur as a luxury. Shelter was the *yurt* or round tent (though originally this had meant the more indispensable surrounding pasture rather than the shelter itself): a framework of willow branches linked by leather crosspieces, covered with layers of felt, three in winter, one in summer, and on the floor sheepskins or woven carpets. Different animals provided different things. Horses, cattle, camels and yaks provided transport, fast and slow, light and heavy, and milk. Sheep and goats provided meat, wool or hair. But horses were eaten, camelhair was used in felt, goats were milked. All animals provided *argal* droppings, used for fuel in a land short of trees except in river courses or on the edge of the taiga.

Different animals had different requirements. Horses ate the top of grass, cattle graze shorter, sheep and goats shortest, so they needed different quantities of space. Camels got something out of *gobi*, desert tussock, where the other animals could not. Species differed in speed, endurance, and capacity to go without food and water. One of the most feared phenomena on the steppe was *dzud*: the refreezing of melted snow at the end of the winter. Horses kicked away snow and ice instinctively but

cattle and sheep did not, and so would die if *dzud* was prolonged. A quarter or even half the herds could be lost in this
way. Equally, unexpected summer drought on the migration
route could be deadly too. All these factors had to be taken into
consideration in deciding the migration cycle. Nomadism was
not haphazard wandering. The nomads went where they expected to find grass. There was always a plan, though, equally,
there always had to be fall-backs, contingency plans. As Lattimore
emphasized, the point about nomads is not that they do move
anywhere, but that they can. The simplest kind of migration was
transhumance: in summer, north, up the mountain to find
pasture out of the sun; in winter, south, down to the plain to
find shelter out of the cold. This was the cycle of the Great
Horde Kazakhs in Semirechie, of the Kirghiz in the T'ien-shan
between Transoxania and Chinese Turkestan and of the Chahar
Aimak in Afghan Turkestan. In these cases, summer and winter
camps (*ailaks* and *kishlaks*) were two hundred miles apart, sometimes only one hundred. Grass and movement were fairly pre-
dictable and the journey took only a month or so each way.
Most Turco-Mongolian nomads, however, out in the dryer,
open steppe, required a more complex cycle: not just A to B,
but ABCD according to four seasons, with ABEF in reserve for
bad years. Cycles of five hundred, even one thousand miles
were regularly followed, especially in Central Kazakhstan and
in Zungharia.

What sort of living did nomadic pastoralism provide? It was a
hard life, a constant battle against a harsh environment and
meteorological uncertainty, but not without positive features.
The food was strong on fats and protein, the clothes were
warm, the yurt was comfortable if not too overcrowded. Life was
varied, not too monotonous. There was much independence
and room for initiative by both genders and all ages. Despite
these features, however, nomadic pastoralism was not self sufficient. As Lattimore said, the pure nomad was the poor nomad.
The nomads needed grain for the carbohydrate element of
diet. It was useful to have iron tools and weapons. It was pleasant to have luxury foodstuffs, like tea and sugar, for oneself,
luxury textiles, especially silks, for wives and daughters. The
nomad needed the sedentarist: the farmer, the artisan or the
merchant who represented them. This gave rise to the trade/
raid syndrome of nomadic pastoralism: buy if the price is right,

take by force or tribute if it is not. The need for contact, originating in the basic technology, was compounded by social structure, and political institutions.

Social Structure

Steppe society was not monolithic: there were differences between the social structure of the Kazakhs and that of the Kirghiz. Steppe society was not unchanging: in the period of world history it was to be modified by the introduction of new religious institutions. In general, however, steppe society operated through both a class system and a family system, both of which may be described as 'unequal egalitarianism'. On the steppe, the only essential means of production was the migration cycle itself, and this was the property of the group rather than any individual. Within the group, however, there were inequalities both as regards animals owned, and as regards status, since human groups are seldom just economic units but provide social distance as well as goods. First, there were the *noyon*, lords, famous families with pedigrees, real and fictitious, and large herds. They chose and advised the *khan* or ruler, generally through a council of four senior lineage chiefs. They organized the migratory movements of the group, assigned pasture to sublineages and individual families, and expected to command military units in time of war. To fulfil these functions they were entitled to call upon the services of the next two subgroups. Second, there were the *arat*, herdsmen, commoners, free men, who owned lesser herds, received pasture, and formed the rank and file of the group. To the *khan* and *noyon*, they owed *qubciri* or intermittent services such as the herding, lending horses or taking messages. Third, there were the *bogol*, slaves, who might belong to either *noyon* or *arat*. Slave is a misleading term because such people enjoyed the use of animals on condition of services to their masters. Certainly they were a disprivileged group, recruited from defeated enemies, war orphans from both sides, oblates to outstanding leaders, but their lifestyle was not so different from that of the *noyon* or *arat*. Movement upwards was not impossible. Some *bogol* stood closer to the *khan* than some *arat* and might rise to become confidential agents and military commanders. Membership of the three classes was unstable, as steppe communities were loose and frequently

recast by war or internal rivalries, but the classes themselves
remained constant and corresponded to some basic imperative
of social distance.

Actually, in daily living, the division *noyon, arat, bogol* was less
important than that between men, women, children. Because
of the need to spread out over the grass, the unit of operation
was small: half a dozen tents, called *aul* by Turks and *arban* by
Mongols; maybe one noble, three commoners, two slaves, a
working community bound by kin or clientage. In these communities, herding was done by children and teenagers, women
processed milk, wool and meat in the *yurts*, while men were
largely idle: at best managerial, at worst drunk, or, in between,
engaging in horse racing, wrestling, archery or collective hunts
with equally idle men of associated *yurts*. In these circumstances,
it has been said, the young worked sometimes, older women
always, and men never! In fact there was some exaggeration
here, because of the different grazing requirements of different
animals. Camels on the *gobi* beyond the grass did not need
much care. Horses, however, required wide grazing and were
kept furthest out on the grass looked after by men. Cattle came
next and looked after themselves. Sheep and goats came closest
and were looked after by women and children. Even in this
redefinition, male work was not demanding and left much time
for hunting, especially deer, with dogs. Partly because of their
economic function, the status of women on the steppe was
quite high and increased with age as they became matriarchs.
Women retained the services of one of their sons as *otchigin* or
hearth-guardian, and played an active role in politics, both
local and supralocal.

Political Institutions

What the function of the state was in the circumstances of
nomadic pastoralism has given rise to two views in Western
scholarship, which may be termed the ecological and the sociological. The first, the ecological view, may be associated with
John Masson Smith.[10] It argued that state power was essentially
irrelevant to nomadic ecology and hence remained weak and
underdeveloped until the time of Chinggis, who introduced
something new. Steppe society operated by small units, *aul* or
arban; the migration cycles and allocation of pasture were

relatively fixed by custom; and state power could contribute nothing except occasional arbitration and disaster relief, for example in a bad case of *dzud.* On the contrary, any increase in state functions over a prolonged period, for example in war, could only disrupt steppe society by its enlarged demand for *qubciri:* services in manpower and horsepower. Steppe society, it is true, easily militarized. Collective hunts were training in cavalry operations. Families and herds could move and act as commissariat. But prolonged militarization was socially injurious. Military imperatives for mobility were not the same as ecological imperatives. If too fast, too concentrated, the herds would suffer and men get parted from their womenfolk. Though booty might be taken, it would be unevenly shared, and the ordinary *arat* might not benefit. Indeed, continuous mobilization of men, animals and resources was impossible in the long run. Groups would drop off and go back to the pastures. The state would dissolve if it overextended itself and the *khan* would find himself without any followers. The nomad state did little, was weak, and even discontinuous. The nomad was a natural anarchist, but a relatively peaceful one, except for a little raiding if trade failed.

The second, sociological view, may be associated with Joseph Fletcher, and in particular with his theory of blood tanistry (from the Celtic word meaning 'succession').[11] Fletcher agreed that nomad states were fissionable and frail, but he thought the reasons for this were not ecological, but political and sociological. Politically, nomad states were fissionable because of an absence of legitimacy and clear rules of succession. Every time a *khan* died, power was up for grabs, the state dissolved and had to be painfully reconstructed. But this practice of blood tanistry, was not just the absence of a system, a kind of constitutional oversight. It was a system in its own right, with deep roots in society. Political instability was sociologically useful. Basically, Fletcher saw steppe society as more violent and frictionful than Masson Smith. Migration cycles conflicted, use of pasture was frequently contested, war was less disruptive and more advantageous to a greater number of people. Indeed, to adult males, status and booty, both acquired essentially in war, were more important than economic loss and gain. Society required status. War conferred status. So the state needed to create violence, internal or external, as well as controlling it. As in some

Mediterranean societies, violence was a form of bonding both within groups and between groups. Blood tanistry acted as a periodic reheroization of society: a revaluation of prestige and pecking order, a redistribution of status and property. In this sociological view, therefore, the state did more than in the ecological view. Negatively it controlled violence, positively it created it. It was not an irrelevance to nomad society. The nomad was compelled to be a political animal, and a violent one, both to himself and his neighbours.

Between these two views no absolute choice needs to be made. The state was not a constant in nomadic pastoralism. Both views may have been right at different times. In a sense, the two views are complementary. The state may have been ecologically minimal and sociologically maximal. Nevertheless, the sociological view seems more in accordance with what is known about the character of steppe politics before and after Chinggis. For Fletcher, Chinggis is less of an anomaly than he is for Masson Smith. The Mongolian explosion can be seen as a megaton version of earlier, smaller explosions, its destructiveness as internal violence externalized. This in turn creates a problem. The fact is that before 1100 steppe societies were relatively unaggressive. Though massive invasions of horsemen from the steppe were feared by sedentary societies since at least the time of Jeremiah, they never occurred. Blood tanistry might explain why this was so, but in that case, something must have happened after 1100 to change the situation. The sociological view has to face the problem why the Mongolian explosion was so late, given the military potential of the steppe.

(2) Oasis Agriculture

Basic Technology

Where nomadic pastoralism involved following water wherever it was to be found, oasis agriculture meant staying with water wherever it was. The essence of an oasis was water and the essence of a prosperous oasis was water intensively applied to agriculture. In pre-modern conditions, intensive irrigation would increase land yields in cereals two-fold or more, as well as supplying textile fibres such as cotton, and high quality fruit, notably grapes and melons. If nomadic pastoralism represented an extreme of dispersal, using every blade of grass, oasis agriculture represented an extreme of concentration, getting the most out of every drop of water. Nomadic pastoralism and oasis agriculture contrasted, but they were alike in their ecological extremism.

The oasis region of Central Asia received little rainfall, even less than the associated steppe to the north. The Central Asian oases, with the exception of deltaic Khiva, were situated to the north of the mountains where they could utilize the water produced by the melting of the snow, deposited on the mountains by the various monsoons and westerlies. Oasis agriculture was based essentially on a form of run-off irrigation, water being tapped in three ways. First, it was tapped by damming or diverting a river, before it joined some larger stream or went off into the desert to die of evaporation, into innumerable irrigation channels, along which villages or farms collected. In Samarkand, it was reckoned that there were 100,000 channels great and small. Such irrigation was tantamount to the creation of an artificial, interior delta, and some rivers like the Zerafshan had a series of them. Second, water was tapped by sinking wells to greater or less depth. Well-sinking was therefore an honoured and skilled profession in oasis communities and wells were particularly important in Ferghana. Third, it was tapped from subterranean and hence non evaporated run-off basins on hillsides, by the underground aquaducts known as *kariz*. Generally driven uphill, with occasional outlets and air holes, *kariz* demanded considerable geological knowledge, tunnelling skill and much labour in repair and maintenance, as did all the hydraulic works. *Kariz* were utilized especially at Turfan.

An example of how these factors combined in a single oasis is supplied by Herat, as described by British intelligence at the end of the nineteenth century.[12] At that time, the oasis covered about one thousand square miles, an oblong one hundred miles by ten miles along an alluvial fan of the Hari Rud, unlike the circular shape familiar from other oases. The population was about 300,000, though in time past it had been 500,000 or even a million: not a high density compared to the 5 million supported by the 3000 square miles of the Chengtu irrigation works in Szechwan or even the 30,000 supported by the 30 square miles of Hami in Uighuristan. Two thirds of the population were rural. Half the cultivated area was irrigated, but this half produced twice or three-times as much grain as the non-irrigated, as well as much fruit and vegetables. Most of the irrigation was by diversion canals from the Hari Rud, but further from the river, *kariz*, wells, and springs were employed in that order of importance. Thanks to the presence of running water, water mills were extensively used for irrigation and corn grinding: windmills, too, thanks to the one hundred and twenty day wind for which Herat was notorious. As a result Herat produced $1^{1}/_{2}$ million cwt of grain for 300,000 population: an affluent 4 cwt per capita plus a 300,000 cwt surplus, stored in large, dry, granaries, which could be the basis of trade, war or political bargaining. The farmer's surplus, as opposed to the oasis', was extracted from him by goods, services, rent and taxes. It provided the basis for the city: the group of artisans, merchants, clergy and officials in which the oasis culminated, its secondary and tertiary activities.

Social Structure

First, there was a dichotomy of villages and town, though the two were not far apart physically. The villages, whether strung out along a canal or nucleated round a dam, well or *kariz* outlet, were unequal communities of middling landlords, often absentee in the town, and small peasant cultivators. Though there was always some state property, before the Mongol conquest, most land was owned privately. There were two forms of ownership: *milk*, lands owned by laymen which paid *kharaj* or land tax to the ruler, and *waqf*, lands owned by religious foundations (mosques, colleges, schools, charities) which, by and large, did not. Landlords, whether individual or institutional, either cultivated the land directly through live-in hired servants, or they leased it to village communities or individuals. Leases were either on a permanent basis, the tenants acquiring a customary right to the land for a fixed ground rent, or, for a term of years for a stated share of the principal crop. There were therefore three kinds of peasant: hired servants, *kadivar*, customary tenants, *raiyyat*, and sharecroppers, *muzari*. The proportions varied according to circumstance. In pre-Mongol times, most peasants were probably *raiyyat*, and most oasis land was held in this way. This was the best status, which amounted to co-ownership. Rent and tax were not particularly heavy, and *kharaj* was paid in the first instance by the landlord not the tenant. But in contrast with the daily equality of lifestyle on the steppe, there was in the oasis a marked inequality of town and country, landlord and peasant. It was a class society.

Second, within the town, of which there was generally one per oasis, there was a trichotomy of politics and culture, trade and work. Most people in the oasis town worked as craftsmen or domestic servants to officials and clergy. Guilds were important institutions through which the ruler levied taxes on industry and through which artisans fended them off. Government in an oasis was frequently alien: from another oasis, from nomads, from some external great power. The sultan or his governor, however, would be wise to consult, and promote, a group of local notables known as the *sadr*: bigger landlords, clergy, larger-scale merchants, people often related to each other who combined money and status. This tripartition was reflected in Central Asian urban topography. Frequently, there was a new city or citadel for the ruler, his governor, his garrison, his tax office, physically separate, often by a few miles, from the native old city of religious foundations, guilds and artisans, with the major market, which served both, and also longer distance trade, in between. Sometimes an ambitious ruler would put an encircling wall around all three: new city, old city and central bazaar. This tripartite division is clearest in Chinese Turkestan, but there are signs of it at Herat. Herat began as a single Persian or Greek gridiron city, but within its walls there gradually developed the Central Asian tripartite division of a labyrinth of small alleys, central covered bazaar, and inner fortress to the side for the ruler. Trichotomy of this kind corresponded to a basic social imperative.

Political Institutions

Unlike the steppe, the role of the state in the oasis was relatively unproblematical. It was considerable, largely economic and generally accepted. The oasis was a tight community bound together by taxes, rent and water. Government of some kind was necessary to make the system work. A good ruler could be positively philanthropic by building dams, canals, bazaars, bridges, religious foundations. Equally, a bad ruler could do so much harm by neglecting essential building, taking too much out of the oasis and spending it elsewhere, or by letting war into the oasis to destroy its accumulated resources. An oasis was the work of centuries. It could be, if not destroyed, at least much reduced in a day. Beyond basic economics too, long distance trade and high culture depended to a considerable degree on the protection and promotion of the ruler. In some circumstances, Central Asian political institutions took the form of a city state, which witnessed both to the necessity of politics for life – and for the good life – and to an underlying sense of oasis community, whatever the class divisions. In the structure of this sense, an important ingredient was the awareness of the contrast of the oasis and the steppe, and the problematical character of their relationship.

(3) The Relationship of Nomadic Pastoralism and Oasis Agriculture

The struggle of desert and town, Iran and Turan, Persian and Turk, is reflected in much Central Asian literature, especially from the sedentary side. Outstanding here, of course, is Firdausi's *Shah-nama*, the Persian epic written under a Turkish ruler.[13] It is not surprising, therefore, that the first scholars to study oasis/nomad relations saw them in terms of *conflict*. This view could be supported by the fact that while oasis agriculture and nomadic pastoralism were mutually exclusive ecologies: the same people could not combine the intensivity of the one with the mobility of the other; yet particular pieces of marginal land could be used either for grain or grass, and so conflict was inevitable. Furthermore, it could be urged, the psychologies of nomad and sedentarist were completely opposed. The nomad had a natural, superiority complex, the sedentarist had a natural inferiority complex. Steppe violence and oasis passivity were bound to conflict.

Nevertheless, a second look revealed important elements of *complementarity*. The nomad needed grain, weapons, and tools: he wanted tea, later tobacco, and luxury textiles, high culture even. Similarly the sedentarist needed meat, wool, transport animals: he wanted fur, leather, high grade carpets whose manufacture began in steppe tents and was only later transferred to oasis workshops. In particular, the camel, the two-humped Bactrian camel, linked the two communities.[14] Camels were bred in the steppe, notably Semirechie and the Tsaidam, but were used in the oasis, or rather between oases, in the caravans which were managed mainly by sedentarists. Ecologically, there was symbiosis between nomad and sedentarist. Politically too there might be cooperation at least. On the one hand, the sedentarist found the best defence against one set of nomads was another set of nomads. On the other hand, if the nomad wanted to organize an empire out of his conquests, it was best done from an oasis with its granaries, money, literacy and unifying religion. The oasis needed government and protection: the steppe could provide both. The steppe lacked administration and education: the oasis could provide both.

Another aspect of the relationship might be termed *compenetration*. Oasis and steppe were physically close to each other, especially in Transoxania, the centrepiece of Central Asia. People moved relatively easily from one to the other. The steppe tended to be overpopulated. Dispersal and fewness were the law of its life and nomad society excluded marginals. If a herdsman's animals fell below a certain minimum through war, disease or *dzud*, then the marginal nomad would have to enter despised sedentary society as an agricultural labourer: a hired servant, *kadivar*, on an oasis estate. The oasis, on the other hand tended to be underpopulated. Except in Chinese Turkestan which seems to have been exceptionally healthy perhaps because of its elevation, there was much tuberculosis in overcrowded townships, much malaria in over-irrigated farmsteads, and in both intestinal parasites and fever epidemics, especially smallpox, the red death, the killer of children. The oasis, thanks to its high death rate, needed immigrants and welcomed the refugee nomad. Not all movement, however, was from steppe to oasis. Some sedentarists went out into the steppe: cameldrivers, carters, merchants, charlatans or doctors, religious enthusiasts, political intriguers, literate scribes; others might be taken there, if *bogol* were in short supply or ransoms needed to pay for imports, ransoms never paid, or, in the case of some girls, never asked. Nor were all immigrants from the steppe marginals. There would also be mercenaries awaiting a return to steppe politics, high born losers in blood tanistry who settled in old age in cities, retired bandits who sought a safer investment for ill-gotten gains. In both directions and at every social level, there was compenetration as well as conflict and complementarity. It formed a strong undertow going on below the surface of history: an invisible background to the invasions, great or small, which strike the attention of the historian and provide his narrative. Compenetration was a hidden constant in the unity of Central Asia in the sense of a group of oases and their associated steppe.

What varied was the degree of compenetration. One aspect of the Mongolian explosion through which Central Asia made its contribution to world history, was an immense increase in the speed and scale of compenetration. Two communities, formerly apart to a large extent in co-existence (another form of relationship) were forcibly osmosed, initially, in simple confusion. With this inflationary big bang, continuous world history commenced. Central Asia, however, had participated in the discontinuous world history which had gone before, and this earlier participation was a factor in the genesis of the continuity.

2 Central Asia and Temporary World Institutions

Continuous world history began with the Mongolian explosion. Before that, world institutions, weak or strong according to whether they operated in two, or more than two, of four primary civilizations, had existed, but they had been temporary. The role of Central Asia in them, however, forms part of the prehistory of our field. It therefore is the subject of Chapter 2. The topic has other points of relevance to the overall theme. First, Central Asia's role in temporary world history shaped its role in continuous world history. Indeed, it is arguable that, without those earlier participations, there would have been no Mongolian explosion and subsequent development of ongoing world institutions. Second, Central Asia's participation in the temporary world institutions raises perennial questions about its function: core or periphery, active or passive, living heart or dead centre? Central Asia, it has been said, suffers from every geographical liability, but enjoys one asset: its central position between the homelands of Europe, Iran, India and China. This centrality has allowed it to be alternately a point of diffusion and a point of convergence. In the following discussion of Central Asia and the seven temporary world institutions in which it participated before 1200, three points in particular will be attended to: its degree of activity or passivity, its relations with the homelands, and its contributions to and receipts from, the world institution in question.

THE INDO-EUROPEAN EXPANSION

In a sense, the Indo-European expansion was not temporary. Today, Indo-European languages are spoken widely in three out of the four primary civilizations. Even in East Asia, English is widely used as the expression of a common scientific and business co-consciousness, which is likely to spread. Central

Asia, however, has been the scene of one of the Indo-European expansion's two greatest setbacks, the other being the loss of the southern Mediterranean to Arabic and Turkish. At one time, Indo-European languages were spoken throughout Central Asia as far east as Kansu in both steppe and oasis. The Indo-European expansion, wherever originating, was a true world institution in that it operated in both the West Eurasian and East Asian primary civilizations. Subsequently, first in the steppe before 1200 as a result of the Avar advance, and then in the oases after 1200 as a result of the Mongolian explosion, Indo-European languages lost their predominance in Central Asia except in Afghan Turkestan and the enclave of Tadjikstan. Indeed, under the double advance of Arabic and Turkish, the Indo-European expansion was confined to the Western Eurasian primary civilization. It ceased to be a world institution until its advance into America in the sixteenth century. In the Central Asian context, the Indo-European expansion may be treated as a temporary world institution.

It is still debated whether Central Asia was a core or a periphery in the Indo-European expansion.[1] One view, which goes back to the first conceptualization of Indo-European by Sir William Jones in 1780 and is still held by scholars such as Marija Gimbutas, sees Central Asia as a core. Central Asia was the origin of a proto-Indo-Europan language. It was diffused by steppe nomads or chariot using aristocracies to the homelands of Europe, Iran and India, where previously non-Indo-European languages, such as Etruscan, Basque, Pictish, Sumerian, Elamite and Dravidian, had prevailed. There it developed into the various branches and members of the Indo-European family by the process of linguistic heterogenization which has been accepted as the dominant model by philologists since Humboldt. Some scholars have even felt able to ascribe precise cultural traits to the proto-Indo-European speaking group: patrilinear, patriarchal, warlike, horse-centred, epic making, logic developing. If some of these characteristics are regarded as pejorative and if language is equated with race, it is possible to arrive at an inverted form of Nazi mythology: the Aryans as the source of all evil.

The alternative view, that of Colin Renfrew, sees Central Asia as a periphery. Central Asia was the product of pastoralists from the west and agriculturalists from the south, but both speaking

Indo-European and both coming ultimately from the west from a point of origin in eastern Anatolia. For Renfrew, the Indo-European expansion was an earlier phenomenon than it is for the other view: 7000 BC rather than 2000 BC. It was also a slower phenomenon. Renfrew associates it, not with the military explosion of a warrior elite, but with the ecological footsteps of Western Eurasian neolithic agriculture and pastoralism, advancing at a glacial mile or so a year, according to the schema of Luigi Cavalli-Sforza which Renfrew adopts. Moreover, while Renfrew accepts the philological orthodoxy of heterogenization over time in his picture of the overall development of the Indo-European languages, he is more sympathetic to the alternative model of homogenization of N. S. Trubetskoy in explanation of actual Indo-European languages, such as the Celtic group.

Another difference between Gimbutas and Renfrew concerns the origin of nomadic pastoralism within their respective time scales. Gimbutas sees nomadic pastoralism as primitive and comparatively early. It was either the direct descendant of paleolithic hunter gathering or the offshoot of an independent neolithic in the middle Volga which emphasized pastoralism rather than agriculture. It existed before the diffusion of Indo-European languages and moved from north to south. Renfrew sees nomadic pastoralism as sophisticated and comparatively late. It was a specialized form of Indo-European ranch pastoralism, just as oasis agriculture was a specialized form of Indo-European extensive agriculture. It was not a cause but a consequence of the diffusion of Indo-European languages and it moved from west to east, from the Ukraine out into the steppe. The first view makes nomadic pastoralism a Central Asian invention. The second makes it an Indo-European introduction into Central Asia. Renfrew, moreover, is sceptical of any independent development of neolithic in Western Eurasia outside the Indo-European mainstream, while Gimbutas postulates it in the middle Volga. Not surprisingly, some of Renfrew's critics, again identifying language and race, have accused him of reviving neo-Darwinian bioethnology: the Aryans as the source of all good.

Where archaeologists differ, it is difficult for a historian to decide between them. Yet decide he must, at least provisionally if the early history of Central Asia, and the baseline for its subsequent development, is to be intelligible. Under this neces-

sity it must be decided that Renfrew's view is the more convincing in the present state of the evidence. First, nomadic pastoralism as it was described in the last chapter, was not a primitive
but a sophisticated mode of ecology. Second, as a mode of
ecology, it was not fully independent of agriculture, extensive
or intensive, and was not possible without its at least tangential
presence.[2] It is unlikely, therefore, to have been derived from
palaeolithic hunter gathering, or a purely pastoral neolithic.
Third, as Renfrew points out, all the early groups to whom
nomadic pastoralism may be ascribed, such as the Cimmerians,
Sarmatians, Scyths, Alans and Yüeh-chih, were Indo-European-
speaking. Fourth, if nomadic pastoralism had been primitive,
early and Middle Asian, then it is surprising that, unlike the
Inuit mode of palaeolithic, it never found its way to America
where, even in the absence of the horse, it could have been
made to flourish. Fifth, once the Indo-European origin of nomadic pastoralism outside Central Asia is accepted, then the
case for the similar introduction of Indo-European languages
in the sedentary sector is strengthened, particularly in view of
the early dates (5000 BC) for agricultural settlements in southern Turkmenistan. Sixth, it would be further strengthened if
Renfrew's hypothesis A, that the Indus river civilization was
Indo-European in speech, is substantiated. Even if he were
forced back on to his hypothesis B of a late Indo-European
introduction following a systems collapse in the Indus Valley
*c.*1800 BC this sequence would not have the significance attributed to it by the core view. Central Asia would remain a periphery, a colony of Indo-European expansion agricultural and
pastoral and Aryan India would be a late colony of a colony, one
of conquest rather than settlement.

Early Central Asia's colonial relations with the homelands
were limited to Iran and Europe. Relations with Iran came first,
*c.*6000 BC, as part of the initial push of Indo-European neolithic
from eastern Anatolia to Media and Parthia. Relations with
Europe came second, *c.*2000 BC, as part of the subsequent push
of nomadic pastoralism, taking off from agricultural settlements
east of the Carpathians. Relations with India, if Renfrew's hypothesis A is correct, would have come not long after those with
Iran, *c.*3000 BC but would have not have been colonial. Renfrew
sees the advance of the Indo-Europeans into India coming
from the Zagros through Baluchistan rather than from the

Kopet Dagh through Afghanistan. It would not have been long, however, before contact between the two arms of the advance was made. Indeed, it has been suggested that Bactria was first developed by Indo-European colonists from the south, from Harappa, rather than from the north or west.[3] Under Renfrew's hypothesis B, which accepts Mortimer Wheeler's original identification of the Indus river civilization as Dravidian speaking, Central Asia's role in the establishment of the Indo-European languages in the subcontinent would be more positive. What that role was, however, is harder to define. The traditional reconstruction of the coming of the Aryans is derived from the *Rig Veda*. This work, it was been claimed, was composed not long after 2000 BC and was collected around 1000 BC, but it was not written down in its present form until the fourteenth century AD, though its existence is attested around 300 BC by a work of exegesis, the *Nirakta* (Etymology) of Yasha.[4] Recent doubts about the possibility of exact oral transmission over long periods of time, however, have called the evidential status of the *Rig Veda* into question.[5] It may have been no more than an archaizing pastiche in reaction to subsequent Iranian contact, or to the development of the *Upanishads*. Though Renfrew does believe in long range oral transmission and accepts the *Rig Veda* as evidence for the second millenium, there is no need to follow him here.

Relations with China are unlikely to have been significant at the time of the first Indo-European expansion. 'China' was then no more than a series of coastal neolithic settlements along the rim of East Asia, many of which may not even have spoken Chinese.[6] Neolithic, it is agreed, was independently developed in Western Eurasia and East Asia, as in Black Africa and Meso-America. At one time, in the so-called Sinocentric model, it was believed that northwest China was the point of diffusion for neolithic throughout East Asia. In that case the question of early Chinese relations with Central Asia and the west was important. With northwest China seen as a point of convergence for other neolithics in China or East Asia, the question becomes more marginal. The Sinocentric model, of course, could be revived with earlier dates for northwest or central Chinese neolithic, or with new sites in eastern Turkestan. In any case, once Chinese and Central Asian neolithics were established, relations between them developed, as is indicated by silk at the Sapalli site in southern Uzbekiston (*c.*2000 BC) and jade at the Chust site in Ferghana. By the end of the Bronze age, if not before, Central Asia was in touch with all four homelands.

In the temporary world institution of the Indo-European expansion, Central Asia was a borrower rather than a lender. In its earliest nucleus, the little Mesopotamia of piedmont and deltas between the Tedjen and Murghab in southern Turkmenistan, it borrowed basic agriculture from eastern Iran. In the steppe adjacent to Khiva, then represented by the Kelteminar culture, it borrowed nomadic pastoralism from eastern Europe. In return, Central Asia made three contributions. First, it is likely that the small oases of the Kopet Dagh run-off were the home of the *kariz*. When it was first settled by agriculture, Central Asia was probably better watered, by both rainfall and river flow than it is now. The *kariz*, or underground aqueduct shielded from evaporation, would have been a later development as communities wanted to expand agricultural areas despite worsening climatic conditions. Although the *kariz* was always secondary to other kinds of irrigation, it was a useful addition to the armoury of intensive agriculture. Subsequently, it found its way as far east as Turfan and as far west as Madrid and Mexico.[7] Second, it was in Central Asia (not necessarily Bactria) that Bactrian camels were first domesticated, i.e. herded and then used for burden and draft. From there, they were diffused to Iran, India and China, though later, in the west, they were replaced by Arabian camels.[8] Though never as numerous as the Arabian camel and only gradually finding an appropriate pack saddle, the Bactrian camel added to the transport facilities of the Indo-European world. Third, Central Asia was the source for that world of turquoise (Nishapur), jade (Khotan) and lapis lazuli (Badakhshan), the raw material for the blue pigment ultramarine. As talismans and status symbols, precious and semi precious stones were an important element in the earliest trade. Philip Kohl has explained the relative underurbanization of Central Asia, Bactria in particular, by its function as a group of mining camps within an already commercially-linked Indo-European community.[9] Central Asia was peripheral, but it had something to offer: vegetable, animal and mineral.

THE ZOROASTRIAN REVELATION

In the second world institution, the Zoroastrian revelation, Central Asia was at the core. After millenia of provinciality, Central Asia unexpectedly moved centre stage intellectually with Zoroaster, the prophet of the 'good relation' of Ahura Mazda. Zoroastrianism is often regarded as a Persian, national, dualist religion, and so it became. In fact, it was originally a universal, Indo-European, henotheistic revelation. Moreover, it resonated beyond the world of Iran to Mongolia and Tibet in one direction and to the Semitic and Greek speaking regions in another. Zoroastrianism can claim to be the first world religion in the sense of affecting two of the primary civilizations.

The date and birth place of Zoroaster continue to be matters of dispute. In the most recent reconsideration, Mary Boyce wrote: 'it seems natural to conclude that the prophet lived sometime between say 1400 and 1000 BC, at a time when his people were perhaps still dwelling in northern Central Asia before moving south in their turn to fix their abode in Khwarezm.'[10] This conclusion ascribes to Zoroaster both an earlier time and a more northerly place than previous interpretations. These had put him not long before the Achaemenids, c.600 BC, and in Balkh or Merv rather than Khiva.

Boyce rested her case on both philological and ecological evidence. Philologically, she argued that the language of the *Gathas*, the earliest stratum of the *Avesta*, and the one which may be attributed most confidently to Zoroaster himself, indicated a northeastern Iranian dialect. Boyce's authority carries weight here, though, as with the *Rig Veda*, there are problems in the late date of the current text of the *Avesta* and its relationship to original composition, collection and oral transmission. Ecologically, Boyce followed the Gimbutas view of Indo-European origins. Thus in discussing the Indo-European polytheism from which Zoroaster emerged as a reformer, she wrote: 'it was ancient nomadism, lived on vast steppes, which gave an especial character to these ancestral gods.'[11] She emphasized the pastoral imagery of the mounted horse. If, however, Renfrew's view of a late, eastern European-introduced, nomadic pastoralism is accepted, then the context at least of Boyce's interpretation is in need of modification, Khiva loses some of its attraction as his location, while the cattle imagery of the *Gathas* might refer only to the subsidiary pastoralism of oasis margins. Renfrew's perspective, therefore, leads one back to both the place and the time of the older view: Balkh or Merv before the Achaemenids. Both views, however, agree in making Zoroaster a Central Asian. He was the first of an unexpectedly long line of intellectual and spiritual leaders emerging from its oases and steppes.

Zoroaster's revelation, as Boyce reconstructs it, was of the essentially moral character of Ahura Mazda, and his consequent preeminence above all other gods. A further implication was the realignment of the Indo-European pantheon from a triple, horizontally stratified, cosmogony to a vertically divided ethical dualism. This message, proclaimed with prophetic fervour, found little acceptance in the homelands, except in Iran, where it became first the house religion of the Achaemenids and then, under the Sassanids, the national religion of the gentry of Fars. Eastern Europe and the Kipchak steppe never received the revelation: another argument against its early Khivan and nomadic pastoralist origin. India rejected it in favour of the old pantheon as modified by Brahmanic ritualism and Upanishad panenhenism. China was to give hospitality, and even military assistance, to the last Sassanid princes, but the Parsee community did not survive the great persecution of foreign religions in 845.

Where the Zoroastrian revelation may have had some impact was in Mongolia and Tibet. L. N. Gumilev believes that the religion of the Mongols in the time of Chinggis may not have been Shamanism, as it has been assumed to have been, but a form of Zoroastrianism: monotheistic, or at least henotheistic, i.e. worship of a single high god.[12] In this view, Kököchu or Teb Tengri, who figured prominently in Chinggis' early history, would not have been a shaman, but a magus. This conclusion is important because the religion, whatever it was, was significant in the genesis and subsequent ideology of the Mongolian explosion. Gumilev further suggests that Bon in Tibet may have been a derivate of Zoroastrianism rather than an autochthonous product. In the Far West, too, Zoroastrianism may have had some resonance. One of the books of the Nag Hammadi collection is called *Revelation of Zoroaster*, but it may just have been pastiche, and the Mithraic freemasonry was a Rhenish rather than an oriental religion.[13]

As a world institution, Zoroastrianism borrowed as well as lent. At one time, it was believed that the Old Testament idea of the Messiah might have been influenced by Zoroaster's notion of the *saosyant* 'he who will bring benefit', the final prophet at the end of the second age of time. The Old Testament, however, had already developed this idea before the Zoroastrian revelation entered Iran with the Achaemenids. Indeed, the order of influence is more likely to have been the other way round: the *saosyant* as a single figure being a later stratum of Zoroastrian thought and derived from the Messiah from the Jewish colonies in Iran, such as Rages. At one time, it was believed that the Zoroastrian cosmogony of the two states (good and evil) and the three times (separation, mixture, separation) influenced the Manichaean cosmogony which was similar except that spirit and matter were superimposed on good and evil. The discovery of the Cologne papyrus, which shows the Elkesaite, Mesopotamian and sub-Christian ambience of Mani, makes this unlikely. Zoroastrianism, like Buddhism, was only on the fringe of Mani's world.[14] The formulation of two states and three times was probably borrowed by the Zoroastrians from him. In another direction, the anti-dualist Zoroastrianism heresy of Zurvanism may have borrowed from the time technology and meta-time ideas which lay behind Taoist alchemy.[15] Indeed, Zoroastrianism might have liked to have borrowed more. In the third century, the Sassanian shahs contemplated taking Christianity under their protection against the pagan Roman empire, but here they were preempted by the house of Constantine.[16] In the last resort, Zoroaster was only a provincial prophet from peripheral Central Asia. Without the substantial borrowing which was denied it, the Good Religion could not maintain itself as a world institution.

THE ACHAEMENID AND MACEDONIAN WORLD EMPIRE

Pierre Briant describes the Achaemenids as ruling the first interregional world empire.[17] Under their Macedonian successors, the empire became even more widely flung, penetrating into eastern Turkestan to the borders of China under Euthydemus I of Bactria (210–190 BC). Since it extended into Africa and had relations with East Asia, it may be regarded as

a world institution in the second half of the first millennium
BC.

The Achaemenid state was complex. As its core was an ethno-class, the Medo-Persian aristocracy. It was bound together by gifts from and loyalty to the king, whose royal favours it extended in a vast web of patronage and dependence. The shah was a warrior rather than a priestly king, and loyalty was demonstrated by accompanying him on campaign with the maximum number of retainers. Hence the huge armies which so impressed Herodotus, but were probably more of a liability than an asset militarily. The real army was the Immortals, an elite corps of heavy cavalry armed with lances, but they were always in danger of being swamped on the battlefield by their own batmen. Although the core of the empire was the Medo-Persian aristocracy, there were no theoretical limits to its subjects. Three different scripts were used in its publications and Aramaic, not Persian, was the vernacular language of state. Colonies of persons were moved from one end of the empire to another for security purposes and its depth of penetration in terms of administration was not insignificant. In religion, the empire was tolerant and Zoroastrianism was only the house religion of the dynasty.

In this empire, Central Asia was a province and more than a province. It included the satrapies of Aria, Choresmia, Sogdiana and Bactria, i.e. Herat, Khiva, Samarkand and Balkh. To the east, the Jaxartes was the frontier, while Ay-Khanoum was the border fortress on the upper Oxus. Ferghana was not part of the empire, nor anywhere in the Tarim basin.[18] In Briant's view, there was no Bactrian kingdom before the Achaemenid conquest: only a congerie of oasis-scale city states. With the conquest, Bactria became a major satrapy with a high tributary contribution and usually a royal kinsman as satrap. Darius I, it has been suggested, came from Bactria, or at least married a Bactrian queen. Balkh was almost a second capital and uprisings had the character of royal usurpations rather than separatist revolts. The royal government was effective. At Ay-Khanoum irrigation was extended. Bactrian troops fought at Plataea and Gaugamela. Bactrian colonists were sent to Armenia, Cappadocia and Lydia. Greek colonists were received in Bactria. When the Western Achaemenid empire fell to the Macedonians, Bessos, the satrap of Bactria, thought it possible to maintain a truncated empire in the east under the title of Artaxerxes IV.

Alexander the Great had other ideas.[19] Persian tradition came to regard him as a half brother of the defeated King Darius III and thus a legitimate Achaemenid. He claimed the whole Achaemenid inheritance and gave indications of wishing to upgrade Bactria vis-à-vis Fars. Thus he founded there an unprecedented number of Alexandrias: Aria (Herat), Arachosia (Kandahar), Sub-Caucaso (Begram), Oxiana (Ay-Khanoum), Eschate (Khojend), Margiana (Merv). Not a marrying man, he married Roxana, the daughter of the local chief Oxyartes, and induced his general Seleucus to marry Apama, the daughter of the local rebel Spitamenes. The number of hyparchs or subsatraps was increased and more confidence was placed in them than in Persians from the west. Though it is fashionable not to credit Alexander with long term plans and with anticipating the future, it is difficult not to see these moves as part of a scheme to make Bactria the eastern turntable of a Graeco-Iranian empire. True, much of the structure was jerry-built and even before Alexander's death was falling apart in the rivalry of Greeks and Macedonians, Persians and Bactrians. Subsequently, however, much of what Alexander envisaged was accomplished, first under the Seleucids, notably Antiochus I the son of Apama who was bilingual in Greek and Iranian, and then under the Graeco-Bactrian kingdoms which lasted down to the end of the second century BC[20] Alexander cannot be dissociated from the Hellenistic world.

Central Asia's chief contribution to the Achaemenid – Macedonian world empire was horses. Specifically, it provided the chargers, the 'heavenly horses' of the Chinese sources, which alone could carry the cataphract of the armoured knight of the Iranian military tradition, a term first used by Polybius and Livy apropos of the Seleucid armies. The large horse was a natural mutant, derived ultimately from a zebra strain, but developed by a selective breeding at certain locations by sedentary populations. In the west, the chief were Thrace, the North Caucasus and Nisaea in Media, but operating on a bigger scale were Bactria and Ferghana. The large horse, with its speed, stability, shock and staying power, was developed as a defence against steppe nomads. It was equally, if not more, effective against sedentary chariots and infantry, and became the basis of both the Achaemenid and Macedonian heavy cavalry. From an Iranian standpoint, Alexander's army was the Immortals minus the batmen and plus better commissariat and an improved lance, the *sarissa*.[21] Mobile and battlefield effective, the Achaemenids went down before it. Yet it needed remounts and replacements, and, by the time he conquered Bactria, Alexander was having difficulties with both the Macedonians and the Greek mercenaries. Bactria must have struck Alexander as another Macedonia: a land of big horses and military gentry, an excellent basis for an army of the east, if its loyalty could be assured, as it might be by the marriage to Roxana.

Subsequently, the heavenly horses of Ta Yuan (Yavan, Yonakas, Ionians, Greeks) became the target for the imperialism of Han Wu-ti (140–87). Following the reconnaissance of Chang Chien from 138, Ferghana was brought under Han suzerainty by the second expedition of Li Kuang-li in 101. By this time, the Greeks had lost their predominance to the nomadic Alans, Scyths and Kushans. Ay-Khanoum fell in 145 and henceforward the Greeks were confined to small kingdoms in the Hindu Kush. The world empire of which they had become the leaders under Alexander was over.

THE BUDDHIST ECUMENE

Buddhism itself was not a temporary world institution but a permanent one. Today, Buddhist philosophy is everywhere appreciated, Buddhist communities exist in all four primary civilizations, and in two of them, three groups of states (Ceylon and Burma, Thailand and Cambodia, Korea and Mongolia) and one incipient superpower (Japan) may be regarded as Buddhist countries. By Buddhist ecumene, however, is meant something more integrated and institutionalized. In the seventh century, in the reigns of emperor Harsha (606–47) and empress Wu (660–705), Buddhism was predominant in the leading homelands of India and China. Central Asia and Southeast Asia were more Buddhist than anything else. An incrustation of monasteries, following similar rules (*vinaya*) dotted the Buddhist space. Within that space, pilgrims, students and missionaries moved freely without sense of unfamiliarity. Everywhere there were the same devotions, the same system of lay patronage, the same sacred language of Sanskrit. Though divided into sects and schools, everywhere there was a high intellectuality, directed to the same critical problem of the relation of thought to reality, and finding the same metacritical solution of the self disclosure of the second to the first in their very disjuncture. The Buddhist ecumene was Mahayana rather than Hinayana, metropolitan rather than provincial, intellectual rather than devotional. It operated through a high level integration of thought and personnel on an international scale.

In this temporary world institution, Central Asia was both passive and active. Buddhism came to Central Asia from India. It was, of course, an Indian religion, though never quite the religion of India, even under Asoka and Harsha. Buddhism first penetrated north of the Hindu Kush under the Graeco-Bactrian kings. Demetrius (190–167) had contact with Indian Buddhism and his successor Menander (167–145) became the hero of a Sanscrit, Buddhist apologetic dialogue, the *Milindapanha*, possibly originally written in Greek. Lévi-Strauss speculated on the consequences if Greek philosophy had entered the service of Buddhism rather than Christianity.[22] In fact, the pro-Buddhist policy seems not to have been popular among the Bactrian Greeks and may have been a factor in the revolt of Eucratides, a cousin of the super Hellenist Antiochus IV, against the Euthydemid house. The revolt divided the kingdom, north and south, and led ultimately to its failure to maintain itself either in India or in Central Asia. The spread of Buddhism, however, accelerated under its successor, the Kushan empire, *c.*100 BC–250 AD. The Kushans, possibly the same group as the Chinese called Yüeh-chih, came from an Indo-European nomadic background. By this time, however, they were more an army in search of a state than a people in arms. They may have contained more Tibetan than Indo-European speakers, though the linguistic status of Tibetan is now in doubt. They gave their patronage indifferently to Buddhists, Zoroastrians and Hellenists, but Buddhism benefited most. It was widely adopted by the oasis aristocracies north of the Hindu Kush, and survived the fall of the Kushans as an ideology of resistance to the Zoroastrian but overly Persian Sassanids. Bamian, one of the earliest and greatest iconographic expressions of the Cosmic Buddha, was built under the Kushans by one such aristocracy.

Even before the fall of the Kushan empire to the Sassanids, Central Asia became actively engaged in missionary exchanges with China.[23] Particularly active were the oases of eastern Turkestan, notably Kucha and Khotan, which became Buddhist in the first century AD. The two centres represented opposite poles of Buddhism: Kucha, Hinayana Sarvastivadin realism; Khotan, Mahayana *prajnaparamita* agnosticism. The first Central Asian missionary to China was the Parthian monk-prince An Shih-kao (Arsak) who arrived at the court of the Later Han at Lo-yang in 147. An was a Hinayanist and he introduced to China *dhyana* meditation techniques, Buddhist magic and Sarvastivadin scholasticism. He was followed in 168 by Lokaksema, a Kushan, who has been variously ascribed to Peshawar, Kashgar or Khotan. He introduced and translated the *Astasahasrika-prajnaparamita*, the basic Mahayana text, and other scriptures which emphasized the new ideal of the Bodhisattva as opposed to the arhat: enlightenment for others rather than oneself. In 220, Chih Ch'ien, a third generation Kushan living in Nanking, made the first translation of the *Vimalakirtinirdesa sutra*, one of the most impressive and vivid of the Mahayana scriptures. In 260, not long after an embassy from the Kushan king Vasudeva, the first Chinese pilgrim, Chu Shih-hsing, went to Khotan and obtained the text of the greater *prajnaparamita* in 25,000 verses, which he sent home for translation. Around 290, another Kushan, Dharmaraksa, born in Tun-huang (Throana), visited Central Asia and then returned to Ch'ang-an, where he translated the *Sadharmapundarika sutra*, the Lotus, the fullest revelation of the Cosmic Buddha. Another Central Asian, Fo-t'u-ch'eng, possibly from Kucha, a Hinayanist, Sarvastivadin magician, acted as chief religious adviser to Shih Lo of the Later Chao dynasty in the period 311–348.

The climax of this Central Asian missionary activity was the arrival in 401 of Kumarajiva, prince of translators and the St. Augustine of Mahayana in China. Born in Kucha, the son of an Indian father and a local princess, Kumarajiva started as a Hinayanist. As a result of visits to Kashmir and Kashgar, he was converted to Mahayana in its extreme, logical Madhyamika form. During his residence at Ch'ang-an from 402 to 413, he not only translated or retranslated the major Mahayana scriptures into what became their authorised versions, but he also

introduced and translated the greatest work of Mahayana scholasticism, the *Mahaprajnaparamitasastra* or commentary on the
greater *prajnaparamita*. Ascribed to the South India philosopher Nagarjuna and expressing some of his views, the book has
a Kashmir background and, if not by a Kashmiri deutero-
Nagarjuna, may have been written by Kumarajiva himself. The
text has to be read at several levels. In form a scriptural commentary, in substance it is a radical deconstruction of
Sarvastivadin realism by the introduction of the Madhyamika
parameter of *sunyata*, 'emptiness', an incomputable surdity like
the square root of minus one. As a third, countertextual level,
however, *sunyata* is in turn deconstructed, so reality again becomes knowable. In this way, the *Mahaprajnaparamitasastra* laid
down the foundations for a less agnostic Buddhist scholasticism
in China.

Central Asia's contribution to the Buddhist ecumene was not
only to bring China into it. It also brought about the characteristic form of Buddhism there: what Zenryu Tsukamoto called
Multiple Buddhism. From Central Asia and Southeast Asia,
China received a variety of Buddhist sects and schools which in
their homelands were mutually antagonistic. The Chinese, receiving these teachings at different times and often initially
with imperfect understanding, saw them as mutually complementary. In the T'ien-t'ai and Hua-yen schools, when it first
becomes possible to speak of Chinese Buddhism rather than
simply Buddhism in China, they devised systems of *p'an-chiao*,
'dividing the doctrine', which arranged the various *sutras* and
sastras in order of time and degree of truth.[24] In this way, the
Buddhist world was provided with an ecumenical scholasticism,
though, of course, rivalry continued between different *p'an-
chiao* systems. In the construction of the Hua-yen system in the
time of empress Wu, an important part was played by Fa-tsang
(Dharmapitaka) whose family was of Sogdian origin. He joined
the Khotanese Siksananda in preparing a new translation of the
basic text of the school, the *Avatamsakasutra*, an improved text
of which was obtained from Khotan by empress Wu. Hua-yen, a
doctrine where *sunyata* was reinterpreted as inter-relationship,
was the last school of Mahayana scholasticism before the Buddhist ecumene was disrupted by irrationalism within and Islam,
Hinduism, Taoism and Confucianism without.

TANG COSMOPOLITANISM

After 600 AD, concurrent with the Buddhist ecumene, there
was another world institution, which may be termed T'ang
cosmopolitanism. After a prolonged period of political division
between 200 and 581, China was reunited first by the Sui and
then, on a slightly different basis, by the T'ang (618–901). To
consolidate their rule, the T'ang emperors, notably T'ai-tsung
(627–50) and Hsüan-tsung (712–56) adopted a policy of making their courts centres of magnetic, secular glamour, especially cosmopolitan glamour. In the past China, stuck away
beyond immense deserts and mountains, had been provincial.
Under the T'ang, thanks in part to the reception of the Buddhist ecumene, this was no longer so. China had created her
own Sinosphere and exported culture not only to Korea, Japan
and Tibet, but also to India and Islam. China could now consider herself metropolitan. For the first time, she was in truth
the *Chung-kuo*, the middle kingdom. Yet under the T'ang, this
was not interpreted in an exclusive, isolationist, xenophobic
sense, but in an inclusive, receptive, cosmopolitan sense. The
T'ang court, the centre of the world, was eager to borrow what
the rest of it had to offer. Such cultural cosmopolitanism required an active, even aggressive, foreign policy to maintain a
flow of contacts, people and exotica. Thus Chinese forces intervened in India after the death of Harsha; China supported a
Sassanid government in exile at Kucha, an oriental Koblenz as
Grousset called it; and Chinese armies crossed not only the
Himalayas, but also the T'ien-shan and the Hindu Kush. China's resonance extended beyond Chinese arms, beyond Eurasia
even. Chinese coins and goods reached Black Africa. Chinese
influence may have reached America via the Aleutians and
Kurosiwo current, though no conclusive evidence has yet
been found.[25] It is this wide diffusion of things Chinese, plus
China's profound receptivity to things foreign, which constituted
between 600 and 750, the world institution of T'ang
cosmopolitanism.

Central Asia was a source of goods and services.[26] Ferghana
and Samarkand supplied large horses for the heavy cavalry to
which China, like the Byzantine east and the Carolingian west,
shifted its military emphasis between 400 and 800. Kucha sent

musicians, instruments and music. Music included dance. The
arrival of the Western Prancing Dance, the Dance of Chash, the
Western Twirling Girls were notable events at the T'ang court.
Along with chargers and choreography, Central Asia supplied
polo ponies, hawks for the chase, furs from Khwarazm, cottons
from Turfan, woollen carpets from Bokhara, jade from Khotan,
lapis from Badakhshan. High fashion owed much of its pa-
nache and many of its status symbols to Central Asia. Samarkand
was *bon chic bon goût* at Ch'ang-an.

On the political and diplomatic side, Central Asia was equally
prominent. It was Sui Yang-ti's failure to perform against
the Turks which gave the T'ang the opportunity to seize the
leadership of the *kuan-chung* aristocracy. Relations with the
Turks, i.e. the steppe nomads of western Mongolia, Zungharia
and Semirechie, dominated the reign of T'ai-tsung. Defence
of Central Asia against Tibet, then an aggressive military
power, dominated the reign of empress Wu and preoccupied
reigns down to the treaty of 821, though Tibet was not always
an enemy. In 648 Tibetan and Nepalese forces assisted Wang
Hsüan-ts'e's intervention in Magadha. In the 660s Su Ting-fang
with Central Asian clients and Tibetan allies, operated in
Tukhara in Afghan Turkestan in support of the Sassanids against
the Omayyads. With independent action by the Tibetans
and their alliance with the Turgesh of Semirechie, Chinese
authority was eclipsed. It was restored and extended by Kao
Hsien-chih's campaigns of 747 and 750 against the Tibetans,
coming from the west across the Hindu Kush, having subdued
the Turgesh. In 750, Kao, *sahib gibal-al Sin*, 'lord of the mountains of China', as the Arabs called him, dominated Central
Asia. Hsüan-tsung, however, pushed on by barbarian generals
and court favorites had allowed his empire to become over
extended. The defeat of Kao Hsien-chih by Ziyad ibn Salih
on the Talas river, an east bank tributary of the Jaxartes, in
July 751; the revolt of the Sogdian frontier marshal An Lu-
shan (Rokshan) in Hopei in December 755; and the capture
of Ch'ang-an by the Tibetans in November 763, spelt the end
of the T'ang *Weltreich*. Though the dynasty survived, partly
through the Central Asian aid mobilized by the Manichaean
diplomat Li Mi, it was within narrower frontiers and contracted
horizons.[27]

THE UNIVERSAL CALIPHATE

As the Buddhist ecumene stood to Buddhism, so the universal caliphate stood to Islam. Today Islam is a world institution operative in all four primary civilizations. Its structure, however, is loose and, except in the Dervish orders, more national than universal. Under the universal caliphate, roughly 650–1000, the Islamic world was more integrated and institutionalized.[28] The caliphs were God's deputies (*khalifat Allah*), not just successors to the apostle of God (*khalifat rasul Allah*). They combined religious and political authority, which only later was devolved, on the one hand, to the *ulema*, the Islamic law doctors, and, on the other, to usually Turkish sultans. The caliphs were *imams*, divinely appointed leaders, *mahdiyyun*, 'rightly guided ones' and their authority exceeded that of the prophet. The caliphate grounded the Islamic community. As late as the twelfth century, al-Ghazzali could say, no caliph, no Islam, no *umma* without an *imam*. Early Islam was not the loose collections of tribes sometimes portrayed. It was a universal, revolutionary, theocracy, Trotskyite rather than Stalinist in its expansionism. The caliphs thought in global terms. In the desert castle of Qusayr Amra, fifty miles to the east of Amman, a fresco, datable to the reign of al-Walid I (705–15) depicts the enemies of Islam. The major enemies were the Byzantine emperor, the shah (in exile at Kucha), and the Chinese emperor, his protector. The minor enemies were the Visigothic king of Spain, the Negus of Abyssinia, and, most likely, because the fresco is damaged, the ruler of Sind.

In this new world institution, Central Asia was both passive and active. It was passive in that, under the universal caliphate, it received its first wave of Islamization. It was active in that, once incorporated into the universal caliphate, it contributed powerfully to its evolution.

The Islamic conquest of Central Asia was hesitant. Even today Islam has a frontier with Buddhism in Zungharia as in Kashmir. The campaign began grandly. Al-Hallaj, al-Walid's viceroy in Mesopotamia, sent Qutayba across the Oxus to conquer the shah, Muhammed Qasim across the Indus to conquer the ruler of Sind, the two to meet up in China, whose governorship was promised to whichever arrived first. Yet the results were meagre. In India, though Sind was conquered, it remained a bridgehead contained by the Pratiharas to the north and the Rashtrakutas to the south. In Central Asia, though Muslim occupation was extended from Merv and Balkh to Bokhara, Khiva and Samarkand, the T'ang empire with its Turkish and Tibetan allies remained the predominant power. Even when the Turks and Tibetans were anti T'ang, they continued to impede the Muslims, as in the battle of the 'day of thirst' in Ferghana in 724. After the Talas river battle in 751, indeed, Tibet assumed the role of leading anti Muslim power, since the T'ang, thanks to the diplomacy of Li Mi, was now allied with the caliphate. Harun al-Rashid's long war with the Tibetans, however, showed no decisive result. Part of Afghanistan was converted, but Nuristan remained pagan till the nineteenth century, and to the east the frontier continued jagged.

The relative failure was not accidental. The paradox, noted by Beckwith, that decentralized Central Asia resisted Islam better than centralized Byzantium or Persia, can be resolved.[29] First, sociologically, early Islam was a protest against centralization, a *club des sans clubs* of outsiders. Where there was no centralized empire, as in Northern India and Central Asia, Islam had to find an alternative sociology. Second, as Bulliet has shown, in these areas, Islam reached the limit of the one hump pack camel, its transportation base to date. In Central Asia and northwest India, the cart had never been replaced by the camel, since two-hump Bactrians were as convenient in draft as in baggage. Beyond Iran, Islam had to adapt itself to a different ecology. Third, politically, the army of Khorasan had to look over its shoulder to Baghdad and Damascus, and must often have felt it was not given sufficient support. No wonder that many were attracted to Shia, to an alternative dynasty, or, eventually, to local autonomy.

Yet if Islam failed in Central Asia as a tornado, it succeeded as a glacier. Gradually it found its new sociology, ecology and politics. From the bridgeheads, support was slowly built up, group by group, oligarchy by oligarchy, especially under the Samanids of Bokhara (874–999), themselves descendants of a Zoroastrian noble of Balkh. In 814, the 'Tibetan' King of Kabul was converted, in the tenth century, Gilgit was captured by the Ismailis, in the fourteenth century, Baltistan by the Twelver Shia. A Bhotia Islam was created. North of the mountains, some of the Qarluk of the Semirechie were converted in the ninth century, the Qarakhanid Ilek khans of Kirghizia and Kashgar followed around 960, the Kazakhs in the fourteenth century. A Turkish Islam was created. Within the oases themselves, Islam ceased to be monoglot and spoke, and wrote, Persian as well as Arabic. Central Asia was now able to take an active role, especially from the reign of Caliph al-Mamun (809–33) whose capital was at Merv.

As active, Central Asia made contributions to three major developments in the Islamic community.[30] First, via its supply of soldiers to the slave armies of the caliphate, particularly developed by al-Mutasim (833–42) the founder of Samarra, Central Asia contributed not only to the rise of Turkish Islam as against Arab Islam, but also, more generally, to a split between military and civil society, power and ideology. This split subverted the universal caliphate, which rested on the unity of these elements. Subsequently, Islamdom oscillated between Shia efforts to remove the division and Sunni attempts to justify it. Neither proved satisfactory in Muslim terms.

Second, Central Asia played a notable part in another disjuncture in Islamdom, that between religion and secular culture. Here a principal figure was the poet Firdausi (941–1020), the author of the *Shah-nama*. Firdausi was born at Tus, the ancient counterpart to modern Meshed, under the Samanids. He wrote his poem at the court of the slave-descended Mahmud of Ghazna, and, on the non-fulfilment of his contract, fled to the protection of the caliph at Baghdad, where he wrote *Yusuf and Zuleika*. He subsequently returned to Tus where he died in bad odour with the clergy. Firdausi is often regarded as a Persian nationalist, puffing the days of the Sassanids, while preferring to ignore the realities of Islam, especially Turkish Islam. In fact, his work is more subtle. Its background is Central Asian: a civilized middle kingdom, set between Turan to the north, the realm of Caesar to the west, the empire of China to the east, India to the south. Though he experienced the usual vicissitudes of Islamic court life, there is little reason to doubt Firdausi's commitment to Islam, or his basic harmony with the society in which he lived. What his life and work asserted, however, and were taken by contemporaries and posterity to assert, was the existence of values other than religious and political ones: the secular values of a heroic, but cultivated, aristocracy. Firdausi's ideal was not incompatible with Islam or Islamic courts. Indeed, it presupposed them as a source of stability and patronage, but they were not its inspiration. Firdausi was a Renaissance man. It was his misfortune, and the misfortune of the many in Central Asia who subsequently pursued his ideal, that such self generating secular values were less sustainable in Islamdom than in Christendom.

Third, Central Asia played a notable part in a specific form of the disjuncture of religion and secular culture: the rise, but relative failure, of philosophy in the Islamic world. Here the principal figure was Avicenna (980–1037), ibn Sina, the first systematic Muslim philosopher. He was born in Samanid Bokhara, lived part of his life in Khiva, and, like Firdausi, had to flee from the intolerable patronage of that oppressive culture-vulture, Mahmud of Ghazna. He died at Hamadan in western Persia. Philosophy in Islam was an affair of the frontier: Central Asia in one direction, Spain in another. On these frontiers Islam had to argue. In Central Asia, philosophy was associated with the *medreses*. These were colleges of higher Islamic studies, which possibly derived from the preceding Buddhist monastic schools of philosophy. Caliph al-Mamun, most Central Asian of the Abbasids, both at Merv and Baghdad, patronized Mutazilite rationalism to counter Sunni legalism and Shia oracularism. Among the Central Asian scholars he brought to the west, was al-Khwarazmi (780–850), the translation of whose algebra was to be the principle source of 'Arabic' numerals in Christendom. Philosophy in Baghdad, developed by Alfarabi, himself of Central Asian origin, on the basis of earlier Syriac translations of Plato and Aristotle, was returned to Central Asia under the Samanids, where it was eagerly seized on and systematized by Avicenna. A medical man and polymath, Avicenna's principal contribution to philosophy was the distinction in metaphysics between existence and essence: the whether and the what. This distinction allowed a more rational discussion of the relation between God, in whom existence and essence were identical, and creatures, in whom they were not. It was, however, a distinction and an enterprise more appreciated in Christendom than Islam. Both Alfarabi and Avicenna were attacked strongly by al-Ghazzali in his *Incoherentia Philosophorum*. Islam did not argue for long, while Christendom continued to do so.

THE NESTORIAN CONNECTION

A striking fact of the period 750 to 1100 was the conversion of nomadic pastoralists to hitherto exclusively sedentary religions. Thus the Khazars were converted to Judaism around 740.[31] In 781 a king of the Turks requested missionaries from the Nestorian patriarch of Baghdad and eighty were sent by the archbishop of Samarkand and the bishops of Bukhara and Tashkent.[32] Some Qarluk Turks adopted Islam in the ninth century and the Qarakhanids made it their state religion in 960. In 763 the Uighurs, then still mainly a nomadic people, adopted Manichaeism. In 864 the Volga Bulgars were reported as Christian, in 922 as Muslim. In 1077, Abdishu (slave of Jesus), archbishop of Merv, informed the Nestorian patriarch that there were 200,000 converts among the Kereits of central Mongolia including their khan. By the thirteenth century, Nestorian Christianity was widely diffused among the Naimans of Zungharia to the west. To the east, both the Khitan and the Tanguts became fervent Buddhists though in scripts different from that of the Chinese. Everywhere the steppe assumed a sedentary patina, and of a particular kind. For in three of the above cases, the Khazars, the Uighurs and the Turco-Mongols, the religion adopted was not the orthodox mainstream of its sedentary homeland neighbours, but a heresy, or a countercurrent, of an international kind: Judaism, Manichaeism, Nestorian Christianity.

The most important of these conversions was to Nestorianism. L. N. Gumilev has recently argued that, while the story of Prester John cannot be taken literally, it does reflect an institutional situation in Inner Asia. The Nestorian connection, as it may be termed to indicate something more integrated and institutionalized than the Nestorian communion, was a world institution. At its widest extent, it embraced both Western Eurasia and East Asia, both steppe and oasis, and even had prolongations in Africa, where Ethiopia, contrary to expectation, had Nestorians as well as Monophysites.[33] Marco Polo is witness to the position of the Nestorian patriarch as *papa alterius orbis*, catholicos of the east. He wrote:

> I should explain that the archbishop of Socotra has nothing to do with the Pope at Rome, but is subject to an archbishop

who lives at Baghdad. The archbishop of Baghdad sends out the archbishop of this island; and he also sends out many others to different parts of the world, just as the Pope does. And these clergy and prelates owe obedience not to the Church of Rome, but to this great prelate of Baghdad whom they have as their Pope.[34]

At the height of his influence around 1000, the patriarch had jurisdiction over twenty archbishops and between two hundred and two hundred and fifty bishops. These included sees in Merv, Herat, Samarkand, Kashgar, Tangut and Peking, as well as Mosul, Damascus, Jerusalem and South India.[35] Nestorianism, though international, was triply a countercurrent: a Christian heresy, a non-Muslim *millet* and a proscribed religion in China.

The context of these conversions may be sought in three sets of circumstance. First, the steppe had been under pressure from the sedentarists. The empire of the Kok Turks, which had embraced most of it east of the Caspian, had been dissolved by T'ang arms and diplomacy. The Khazars were losing ground to the caliphate in the Caucasus, but feared to become simple clients of the basileus. The Uighurs, thanks to the diplomacy of Li Mi, were allies of the T'ang, but were threatened by the Tibetans who took Urumchi in 789. In the Far West, Charlemagne overthrew the Avars in 799. Everywhere the isolation of the steppe was being broken down. Second, existing institutions proved inadequate to absorb what had been opened. The Buddhist ecumene lost its universalizing rationalism and succumbed to parochial irrationalisms: Tantric occultism, Pure Land evangelism, Ch'an illuminism, neo-Hinayana fundamentalism. T'ang cosmopolitanism was shaken by the provincialist rebellion of An Lu-shan and by the new ethnocentric Confucianism of Han Yü.[36] The universal caliphate surrendered its spiritual authority to the ulema, its political power to sultans and resigned itself to being a point of arbitration in an *Islam des patries*. The steppe, suddenly colonized, was equally suddenly decolonized. Third, as the colonial order disintegrated, the merchant communities which had provided east–west links within it: the Jewish Radhanites, the Nestorian Syrians, the Manichaean Sogdians; had to find new customers and patrons. They found them in a new north–south trade which linked the steppe to the sedentary world, and provided it with the right degree of contact, both commercial and cultural. For steppe rulers, and more particularly their women folk, who were the chief consumers of goods commercial and cultural, adoption of a foreign yet international heterodoxy combined outside contact at the level of society, with continued independence at the level of the state. Conversion to Judaism, Manichaeism and Nestorianism was an expression of voluntary recolonization.

The consequences were considerable, at least in the case of Nestorianism. For Judaism on the Kipchak steppe did not long survive the fall of Itil to the Rus in 965 and Manichaeism among the Uighurs was overlaid by Buddhism as they sedentarized after 840. Nestorianism, however, was boosted by the arrival in Central Asia in the early 1130s of the exiled Khitan empire-builder Yeh-lü Ta-shih. Yeh-lü Ta-shih had no wish to be a Prester John, an eschatological Christian King. By background he was a Buddhist. Most of his initial supporters were shamanists, for whom he had the appropriate sacrifices performed. The empire of Kara Khitai he constructed was religiously mixed and ideologically tolerant. If he was inspired by anything, it was by the afterglow of T'ang cosmopolitanism which had already animated Li Yuan-hao, the Tangut founder of Hsi-hsia. Yet there were enough Nestorians in his state to make it inevitable that, in conflict with the Muslim Seljuks, he would be cast as a Christian king, to the extent that he gave his son the eschatological name of Elijah (I-lieh). Otto of Freising did not invent the story of Prester John, nor, as Gumilev suggests, did the Templars as propaganda for the Second Crusade. It was a Central Asian gloss on Yeh-lü Ta-shih's defeat of Seljuk sultan Sanjar at the battle of Qatawan in September 1141. The gloss projected a future: a Christian counter-revolution against Islam under steppe leadership within the Nestorian connection. In the meantime, the Nestorians provided the steppe with a corps of literate people, a supratribal sense of identity, and horizons wider than Central Asia. These innovations not only laid the foundations for new institutions on the steppe, but encompassed them with explosive conditions. Those institutions and that explosion will form the subject of the next chapter.

Part II
Central Asia as Active

3 The Mongolian Explosion and the Basic Information Circuit, 1200–1300

World history, like history generally, it seems, began with a big bang: the Mongolian explosion of Chinggis Khan and two generations of his successors in the thirteenth century. As in some cosmological models, too, the explosion, which originated outside the area in Mongolia, was inflated to fireball dimensions by its passage through Central Asia. A Mongolian explosion became a Central Asian super-explosion which united Mongols and Turks in an unprecedented mobilization of nomadic cavalry. This mobilization then launched itself against the homelands of China, Islam, India and Europe, with varying degrees of penetration. Even those parts of the world not penetrated by the Mongols were affected by them. Thus, by being spared the Mongols, Western Europe, Mamluk Egypt and Japan were given their chance in their respective geopolitical spheres. Moreover, beyond those spheres, both the Christian expansions into America and the Islamic expansion into Black Africa and Southeast Asia, may be related to the effects of the explosion. The Mongolian explosion broke down barriers. It was the first global event. It ended isolation. As it cooled, there was produced out of its initial confusion, the first of the permanent world institutions: the basic information circuit. Contained in its memory, was both a new conceptualization of the world and a wealth of intelligence about other places and peoples, unexampled in the ancient or medieval worlds of any of the primary civilizations before. This chapter, and its four successors will consist of three parts: events in Central Asia, their impact in the homelands, and their role in the construction of a world institution.

THE MONGOLIAN EXPLOSION IN CENTRAL ASIA

The Mongolian explosion did not begin in Central Asia. It began in the east of the Mongolian People's Republic in the pastures between the Onon and Kerulen, tributaries, direct or indirect, of the Amur. Its force was first directed not west, but south against the Turco-Tibetan Tangut kingdom of Hsi-Hsia in Chinghai, and east against the Sino-Jurchen empire of Chin in Manchuria and north China.[1] It was, however, only in Central Asia that the Mongolian explosion acquired full power and assumed its character as a global event. Two aspects need to be considered: the course of events and the reasons why.

Course of Events

The name Mongol referred originally only to one small group among the eastern steppe nomads more generally termed Tatars. The *Yeke Mongghol Ulus*, the Great Mongol State, began as a tribal confederation. The term tribal is question-begging. The precise mix of kinship, pseudo-kinship, clientage and function in the various groups on the steppe is obscure. So too is the process whereby Chinggis confederated them. Much of the evidence is provided by a single, difficult text, the *Yüan Ch'ao Pi-shih* or *Secret History of the Mongols*.[2] It is difficult, first, because, although originally written in the middle of the thirteenth century in Mongolian using the Uighur alphabetical script, it is only extant in an interlinear version of the Ming period, in which the Mongolian, now written in Chinese characters used phonetically, is accompanied by a gloss in Chinese. If the text is doubtful, so too is the author's intent. The common view has been that the work was an official history for the use of the governing class, restricted rather than secret. Gumilev, however, has suggested that it was a piece of propaganda by a group of conservative grandees, old companions of Chinggis, but now out of place in the courts of his sons. The book was intended to show that it was they and not the dynasty which had made the state.[3] If exegesis is divided, so too is hermeneutic. Barthold and Vladimirtsov saw Chinggis as the leader of a counter-revolution, of an aristocracy, which accepted radical political reconstruction to save its social predominance from the insurgency of commoners. Gumilev, however, sees Chinggis as the leader

of a meritocracy, 'people of long will' – commoners, clan outsiders, declassés, even slaves – who wanted to enter the aristocracy rather than subvert it, and did so via the political and
military reconstruction which followed Chinggis' election as
Khan in 1182 and Great Khan in 1206.

Chinggis' unification of the Tatars took place in three stages.
First, he reestablished his father's ascendancy over a group of
eastern *oboghs* or clans, which had collapsed on his death in
accordance with the principles of blood tanistry. This he did,
against the clan elders, by building up a personal retinue *nüker*
of marginals and outsiders. Next, in a long period of in-fighting
between 1182 and 1202, which included as much politicking as
actual fighting, Chinggis established first his ascendancy within,
and then his rule over the Kereit Tatars of Central Mongolia,
hitherto the predominant element on the steppe. Third, between 1204 and 1208, he extended his rule to the Tatars of the
West and North, the Naiman and the Merkits. Chinggis' state
now included the northern parts at least of Zungharia. From
1209, it also included, as a satellite, the now largely sedentarized
Buddhist Uighur kingdom of Bishbalik (Urumchi), the Turfan
depression and some of the oases of the Kansu panhandle.

It was friction between the Uighurs and the Tanguts in this
last area which led Chinggis into his first campaign outside the
steppe, that against Hsi-Hsia in 1209. It was not particularly
successful. The Mongol light cavalry defeated the Tangut armoured knights, but could not capture their capital Ninghsia,
which defended itself by flooding its irrigation channels. In
1210 the Hsi-Hsia ruler sent a daughter to Chinggis and the two
states concluded an alliance. In 1211, Chinggis embarked on
his second campaign outside the steppe, that against the Jurchen
Chin. Though the Mongols had grievances against the Jurchen
in eastern Mongolia, it was not these which occasioned the war,
but the alliance with the Tanguts, with whom the Chin had long
been in conflict in Kansu. Again, the campaign was not particularly successful. Though this time the Mongols did capture the
Chin northern capital of Yen-ching (Peking), it was largely
through the assistance of the Khitan, who took the opportunity
to revolt against their former vassals and current masters. The
Chin state was not destroyed. It simply recentred itself around
its southern capital of Kaifeng. In his first two campaigns outside the steppe, Chinggis appears less as a conqueror than as a

mercenary. Had he died in 1215, he would have left a mark no greater than that of the Tibetan emperors of the seventh and eighth centuries. Moreover, his state, despite its novel bureaucrat elements, would probably have dissolved in accordance with the principles of blood tanistry. No doubt this was what the Hsi-Hsia and Chin rulers expected.

The position was changed radically by Chinggis' campaigns in Central Asia between 1218 and 1223 against first the kingdom of Kuchlug, the usurper of Kara Khitai, and then against the empire of Khwarazmshah Muhammed and his son Jalal ad-Din. By these campaigns, not merely were two mighty states completely destroyed, but the Mongol war machine added to itself the manpower and horsepower of Zungharia, Semirechie and Central Kazakhstan. Among the sedentarists to the south, through the recruitment of military engineers, sappers and disposable labour, it acquired the capacity to take cities, not just episodically, as with Yen-ching, but regularly. Moreover, the entry into Central Asia put the Mongols into a new ideological perspective. To his Muslim enemies, Chinggis could represent himself as the Wrath of God, part of the Nestorian or even Zoroastrian eschatology, a crusade come out of the east. To his Turco-Mongolian supporters, Chinggis who was not personally a Christian though many of his family married Nestorians, could represent his empire as lived epic, a version of the Alexander Romance which was known on the steppe. Alternatively, the conquests could be seen as a colossal secular trip parallel to the drug-induced *ecstasis* of the shaman. Both in material and in morale, the Mongolian explosion was inflated in Central Asia into a capacity for total war and universal conquest.

Eastern Turkestan, the remainder of Zungharia and most of Semirechie came into the hands of the Mongols as a result of the campaign against Kuchlug, 1216–1218.[4] Kuchlug was the son of the Naiman Khan Tayang who had opposed the extension of the Chinggisid confederation to Western Mongolia. After his father's defeat, he fled, no doubt with a considerable number of nomad supporters, to the court of the gurkhan at Balasaghun on the Chu river below Issik Kul. Here he soon enjoyed high favour. At this time, Kara Khitai was subject to considerable strains, both between its nomad and sedentary sectors, and within them, between rival religious communities: Muslim, Nestorian, Buddhist. Kuchlug first supported the gurkhan, but then joined with his enemies to partition the empire with Muhammed of Khwarazm. In the east, Kuchlug, originally a Nestorian, turned Buddhist and attempted to consolidate by the forcible conversion of both Muslims and Christians. It was their grievances and appeals which gave Chinggis his opportunity of intervention. Kuchlug's state fell apart at the first touch and the Mongol troops of Jebe-noyon were generally welcomed as liberators in both the oases and the steppe. Paradoxically, Chinggis' first real conquest was a relatively peaceful one.

Western Turkestan, the remainder of Semirechie, and the Central Kazakh steppe came into the hands of the Mongols as a result of the campaign against the Khwarazmshah Muhammed, 1218–1220[5]. The brief Khorezmian empire was an impressive structure. It stretched from the Tigris to the Syr, but it was jerry-built and based on too narrow foundations. Given time, it might have consolidated itself as an eastern version of the Ottoman empire, but Muhammed unwisely provoked Chinggis to war by interfering with trade and executing ambassadors. To Muhammed, Chinggis must have seemed a second Yeh-lu Ta-Shih, a new gurkhan. He had just disposed of one gurkhan, should he not dispose of another before he had time to consolidate, and thus prove himself superior to Seljuk Sultan Sanjar in similar circumstances? However taken, the decision was disastrous. Muhammed's empire, while it did not fall apart as Kuchlug's had done, proved incapable of resisting the Mongol blitzkrieg. This time the conquest was anything but peaceful. A battle was fought in the upper Syr valley, Khojend and Otrar, lower down, were destroyed. In the Amu valley, Bokhara, though it surrendered, was sacked, depopulated and set on fire, and Samarkand, higher up the Zerafshan, was similarly treated. Urgench, the original base of the Khwarazmshah, was more systematically devastated, the river being diverted to flow over the debris. This most decisive of Chinggis' campaigns initiated a new style of mobile and destructive warfare. As the explosion inflated, the civilized world, as represented by eastern Islam, was now thoroughly alarmed.

Afghan Turkestan, and the transhumant country to the south, came into the hands of the Mongols as a result of the campaign against the Khwarazmshah's son Jalal ad-Din, 1220–1222[6], This second campaign had a different character from the first. Although Jalal ad-Din was acting as the heir of his father, what he was leading was no longer an elite Turkish tribal military oligarchy, but a mass Persian urban cilivian *Jihad* supported by Afghan mountain *mujahidin*. The Mongol campaign, therefore, was directed against the civilian population, especially the sedentarists. It was prosecuted now by calculated horror, an attempt to blot out urban life, extermination rather than simple depopulation. This was the treatment meted out to Balkh, Bamiyan, Herat, Merv and Nishapur. It is graphically described in the pages of Juvaini, no doubt on the testimony of eyewitnesses (Juvaini was born in 1226 and wrote in 1252):

> Therefore Chingiz-Khan commanded that the population of Balkh, small and great, few and many, both men and women, should be driven out onto the plain and divided up according to the usual custom into hundreds and thousands to be put to the sword . . . When Chingiz-Khan returned from Peshawar and arrived at Balkh, he found a number of fugitives who had remained hidden in nooks and crannies . . . He commanded them all to be killed . . . And wherever a wall was left standing, the Mongols pulled it down and for a second time wiped out all traces of culture from the region.[7]

If not immediately massacred, as at Merv and Nishapur, the civilian population of one city was driven on to become a human battering ram against the next. No doubt there were always some survivors, and, except at Bamiyan and Balkh, urban life, eventually revived, but it was warfare of unprecedent ferocity for the middle ages. In Eastern Turkestan, Western Turkestan and Afghan Turkestan, the Mongolian explosion inflated itself to a fireball, attempts to quench it simply adding fuel to its flames.

In Chinggis' time, the Mongolian explosion was not yet a global event. When he died in 1227 during a successful campaign against Hsi-Hsia which had refused to join him in the West, its conquests were still confined to Middle Asia. What made it a global event, was that these conquests were pursued for two more generations by Chinggis' sons and grandsons to include large parts of the homelands within the Mongols' embrace. In 1227, many must have expected that the conquests would cease and that the *Yeke Monggol Ulus* would dissolve. In fact, its institutional character already made this unlikely.

The reasons why behind the course of events show how this was so.

The Reasons Why

Three things call for explanation: Why was there an explosion, why was the attack so strong, why was the defence so weak?

Why was there an explosion? First, there is the explanation in terms of Chinggis himself. This was the view of the Mongols as expressed in the *Secret History*, though possibly, if Gumilev is correct, with reservations in favour of his early companions. Similarly, Juvaini and the Islamic tradition, influenced by Firdausi, saw Chinggis as a second Alexander: the Syr battle being Issus, the pursuit of Muhammed that of Darius III, the destruction of Balkh that of Persepolis, etc. Writers in the West too have wished to see the Mongol khan as a *grand chef*, a military leader of genius.[8] In fact, Chinggis was a canny steppe politician rather than a great captain. He was semi-retired at the outset of the campaign against the Khwarazmshah, which was planned by his *keshig* or general staff cum commissariat. Chinggis was a sober man, not a charismatic leader, though admittedly in old age, astonished by his own success, he construed his career as divine predestination to world power: but a second Cyrus rather than a second Alexander.

Second, there is the climatic explanation: the Mongols were driven from the steppe by ecological change. Exponents of this view, initiated by Ellsworth Huntington have, however, been divided as to what this change was and how it operated.[9] Huntington believed the change was increasing desiccation. It operated by injuring the nomad economy. It reduced the amount of pasture and number of animals and so drove the nomads to seek livelihood outside the steppe. This view is not supported by the best climatic history. Moreover, it does not explain why the nomads moved south rather than north, since increased desiccation would have turned the south Siberian marshes into good grazing. Gareth Jenkins, better supported by climatic history, thought the injury to the nomad economy was done by a period of colder and wetter weather, which increased the *dzud* phenomenon. Gumilev, however, while agreeing the colder and wetter weather, believed that it benefited the nomad economy. It increased the amount of pasture and the number of animals and so made raid more effective than trade. All the climatic explanations, though, have to explain the fact that the Great Invasion of the thirteenth century was preceded by the Little Invasions of the tenth to twelfth centuries: the Khitan, Tanguts, Jurchen and Kara-Khitai; which took place in what must be admitted to be different climatic conditions. Neither facts (were animals diminishing or increasing?) nor interpretations (do nomads invade when they are badly-off or well-off?) can be regarded as established. Moreover, Le Roy Ladurie's law, that climatic fluctuation only intensifies conjuncture but does not initiate it, still stands.

Third, there is the institutional explanation. Its leading exponent was Karl A. Wittfogel, more convincing here than in his macrohydraulic theory of Chinese bureaucratic empire.[10] Wittfogel emphasized the novelty of the Mongolian explosion and its discontinuity with previous, less explosive, nomadic empires, such as those of the Hsiung-nu, Huns, Avars, Kok Turks, etc. He quoted Sui emperor Yang-ti about his Turkish enemies that 'their troops were not drawn up in orderly ranks', a contrast to what all contemporaries reported of the Mongols.[11] The difference, he argued, was due to the introduction to the steppe by Chinggis of the *ordo* system. The *ordo*, from which the word horde is derived, was a reorganization of nomad society out of its natural kinship or pseudo-kinship groups into decimal units – 10s, 100s, 1000s, 10,000s – headed either by members of old aristocratic clans or new, meritocratic, 'men of long will'. The *ordo* came to the steppe directly from the Khitan Liao, indirectly from the Uighurs, many of whom Chinggis incorporated into his central secretariat. The introduction of the *ordo* made the nomadic state more bureaucratic and gave it greater purchase on its society. Nomad society was anarchic, whether one takes the Masson Smith or Fletcher view of the state on the steppe. The *ordo* counterbalanced this anarchism and gave the nomads discipline both on and off the battlefield. It meant that campaigns and battles could be planned, that success was no longer dissipated in haphazard looting, that pressure could be kept up remorselessly till total victory. What the party was to modern totalitarianism, the *ordo* was to the Mongolian explosion. Its introduction was Chinggis' principal contribution to Mongol power. He was a Lenin rather than an Alexander.

Fourth, there is the ideological explanation, emphasized latterly by Gumilev. The partial conversion of steppe peoples to sedentary religions, albeit heretical and marginal, gave them new links to the sedentary world and a less particularist perspective. It meant that the nomads could figure in the dreams and nightmares of others and could see themselves as part of universal dramas: epic, shamanist, Zoroastrian, and, especially, Nestorian. Chinggis was not a Christian. He and his companions held to the old Mongol henotheism of Heaven, Tengri, sometimes named Qormusda, Ahura Mazda. But many of his supporters, and particularly their wives, were Christians, and Muhammed the Khwarazmshah deliberately billed Chinggis as a second Prester John, when he challenged him to another, and it was hoped different, Qatawan. Universalist ideology, crusade and counter-crusade, *jihad* and anti-*jihad*, was the field from which the Mongolian explosion inflated itself to the proportions of 1222.

Why was the attack so strong? First, superiority of horsepower. Already in the seventh century Sui Yang-ti had noted that 'The reason for the superiority of the Turks is that they rely primarily on mounted archers'.[12] Calculating from later figures, it may be estimated that in 1200, Inner Asia contained half the world's horse population of around twenty million. By 1220, as a result of the unification of Mongolia, Semirechie and Kazakhstan, most of these were controlled by the Mongol state. Mongol armies were not large: 100,000 in a major expedition; and they were not specially well armed. What they had was remounts, 10–20 per soldier, which gave them mobility on campaign and staying power on the battlefield. The Mongol armies were not invincible. Masson Smith has indicated their limitations: amateur character, short-range bows, dependence on pasture, delays imposed by grazing and the needs of camp followers.[13] Yet, against equally amateurish, unprepared enemies, without abundant remounts, the Mongol blitzkrieg, able to move twice the speed of sedentary armies (thirty miles a day) and on the battlefield to charge again and again, was highly effective. Second, there was calculated terror against the sedentary population, so that, as in the Holocaust and the Gulag, it allowed itself to be massacred. Juvaini describes how at Merv, the Mongols decided that 'the whole population, including the women and children, should be killed, and no one, whether woman or man be spared. The people of Merv were then distributed among the soldiers and levies, and, in short, to each man was alloted the execution of three or four hundred persons'.[14] Jalal ad-Din might argue that, though the Khwarazmshah had lost a battle, Iran had not lost the war, but the civilian population was too cowed to listen.

Why was the defence so weak? Behind inferiority in horsepower and civilian demoralization was political division. Barthold emphasized this in his account of the fall of the Khwarazmshah.[15] The shah was a Turk, most of his subjects were Iranians. He was only the second ruler of his dynasty, whose base was a clan and a city. He was at loggerheads with his mother, the royal aristocracy, and rival clan chiefs. He had quarrelled with both the caliph and the leading dervishes. He was known to be both anti Christian and anti Buddhist. Islamic society had divorced itself from secular politics. The state lacked legitimacy and only gained it in a *jihad* which was declared against the Mongols too late. Iranians thought they could sit out a Turco-Mongol war. Similarly, Kuchlug's state was both new and divided between Christians, Muslims and Buddhists. In North China, the Chin were a conquest dynasty who had not long displaced the Sung. In Chinghai, Hsi-Hsia represented Turks ruling over Tibetans. Nowhere was society fully behind the state. Rulers could not mobilize, had no reserves, and could not sustain defeats. States collapsed and society, directly attacked, became non-viable. As in the totalitarian revolutions of the twentieth century, there was a consequent flight from society, towards a new state which could only, in the circumstances, be that of the Mongols. The Mongols found collaborators. Thus Juvaini, son of a long line of financial administrators from Nishapur in Khorasan, found himself enrolled in the new Mongol regime. He wrote his history in Persian primarily for his fellow collaborators to explain what had happened and to justify it in Islamic terms. In Nishapur even cats and dogs had been killed by the Mongols. The will of Allah was sometimes hard to understand.

THE MONGOLIAN EXPLOSION IN THE HOMELANDS

Inflated by its passage through Central Asia, the Mongolian explosion was further inflated when, in the time of Chinggis' sons and grandsons, it passed into the homelands of China, Islam, Europe and India. This inflation was due, not as the earlier one to an increase in the scale and ferocity of war, but to the mobilization of men, money and material from the conquered territories. This mobilization was pursued particularly by Chinggis' grandson, the Great Khan Möngke (1251–59).[16] It gave a new impetus to the Mongolian explosion, which carried it far into the homelands: the whole of China, two-thirds of Islam, half Europe, a slice of India and much of peninsular Southeast Asia. If one considers people rather than area, more was conquered by his successors than by Chinggis. It was the interconnection of people which laid the foundations for the first of the permanent world institutions, the basic information circuit.

In passing from the heartland to the homelands, the Mongol machine changed its character. First, it had now not only to organize nomad war, but also to administer sedentary territory. Second, even in 1227 but still more by 1300, the empire was now so large, that time and distance made some element of subsidiarity inevitable. Nevertheless, efforts were made to maintain the empire in at least some respects as a single unit, and these achieved a surprising measure of success down to the beginning of the fourteenth century. The empire did not lose its unity with Chinggis. On the contrary, especially under Möngke, it acquired greater solidarity than ever before.

Chinggis died in 1227. In accordance with his wishes, his second son Ögödei was elected Great Khan at a *khuraltai*, or assembly of notables, held in 1229. This was a striking departure from both blood tanistry and sedentary primogeniture. At the same time, the empire was divided formally between Chinggis' four sons. Empire, but what was it? Fletcher described it as a polity imposing a *pax*. It consisted of a score of Mongol *oboghs* or clans subsumed into decimal units, of which the largest was the tumen or 10,000, their grazing lands, and a skeleton central secretariat and general staff. This last controlled an army in occupation of wide sedentary areas in Central Asia which were used for looting and requisitioning. It was less a state than a consortium.

The formal division followed nomad rules of inheritance. Each son (or his heirs, for Jochi was dead) received a group of people from each clan, his *ulus*; a corresponding amount of

grazing land, his *nutugh*; and a right to a share, *inju*, in the still
to be collectively administered spoils of the sedentary areas –
things, people, taxes. Ögödei, as Great Khan, received not only
his own *ulus*, *nutugh* and *inju*, but also the central secretariat
and general staff, with the right and duty of administering and
extending the conquered possessions in the common interests
of the consortium. Geographically too, the division followed
steppe practice. Tolui, the youngest, as *otchigin* or hearth guardian, received the original nucleus: northeast Mongolia and the
core of the army. Ögödei came next with northwest Mongolia
and Zungharia. Chaghadai, the second eldest, received
Semirechie and Central Kazakhstan. Jochi, the eldest, was assigned the lands of the Far West: the Kipchak steppe and the
pastures along the Volga. The south: the sedentary lands of
north China, the three Turkestans and Khorasan, remained the
common possession of the empire. Under Ögödei (1229–41)
and his son and successor Güyüg (1246–48), central administration was lax, and was possibly in danger of breaking down. It
was reasserted, however, by Möngke, with standardized procedures for census, taxation, mobilization and communication
throughout the empire now greatly expanded into the homelands. This expansion was begun by Ögödei, surcharged by
Möngke, and finalized by his brother, and successor as Great
Khan, Khubilai (1260–94).

China

In terms of people, especially educated people, the conquest of
China was the greatest achievement of the Mongolian explosion. It was as if Soviet power had gone on from the occupation
of Eastern Europe to that first of Western Europe and then that
of the United States.

The conquest took place in three stages. First, under Ögödei,
an amiable, spendthrift but effective alcoholic, the still substantial remains of the Jurchen Chin kingdom, with a population of
20–30 million, were absorbed. It was not an easy campaign. The
Mongols were aided both by the Southern Sung and by divisions within Chin. Some of the Jurchen elite had sinicized,
others maintained identity through a separate script, and some
favoured joining the Mongol consortium. Sinification had not
gone far enough to conciliate the Chinese, whose hostility ex-

pressed itself in the new Ch'uan-chen movement of Taoism. Already in Chinggis' time, the Mongols attempted to win over this movement in the person of its leader, the adept Ch'ang-ch'un. Kaifeng, the Chin capital, finally fell after a long siege in 1234. Second, under Möngke, a dour contrast to his uncle, though hard-drinking and still more effective, the Mongols occupied the northern and more populous half of Szechwan, in a difficult and inconclusive campaign against Southern Sung between 1257 and 1259. The sophisticated Sung defence, based on walled cities and river power, proved hard to penetrate. In August 1259, besieging the key river junction of Ho-chou, Möngke, along with many of his army, died of dysentery or cholera. Third, under Khubilai, who combined features of both his brother and uncle, Great Khan now but facing rebellion from the heartland, the Mongols conquered Southern Sung in a long and hard fought campaign between 1268 and 1279. Though the Mongol army could now draw on Muslim military engineers and Chinese explosives, its victory was due as much to divisions within the Sung as its own strength. Resistance was subverted by bureaucratic factionalism, reluctance to pay for high tech defence, the defection of the fleet, tension between town and country, the personality of the Sung prime minister Chia Ssu-tao. Its greatest achievement, the conquest of Southern Sung showed that the Mongolian explosion was losing force.

The Yüan dynasty, the government established by the Mongols in China, was a mass of contradictions.[17] One of the most expensive regimes in Chinese history before the Communists; it may have absorbed fifty per cent of GNP; it made little difference to the Chinese economy. In origin a steppe regime, it moved away from nomadic light cavalry to heavy cavalry on the model of Iran and the T'ang, with the secession of the heartland. A centralized structure at the start, the regime fragmented into regional machines, so that foreigners like Marco Polo and Rashid al-Din regarded it as a collection of kingdoms rather than a single state. Hostile to the Confucian scholar gentry, who it excluded from power by discarding the examination system, and looking for support to non-Confucian clerks, Chinese Taoists and Tibetan Buddhists, the Yüan dynasty found that class its most loyal defender against populist sectarianism. International in personnel and expansionist in outlook, its activities were increasingly confined to China, whose language it did not bother to learn and among whose people it never found full acceptance.

In these contradictions Muslims from Central Asia played significant, generally civilian, roles. Along with the Christian Alans from the north Caucasus who were in charge of heavy cavalry, they were ranked as *se-mu* or assistant conquerors. They assisted especially in the central financial administration, in the *ortaq* or tax farming consortia, as trade commissioners in coastal cities, and as calendrical experts in the board of astronomy. Both Ögödei and his wife Töregene, who was regent from 1241 to 1246, had Muslim confidants. For twenty years Khubilai used Ahmad, a Muslim from Tashkent brought up in the *ordo* of his favourite wife, as his finance minister. He made his son Masud procurator of Hang-chou, the former Southern Sun capital and the largest city in the world. It was Muslim Uighurs Abd ur-Rahman and Sharif ad-Din who first put in bids to farm the taxes of north China. Non-Muslim Central Asians also played a part. Arigh Khaya, one of Khubilai's best generals and conqueror of Hu-kuang, was a Uighur. He was given one of the Great Khan's daughters in marriage and his son Esen Temur was one of the commanders in the second Vietnam expedition of 1287. Without Central Asian expertise, the Mongols might not have been able to mobilize the immense resources of their conquest.

Islam

The penetration of the Islamic homeland was the work of Möngke. In 1253, he dispatched his brother Hülegü to become the first Il-khan, or subordinate ruler, of Persia, 'from the Amu-darya to the extremities of Egypt', as Rashid al-Din put it. The expedition was thoroughly prepared, men and material being mobilized from the whole empire. Möngke, it was said, brought the world against the Abbasid caliphate. In 1257, Hülegü suppressed the Assassins of Alamut, the extremists of the Ismaili Shiites. He thus established his providential credentials in the eyes of Sunni orthodoxy, at least to Juvaini's satisfaction. Having masked his sacrilege, he captured Baghdad in January 1258 and ended the caliphate there. Next, he marched on Syria via the Mosul to Antioch corridor, capturing Aleppo in January

1260, Damascus in March. In April, Hülegü left the campaign on hearing of his brother's death at Ho-chou, leaving his general Kedbuqa to complete it with the capture of Jerusalem and the invasion of Egypt. It was not to be. On September 3, 1260, at the battle of Ayn Jalut, Kedbuqa, already in difficulties with supplies and pasture, was defeated by the heavy cavalry army of the Mamluks of Egypt. In itself Ayn Jalut was not very significant. The Il-khans remained the greatest power in the Levant, indeed were only at the beginning of their ascendancy. But it revealed the limitation of the Mongols in uncongenial terrain and against properly organized enemies. It showed, like Khubilai's campaign against the Sung, that the Mongolian explosion was losing its force.

Of all the homelands, Islam sustained the greatest institutional damage from the Mongols. First, the caliphate was crippled. Although restored by the Mamluks in Cairo and later transfered to Constantinople by the Ottomans, it never again held in the Islamic community the position it enjoyed before 1258. Nevertheless, the impact should not be exaggerated. The universal caliphate had long been eroded by jurists and sultans. It did not hold the place of the Papacy in Christianity, the centre whether by attraction or repulsion. With the rise of *ulema* and *sufis*, Islam had Judaized or Protestantized. It was a community rather than a church, which could live without a central institution. Second, internationalism was crippled. One reaction to the Mongols was the rise of Islamic political radicalism, associated first with the Syrian neo-Hanbalite jurist Ibn Taimiyya who died in 1328. If Juvaini argued that non-Muslim rulers could serve Providence, Ibn Taimiyya argued that Muslim rulers, indeed the *ulema*, could betray it. In opposition to both *ulema* and *sufi* traditionalism, he called for a radical re-Islamization of politics and the state, based on the letter of the Koran, a new fundamentalism. Among those targeted by the radicals as bad Muslims were many Central Asians in the service of the Il-Khans, conspicuous among them Juvaini, who became procurator of Baghdad. Muslim political radicalism rejected participation in a non-Islamic world order. The divisions it fostered and the attitudes it involved were possibly to do the Muslim community more damage in the long run than the injury done to the caliphate. Radicalism was not overly anti-modern, but its rejection of full participation in a non-Muslim

world order placed limitations on the amount of modernization it could absorb. Islam was artificially narrowed, excessively
politicized, and made less receptive than it need have been.[18]

Europe

Although Mongol forces brushed with the princes of Rus at the
battle of the Kalka river in 1223, the real penetration of Europe
by the Mongols came with the western expedition, organized by
Ögödei on a pan *ulus* basis, between 1235 and 1242. Batu, son
of Jochi, as Il-Khan of Kipchak, was nominal commander in
chief; Chaghadai sent his grandson Buri; the house of Tolui,
now headed by his formidable widow the Nestorian princess
Sorqoqtani Beki, sent Möngke; and Ögödei sent his heir, Güyüg.
But the real commander of both the *ulus* units and the core
contributed by the centre was the veteran marshal Subetai. The
campaign is usually seen as a walkover. Western Europe was
only saved from conquest by the death of Ögödei in 1241. True,
the Mongols took Ryazan in December 1237 and Vladimir in
February 1238; destroyed Kiev in December 1240; defeated
Henry of Silesia and the Teutonic Knights at Liegnitz on April
9, 1241 and Bela IV and the Templars at Mohi on the Sayo river
on April 11; and touched the Adriatic in 1242. Kiev, however,
was no longer the strength of Rus, the battles were hardly
fought and costly, and the Mongols, aware of the capabilities of
well-led townspeople, may not have found the view from the
Adriatic into Lombardy inviting. Batu will have realized that
only another pan *ulus* expedition would overcome the resistance of the West. Since he had already quarrelled with Güyüg
and Buri, that would be at the expense of his power as much as
that of the Europeans. No such expedition was launched. Batu
contented himself with what he had: predominance over northeastern Rus, which he consolidated in a limited, private campaign in 1252. Like Khubilai's campaign against the Sung, like
Ayn Jalut, Ögödei's western expedition showed that the Mongolian explosion was being slowed by external military resistance and internal political gravity. The knights had saved Europe.

The impact of the Tatar Yoke in Russia is controversial.[19] As
with the Yüan in China, one is tempted to say that it was heavy
but made little difference. Many of the changes attributed to it,
such as the shift in Russia's centre of gravity from Kiev to

Moscow, were already in train before it. Autocracy, in the sense of the personal power of a monarch in a bureaucracy, was not a Mongol practice. On the contrary, the Khans of the Golden Horde were increasingly ruled by an aristocratic council.[20] So the tsars cannot have learnt autocracy from them. No doubt, the 'special relationship' with Sarai was a factor in the rise of Moscow to preeminence among the principalities of Rus. It was probably less important, though, than Moscow's capture of the metropolitanate of Rus. In 1251, Metropolitan Cyril, newly consecrated in Nicaea, preferred the protection of Alexander Nevsky to that of Daniel of Galicia-Volhynia, because of Daniel's pro papal orientation. Moscow rather than Lviv or Vilnius became the centre of orthodoxy in Russia. This advantaged its ruler especially when, with Byzantine acceptance of papal supremacy at the second council of Lyons and again subsequently at the council of Florence, orthodoxy in Russia became increasingly ethnocentric. Moscow made itself rather than was made by the Mongols. The secular, personal character of its lay government may only have developed as counterpoint to the religious, impersonal character of the metropolitanate. Ivan the Terrible and the Muscovite political tradition of despotism tempered by assassination cannot be blamed on the Mongols.

India

Mongol penetration of India was limited, it is argued, because climatic conditions were unsuited to steppe horsemen. This is at best a half truth. Similar conditions did not prevent the Mongols from operating successfully in South China. In fact too, the Mongol penetration was not so limited. Besides the initial campaign of 1222 in pursuit of Jalal ad-Din, there was a raid in 1248, another in 1285, and six between 1297 and 1308, of which that of 1303 involved a siege of Delhi. Moreover, in considering Mongol activities in South Asia, one should not forget Khubilai's conquest of the Southeast Asian kingdom of Nan-chao in 1232–3, and his subsequent campaigns against Vietnam and Burma. Yunnan was not yet part of China and its occupation is not plausibly interpreted as a preliminary flanking movement against the Sung. More likely, the campaigns were directed towards a back door to India, to the creation of another Il-khanate in Southeast Asia for Khubilai, who was initially, like Hülegü, only a younger brother. The campaigns, furthermore, were not without impact on the life of the area. They precipitated the descent of the Thai speaking peoples: the Shans, the Siamese and the Laotians; from the mountain backdrop into the Southeast Asian lowlands. If Mongol penetration of India proper was limited, it was not due to the climate, but to the vigour of Indian resistance under rulers like Balban and Ala ud-Din Khalji and the inadequacy of the Mongol staging areas: the Chaghadai *ulus* which was too unstable politically, and Afghanistan which was never fully conquered. In India, as in the other homelands, the Mongolian explosion died away for a mixture of internal and external reasons.

THE BASIC INFORMATION CIRCUIT

As the Mongolian explosion cooled into the *Pax Mongolica,* it left behind, to varying degrees in different places, the first of the modern world institutions: the basic information circuit. The notion of information is currently being used in a number of disciplines.[21] Thus the universe, it is said, runs on information. Information is constituent. It is negentropy. Things are what they know. Institutions are effective to the extent that they acquire and process information. Information is the ultimate resource. Without it, nothing can be made. With it, everything can be made. The world is the hardware of which information is the software. In such ideas, the basic information circuit finds its connotation, which gives all three terms a strong sense. Information in-forms: it is morphogenetic. Circuit is more than repository: it is exchange. Basic is more than elementary: it is foundational.

The basic information circuit denotes not simply a greater diffusion of information between nomads and sedentarists in Central Asia, between the homelands beyond it, and between the four primary civilizations beyond them. It denotes also an integration of information, so that elements became components, facts became evidence, and in this way a unified picture of a single world was assembled. This integration was not just discovery: who knew what when about whom. It was the emergence of a unified conceptualization of the world, with the geographies, histories and cultures of the parts coordinated with each other. Such unification went furthest in Europe. It became a reason for the eventual dominance of the world order by the Europeans. Similar unification may also be found to a lesser extent in China, to a lesser extent again in the Islamic world. This distribution of information was novel. Before 1200, Europe was the most provincial of the homelands, Islam the most international, while China knew more about Christendom than Christendom knew about China. By 1300, Christendom knew most, Islamdom least, with China still in the middle. To indicate the new integration of information and its different levels, two or three texts from each of the homelands will now be examined.

Europe

The first witness is Marco Polo's *Description of the World* (In French, its original language, *Divasement dou Monde*), popularly known, on the continent, as *Il Milione,* and, in England, as *Travels of Marco Polo.* The text, however, is much more than a travel book.

Il Milione was published *c.*1308. It was immensely popular from the start. There are 119 early manuscripts, all slightly different. From French, it was translated into Latin, Italian and most European languages including Irish. It was the first international vernacular best seller. This was not its only intellectual significance. First, it represented a vast increase in Europe's factual information about Central Asia and China. What had been science fiction: god-headed men, giants, Gog and Magog, now became science fact in the empire of Kubla Khan. Second, it represented a considerable advance in theoretical geography. It was not a travelogue. Polo has been criticized for not making clear where he had been and where he had not. It was a *Description of the World,* a Christian topography, organized according to blocs of territory and religion. For, as Olschki first showed, Polo was not a merchant or an explorer. He was a papal ambassador. His book is the report he might have written for Gregory X. This was recognized by the Dominicans of Bologna when they translated it into Latin from Rustichello's (Polo's ghostwriter) French.[22]

These two advances, in fact and interpretation, correspond to the distinguishing marks of European thought: greater empiricism, more theory. *Il Milione* was a genuine work of science. It was a product of the age of Albertus Magnus and Thomas Aquinas when science, via the revival of Aristotle, was first conceived. It was an intellectual response to the explosion of the Central Asian heartland. It gave Europeans a new global sense. It made Europeans think about the size of the earth, the length of degrees of latitude and longitude, the possibility of a quicker way to China. Although a product of Aristotelianism, it helped to discredit Aristotelian ideas, such as the uninhabitability of equatorial zones and the absence of inhabited Antipodes. In effect, it hypothesized Australasia. Polo was an intellectual precondition to both the Great Discoveries and the meta-Aristotelian scientific revolutions, alike based on the dialectic of theory and fact.

A second text indicative of the integration of information is the report of the Franciscan missionary Odoric of Pordenone.[23] Odoric went east in 1316. On his return, shortly before his death at Udine in 1331, he dictated a narrative of his travels. This exists in 73 manuscripts, and, after *Il Milione*, it was the most popular of the new texts. Unlike *Il Milione*, Odoric's book really is a travelogue, but an unusually acute and wide ranging one. He tells us that women are better treated in Christendom than in Baghdad; that at Bali there is an ocean current which carries ships south to destruction; that Chinese women are the most beautiful in the world; that Shensi-Kansu supplies chestnuts and rhubarb. Odoric liked figures. There were 700 souls on the junk which took him from Java to Zaiton. Canton was three times as large as Venice, Zaiton twice as large as Bologna. There were 2000 cities in South China larger than Treviso or Vicenza. In Hang-chou, 10–12 households lived in a single apartment block. Yang-chou produced in salt revenue 500 *tumen* of *balis*, i.e. 5 million, which equals 7,500,000 florins. Behind these characteristics, one can see another European intellectual tradition: the Franciscan. Minorite philosophers emphasized the particular: *haeceitas* (thisness), *cognitio intuitiva singularis* (intuitive knowledge of the individual), whether conceptual or empirical, as exemplified in the rival philosophies of Scotus and Occam. Odoric, like the Franciscan archbishop of Peking, John of Monte Corvino, was probably one of the *Spirituali* and may have gone east to ecape the persecution of the Conventuals. We are in the world of *The Name of the Rose*.

A third text in this connection is Pegolotti's *La Pratica della Mercatura*.[24] It was written around 1340, but, although occasionally copied, was not published till 1766. If Polo stands for Dominican universalism and Odoric for Franciscan immediacy, Pegolotti stands for the mercantile pragmatism which sought to exploit the opportunities of the *Pax Mongolica*. Odoric, talking about Hang-chou, remarks that 'I have met at Venice people in plenty who have been there' and in 1951 at Yang-chou, the tomb of Catherine Viliani, the wife or daughter of a merchant who had died in 1342 was discovered. Pegolotti himself may never have gone to the east. He was an executive of the Florentine Bardi company, who spent much of his career at Famagusta in Cyprus. His work is a commercial handbook, replete with prices, measures, costs, distances and intended, no doubt, for the education of the griffins. He was particularly interested in textile raw materials: the English woolclip from the Cistercians and Premonstratensians, and silk from China via the northern land route – Tana, Astrakhan, Urgench, Otrar, Almalik, Kan-chou, Peking. However, he cast his net wide. He has much information about the salt trade in the Mediterranean. All spices he tells us, are available at Tabriz, canar silk can be bought in the plain of Karabagh, the best aloes come from Socotra. China supplies rhubarb as well as silk. Behind Pegolotti is a third European intellectual stratum: that of the accountants – double entry bookkeeping, letters of credit, currency exchange and eventually the adoption of Arabic numerals. It was not a world concerned solely with profit. What moved Pegolotti was that mixture of curiosity about commodities and delight in risk management which has always characterized the true businessman. Profit, no doubt, was the condition, but it was not the cause. Pegolotti, Odoric and Polo belonged to a single intellectual community.

China

In China, the integration of information provided by the Mongolian explosion and *Pax Mongolica* was less complete than in Europe. This was partly because it was less novel. Going back to the Han, there was a tradition of writing about Inner Asian barbarians. From the Southern Sung, there began to be a tradition about maritime barbarians, as instanced by the *Chu-fan*

chih (treatise on the various barbarians) of Chao Ju-kua, customs commissioner at Zaiton, of 1225.[25] The *Chu-fan chih* is
impressive. Chao Ju-kua knew about the caliph in Baghdad, the
patriarch in Antioch, the sultan in Cairo. He describes the
Pharos in Alexandria, Mount Etna in Sicily. He was interested
in spices, particularly the aromatics of Southeast Asia. Such
information and such literature, however, tended to innoculate
the Chinese against further curiosity. Moreover, Chao's book
was not widely diffused.

The nearest equivalent to Marco Polo in China is Ma Huan,
the author of the *Ying-yai sheng-lan* (The Overall Survey of the
Ocean's Shores) published in 1451.[26] Ma Huan was secretary to
the eunuch admiral Cheng Ho and accompanied him on his
oceanic voyages. His book brought the *Chu-fan chih* up to date
in the light of information acquired since 1225. Like the *Chu-
fan chih*, the *Ying-yai sheng-lan* is impressive. There are good
accounts of Chinese trade at Calicut, of Ormuz as an international emporium, and of Mecca as a religious centre. There is
little sense, however, of the discovery of a new world: none of
Marco Polo's wonder. China was a victim of its own degree of
advance. There is less theory than in Polo, less acuteness than
in Odoric, less concrete detail than in Pegolotti. Ma Huan's
book did not have the reclame in China of *Il Milione* in Europe.
He seems to have had difficulty in getting it published, and the
editio princeps of 1451 has been entirely lost, so probably was not
large. Certainly the book never entered the mainstream of
literature in the way *Il Milione* did. Moreover, the information it
contained did not go beyond the Islamic world. There was no
revelation of Christendom to China as there was a revelation of
Cathay to Europe. Both the challenge of, and the response to,
the outside world, was more muted in China than in Europe.
Consequently Europe was more globalized than China.

A second relevant text is the *Hsi-yü fan-kuo chih* (treatise on
the foreign states of the western regions) of Ch'en Ch'eng;
published in 1415.[27] Ch'en Ch'eng was a diplomat from Kiangsi
who went on three missions to the Timurids in the first half of
the fifteenth century. He died in 1457 and his reports became
the basis for the section on Central Asia in the *Ming-shih* published in 1690. In these reports, Timurid Central Asia was well
observed, especially Herat. Beyond Herat, Syria, the Ottoman
empire, Medina and Mecca were only dimly perceived, and

nothing west of that. New information might be acquired by the land missions: that Herat was powerful, practised endogenous marriage, lived luxuriously, and produced salt. But these disjointed facts were given no kind of perspective, and made little impact, partly because China had known about Central Asia for a long time. Ch'en Ch'eng's reports did not have a wide diffusion. By the twentieth century, indeed, they were regarded as lost, till rediscovered in Tientsin in 1934. Ch'en Ch'eng's account of Herat did not and was not intended to alter Confucian horizons in the way Polo's account of Hang-chou was intended to and did alter those of Christendom. China already knew too much. Her participation in the basic information circuit, whether by sea or by land, was therefore limited.

Islam

Paradoxically, Islamdom, most affected by the Mongolian explosion and already spread over three continents, participated even less than China in the integration of information. The resolution of the paradox is that the Islamic world was too vast to be much impressed by anything outside itself, whether in Europe, China, or later in America. Islam had unrivalled sources of information about the rest of the world, but she did not care to make use of them. With his suggestion that non-Muslim rulers could play a part in Providence, Juvaini was groping for the idea of a secular world order, distinct from the religious world order. But this was a difficult notion for Muslims, particularly in the stream of Ibn Taimiyya and in the context of the growing power of dervishism and fundamentalism. Moreover, without printing it was difficult for any information, whether old or new, to be integrated effectively.

The equivalent to Marco Polo in Islam is Ibn Battuta, the Moroccan jurist who between 1325 and 1355 travelled 75,000 miles in Africa, Europe and Asia. Few before his time had seen the Niger, Nile, Volga, Indus, Ganges, Yangtze and Huang-ho. As a travelogue, Ibn Battuta's text is superior to Polo's. He had travelled more widely and there are fewer digressions about things and places not directly observed. Ibn Battuta was more empirical than Polo, but by the same token, he was less theoretical. His real interest was himself: his adventures, the money he made and lost, the princely favours he received and forfeited,

the wives he married and discarded. Where Polo was a papal
diplomat, Ibn Battuta was simply a wandering *alim*. On his
return to Morocco, the king insisted that he dictate an account
of his astonishing travels. The editor, to whom he dictated, Ibn
Juzai, commented: 'This Shaykh is the traveller of our age; and
he who should call him the traveller of the whole body of Islam
would not exceed the truth'. Yet, unintended by Ibn Juzai,
there is criticism in this remark as well as praise. Ibn Battuta was
too tied to Islam. His sympathy was not enlisted by what he saw.
He was moved more by wanderlust than intellectual curiosity.
Moreover, within Islam, his impact was not great. His manuscripts remained, half lost, in the Maghreb, until they were
rediscovered in the nineteenth century by European scholars.
Ibn Battuta's very excellencies prove the lesser receptivity of
Islam to the basic information circuit. He did not achieve even
the limited, minority interest of Ma Huan and Ch'en Ch'eng in
China.

Similar considerations apply to a second Islamic text, the
Jami al-Tawarikh, or universal history, of Rashid al-Din, com-
piled *c*.1310.[28] A converted Jew, Rashid al-Din was vizier to the
Il-khan Oljeitu (1304–16). Like Juvaini, Rashid al-Din was a
collaborator. He belonged, however, to a later generation when
Persia was regaining its prosperity and the Il-khan had been
converted, so that there was less need for apologia or justification of God's ways to men. If Rashid al-Din continued Juvaini,
it was because he was interested in the subject. Consequently he
could widen his horizons and paint on a broader canvas. Part
one of his work was a history of the Mongols down to Ghazan
the greatest of the Il-khans. Part two was a history of the peoples
the Mongols were in contact with. Part three gave genealogies
of the ruling houses of the Arabs, Jews, Mongols, Franks and
Chinese. Rashid al-Din's scope was amazing. In global consciousness, he equalled Polo, if not exceeded him. Moreover,
he was no mere chronicler. He had a good grasp of the institutional basis of politics, in particular the significance of blood
tanistry and the power of dowagers, like Sorqaqtani Beki, in
succession disputes. Yet, like Ibn Battuta in geography, Rashid
al-Din in history had little impact on the Islamic mind. His
diachronic narrative form was followed rather than his
synchronic analytical content. It was not his text which was
defective, but the intellectual context in which it was launched.

Like his master Oljeitu who was by turns Christian, Shamanist, Buddhist, Shiite and Sunni, Rashid al-Din was of uncertain orthodoxy. In his lifetime, he was accused of rationalism, crypto-Judaism, or of being an Ismaili Assassin. In a world increasingly dominated by the Ibn Taimiyya concept of Islamic orthodoxy, Rashid al-Din's wide lense was unlikely to receive much use. Many of his works remained unpublished.

By the end of the thirteenth century, the basic information circuit was unevenly spread: thickest in Europe, less thick in China, least thick in Islam. In Europe, it lay deepest on the Paris–Naples axis established by the Papal–Angevin alliance against the Hohenstaufen, with Lyons, where two outward look-ing ecumenical councils were held, approximately half way between. Though intellectual receptivity and political context conditioned its varying depth, everywhere it was only a deposit, a precious stardust, left behind in a few institutions and indi-viduals after the Mongolian explosion had died away. In Mon-golia itself, Karakorum, the epicentre of the explosion, to which so many embassies, merchants, forced labourers, adventurers had come, from which so much intelligence had been derived, was half deserted as political power on the steppe moved to Bishbalik and Almalik. It had been an artificial city, anyway, a point in time rather than space. Elsewhere the new integration of information as yet made little difference. Even in Europe, it did not yet truly inform, it was not yet substantially morphogenetic. Most people who read Marco Polo read him as Mandeville: science fiction rather than science fact. According to tradition, the Venetian was begged on his deathbed to re-pent of his inventions. Yet the dust was radioactive and over time was to initiate profound changes in European society and culture. If Europe came to dominate the world, it was possibly because Europe first perceived there was a world to dominate. There is a straight line from Marco Polo to Christopher Columbus, the eastward-looking Venetian to the westward-look-ing Genoese, the protégé of Dominican scholasticism to the protégé of Franciscan millenarism. Yet the line could easily have been interrupted or not pursued, particularly in view of the irruption of the next world institution to which Central Asia was to make a major contribution: the microbian common market.

4 The Chaghatai Khanate and the Microbian Common Market 1300–1370

Under the Chaghatai khanate, the Mongol successor state ruled by the descendants of Chinggis' second son Chaghadai (the change from d to t signifies the transition from Mongolian to Turkish), Central Asia enjoyed a rare period of political unity. It was not an unqualified unity. State, society and culture were all deeply divided. Expected to be the strongest of the successor states, because of its centrality, the Chaghatai khanate turned out to be the weakest. Yet it survived longer than any of them only dying in 1930 with the abolition of the vestigial khanate of Hami.[1] The strength was not illusory. Between the end of the Mongolian explosion and the rise of Tamerlane, it made a major contribution to the formation of a second, modern, world institution: the microbian common market.[2] This unification of disease patterns, by the generalization of bacteria and viruses previously isolated, intensified pathological pressure on humankind. It was an ecological disaster unparalleled since the neolithic revolution. It killed far more people over a longer period than the Mongolian explosion. Yet in the end, its effect, too, was positive. Cross-fertilized with the basic information circuit, it produced, in quarantine and innoculation, instruments which first checked the advance of death and then rolled back its frontiers in the nineteenth century Pasteurian revolution. In quarantine, Central Asia was only part of the enemy. In innoculation, it was an ally, one of the roots of its first successful form: vaccination.[3] The chapter follows the pattern of the last: events in Central Asia, their impact in the homelands, and their role in the construction of a world institution.

THE CHAGHATAI KHANATE IN CENTRAL ASIA

The character of the Chaghatai khanate was shaped by its origins. Under the procedures on the death of Chinggis, the nomads and their pasture were divided between his four legitimate sons or their heirs, while the sedentary people and territory were held in common under the trusteeship of the Great Khan. Rashid al-Din says that Chaghadai was given nomads mainly from the Barlas and Jalayir *oboghs* and that their *yurt*, which then meant pasture rather than tents, stretched from Altai of the Naiman to the Oxus. Juvaini, thinking more in sedentary terms, says: 'Chaghatai was a fierce and mighty khan. When the lands of Transoxania and Turkestan were subjugated, his camping grounds and those of his children and armies extended from Besh Baligh to Samarqand, fair and pleasant places fit to be the abode of kings.'[4] The khan, however, continued to nomadize: 'In spring and summer he had his quarters in Almaligh and Quyas . . . The autumn and winter he spent in Marauzik on the Ila.' The pastures of Semirechie and central Kazakhstan were his personal inheritance, probably part of Zungharia too. The rest of Zungharia to the east belonged to Ögödei, while to the west the Kipchak steppe belonged to Jochi. To the south, in the sedentary lands, Chaghadai, like his brothers, only had a share, *inju*, in the usufruct. The administration remained in the hands of the Great Khan, who appointed as first procurator, Mahmud Yalavach. He was a Muslim from Khiva who had already joined Chinggis before the conquest of the Khwarazmshah. He was responsible to the central secretariat in Karakorum headed by Chinkai, a Nestorian Uighur. Gradually, however, the central secretariat ceded its functions to the local khanates. In this repartition, Chaghatai obtained most of sedentary Central Asia, but not all. Khiva went to the Golden Horde and Herat went to the Il-khanate.

The regime so established may be termed an *inju* state. At its core was a group of Mongol clans or *oboghs*, or, more accurately, parts of clans since further parts were to be found in the other Mongol successor states, plus their Turkish auxiliaries and allies, the *tamaci* troops, all arranged in units of 1000 and 10,000 according to the *ordo* system.[5] They were entitled to a share, *inju,* of the common imperial sedentary possessions. Gradually, however, the term *inju* came to mean not only share, but those who shared. Moreover, it was extended from the original nomad clans and associates to their sedentary collaborators: the tax farmers, notables, merchants who acquired the language of the conqueror and became identified with him. This language was increasingly Turkish. The Mongol *obogh* was never a pure kinship unit. Only the leading lineages were genuinely interrelated and only they properly used the *obogh* name. The rest, commoners and slaves, were clients or retainers rather than relations. They took the *obogh* name temporarily, but could transfer, or be transferred, to another. The *obogh* was open ended. As the Mongol army expanded, replaced casualties and formed auxiliaries, it recruited other nomads, ex enemies or ad hoc friends, who, in Semirechie and Central Kazakhstan, spoke Turkish. By 1300, the commoners and slaves of the Chaghatai *ulus* were Turkish speaking rather than Mongolian. The nobles, *noyon,* especially those of actual Chinggisid descent, kept up Mongolian longer, but they too lapsed eventually and Turkified. It was Turkish therefore that the collaborators learnt, and Turkish that they passed to the people of the oases generally. It was in the Chaghatai period that the three Turkestans became what they are named: lands of Turkish-speaking peoples, a process which went least far in Afghan Turkestan, much of which belonged to the Il-khanate. In the *inju* state the Mongol polity was redefined. It became a Turkish-speaking consortium of nomadic conquerors and sedentary assistant conquerors, ruling over an Iranian populace fast losing its language. Established by force initially, by survival, habit and the arguments of people like Juvaini, the *inju* state gradually acquired minimum legitimacy, at least among the *sadr,* the notables.

It did not acquire stability. The *inju* state fulfilled no real need of either the nomadic or sedentary populations, but it imposed crippling burdens on both. Thanks to the *ordo,* the temporary near invincibility of steppe cavalry, and the divisions of its enemies, the *inju* state was politically and militarily strong, but, sociologically and ecologically, it was weak. Unless steps were taken to counteract its parasitic, predatory character, it would in the long run be deserted by both the nomadic and sedentary populations.

At first sight, the nomadic population had everything to gain from the *inju* state: booty, pasture, slaves, jobs, right to tax, status. Surely the Mongol conquests were the fulfilment of every nomad's dream? No, because the costs of the empire were high and disruptive to the nomad way of life. Nomadic pastoralism only needed minimum government. Government was marginal and intermittent rather than essential and permanent. It was required only in an emergency – a feud or a famine – or in the periodic social reshuffling of blood tanistry. The principal tax, *qubciri*, the right to levy herds and conscript people, was always occasional, irregular and for a specific purpose. Any attempt to make levies or conscription permanent and regular threatened to push herds and manpower below the safety level for individual families. But the Chinggisid empire proclaimed a permanent state of emergency, while it eliminated the safety valve of blood tanistry. The incessant levy of men and beasts was just tolerable in war, with all the excitement, community feeling and booty. It became intolerable after the conquest. The khan still needed garrisons in sedentary areas and on frontiers. He still needed horses, above all for the *yam* or postal service, which bound the empire together. These things had to come from the ordinary nomad. But garrisons and postal stations were incompatible with the nomadic way of life, which demanded independence and mobility. Once the war was over, the ordinary nomad got little else out of the empire. It became a costly irrelevance benefiting only an oligarchy of courtiers, officeholders and mercenaries, Turkish-speaking now rather than Mongolian. So nomads, and perhaps especially their mothers and wives, began to drop out, drift back to the steppe, renomadize, join factions, recreate blood tanistry. Political and social imperatives parted company. The khan found himself abandoned by his followers.

The oasis was not anti-government. Government was essential: for irrigation, defence, culture, perhaps long distance trade. Taxes on land and business were permanent and regular and were accepted as a necessary evil. The *inju* state, however, in addition to these traditional sedentary taxes, also imposed the nomad *qubciri* system of intermittent exactions of men, animals and services. It was not so much the exact amount that was objected to as the method of raising it. The unpredictability and unevenness struck at the rhythms and solidarities of oasis life both urban and rural. Although rulers like Möngke, and officials like Mahmud Yalavach and Juvaini, tried to rationalize procedures and eliminate irregularities, the bias of the system remained. It threatened to kill the oasis, and the fact that it was imposed by non-Iranians and non-Muslims, or bad Muslims like Juvaini, did not make it easier. Just as the nomads seceded, the sedentarists, and perhaps especially their womenfolk, began to go underground. They joined mafias, chapels, unions, leagues, which organized non-cooperation, absenteeism, strikes, disappearance, no-go areas. Individually weak, the sedentarists began to discover they were collectively strong. The mass element which had not been organized against the conquest, began to be organized against the occupation. Political and social imperatives parted company. The khan found himself abandoned by his subjects.

Already in the thirteenth century two episodes revealed the danger to the Chaghatai state of these two oppositions. First, in 1238, there was a revolt of Bokhara townspeople under Mahmud Tarabi. A sieve-maker by trade, he was encouraged by his sister, who later abandoned him, to become a magician, protegé of dervishes, and champion of *jihad*. The result was an urban, lower class revolt against the Mongols, their upper class collaborators, and the exactions of the *inju* state. Juvaini tells us that after a victory over the local Mongol forces, 'The people of the country districts, issuing forth from their villages, fell upon the fugitives with spades and axes; and whenever they came upon one of their number, especially if he was a tax-gatherer or landowner, they seized him and battered in his head with their axes.'[6] Inevitably, the revolt was crushed, but it needed the main Mongol army to do it, and Mahmud Yalavach had to intercede personally with Ögödei to avert an old style general massacre. Second, in 1266, when the Chaghatai khan Mubarak Shah moved his headquarters from the steppe closer to Samarkand and adopted Islam, he was abandoned by half his followers as a bad nomad. An anti-khan was elected and a *khurultai* took an oath to maintain the nomad way of life. The schism was eventually composed, but it revealed the state/ nomad split, just as the Tarabi revolt revealed the state/ sedentarist split. The next khan Barak took care to be more nomadic. The basic problem, however, remained. The *inju* state meshed neither with nomadic pastoralism nor with oasis agriculture. It rested on force not utility. State and society were in conflict. Pacification might be achieved, but not stability.

The Chaghatai khans were not able to devote their full attention to domestic problems. Situated in the middle of the three other khanates, they were bound to be involved in foreign politics. Where they might have hoped to become the arbiter and the strongest, in fact they became the pawn and the weakest. The loss of Khiva to the Golden Horde and of Herat to the Il-khanate was both cause and consequence of this weakness.

Chaghadai himself had a fairly long and successful reign (1227–1242). Juvaini represents him as a conservative nomad, a stickler for the *yasa*, Mongol customary law as modified by Chinggis, and hostile to Islam. He forbade halal slaughter and ablutions in running water, at least for his nomadic subjects. However, he had Muslim ministers and a physician, and he did not interfere with the administration of Mahmud Yalavach in the south. He seems to have favoured a kind of apartheid: the *yasa* for the nomads, the *sharia* for the sedentarists. This was no solution to the long term problems of the now mixed population of the *inju* state. Chaghadai simply masked them by his prestige and uprightness. Though Juvaini says that 'he was ever engaged in amusements and pleasures and dallying with sweet-faced peri-like maidens', he was one of the few members of the immediate generation after Chinggis not to succumb to the temptations of Chinese hard liquor.[7] He remained on good terms with the Great khan Ögödei.

Chaghadai died just before or just after Ögödei. His eldest son Mütegin had been killed at the siege of Bamiyan (this was one reason for its total destruction), so Chaghadai's widow, a Qunggirat princess, a member of one of the fourteen original Mongol *oboghs* and a relative of Chinggis' empress Borte, placed on the throne his son Qara Hülegü, with the consent of Töregene, Ögödei's widow and regent of the empire. When Güyüg became Great Khan in 1246 and obtained full authority following the death of his mother two to three months later, he replaced Qara Hülegü with his uncle Yesü-Möngke, another of Chaghadai's sons. According to Juvaini, he was an incapable ruler: 'Now Yesü was constantly carousing; he was ignorant of sobriety and made intoxication a habit, drinking wine from morn till eve.'[8] Nevertheless, he kept good ministers, notably the Muslim savant Baha ad-Din Marghinari from Ferghana, and his reign too was relatively successful. In 1248, however, Güyüg died, and after the regency of his widow Oghul Ghaimish, was succeeded in 1251, not by any of his sons or other members of the house of Ögödei, but, in what amounted to a political revolution, by Möngke, son of Tolui. Yesu-Möngke was on the wrong side. He was deposed and, along with his ministers, executed by Möngke, who replaced him with Qara-Hülegü once more. He, however, almost immediately died, and for the next ten years real power passed to his widow Orqina as regent for his son Mubarak Shah. She was the daughter of an Oirat or west Mongol prince who had married one of Chinggis, daughters. She therefore combined two lines of prestige as well as obviously possessing considerable political ability.

The accession of Möngke meant a reassertion of Mongol central power. The expedition to the west under his brother Hülegü to establish the Il-khanate of Persia temporarily reduced Central Asia to a mere rear area. Möngke's financial reforms, carried out in Central Asia by Masud son of Mahmud Yalavach, were designed to make taxation more regular. It was an attempt to adjust the fiscality of the *inju* state to suit both nomads and sedentarists. In 1259, however, with the campaign in the west still incomplete, Möngke died on his eastern expedition against the Southern Sung.

This time there was a fully disputed succession, which divided the Chinggisids for nearly thirty years. In Karakorum, Möngke's youngest brother, the *otcigin* Arigh Böke, was elected by a *khurultai* managed by the late ruler's prime minister, the Nestorian Bulghai Aga. In Shang-tu in Inner Mongolia, at a rival *khurultai*, Khubilai, would-be Il-khan of Southeast Asia and now commander on the Yangtze front against the Sung, was elected by the army of central China. In this struggle, Arigh Böke had the support not only of the central government and the reserves, but also of Möngke's army of West China, twice the size of Khubilai's originally, though badly reduced by cholera or dysentery. Orqina supported Arigh Böke. She attended the *khurultai* which elected him. Indeed, Rashid al-Din says that she proposed his election. In his cause, she agreed to marry Alghu, Qara-Hülegü's cousin, who was sent to the Chaghatai khanate to mobilize its resources on his behalf. He, however, double-crossed Arigh Böke. He joined the very murky politics whereby Khubilai, enlisting the remnant of the house of Ögödei in Tangut and Zungharia, forced his brother to surrender in 1264. Orqina, however, seems to have retained control in Central Asia, and, after the death of Alghu in 1266, put her own son Mubarak Shah back on the throne. He was much opposed by the nomads and Khubilai did not trust him. Eventually he had him replaced by his cousin Barak, Orqina having by this time died. She was in many ways the real creator of the khanate. She had maintained its existence in a difficult period and it was under her that the administration of the sedentary territories passed from Karakorum to Almalik.

Barak (1267–1270) was very much a nomad. Although appointed by Khubilai, he joined the new revolt against him in Mongolia of the Qaidu grandson of Ögödei. Khubilai never succeeded in mastering this rebellion which in effect separated Mongolia from the rest of the empire. In 1269 Barak went to war with Khubilai's ally the Il-khanate in an old style looting campaign, even plundering his own cities of Samarkand and Bokhara en route. This was absurd as even he seem to have realized. It was clear that some compromise between the nomads and the sedentarists must be attempted.

It was attempted first by Barak's son Tuva in a long reign from 1274 to 1307. On the one hand, to gratify the sedentarists, he promoted trade by founding the city of Andijan in Ferghana on the way to Kashgar and the east. He arranged that business taxes be paid indirectly by the guilds, instead of directly to officials, thereby reducing friction. On the other hand, he remained a non-Muslim, a soldier, who made conquests in Afghanistan and a series of raids into India, a new booty area, untouched so far by the Mongols. This policy of peace at home, war abroad, perhaps copied from Khubilai in China, was later pursued more systematically by Tamerlane. It was an enterprising policy, but in Tuva's hands, it was not much more than improvisation. Moreover, throughout his reign Tuva had to manoeuvre between Qaidu and Khubilai as well as maintain a front against the Golden Horde and the Il-khanate.

More institutional was Tuva's son Kebek, who was the power behind the throne of several khans between 1307 and 1318, before becoming khan himself from 1318 to 1326. Not a Muslim himself, indeed helping to depose a khan who tried to convert, and so pleasing to the nomads, he standardized the currency to conform to those of the Il-khanate and Golden Horde (the word kopeck has been derived from his name) and built a palace near Samarkand, so pleasing the sedentarists as well. He attached the various *tumen* of his army to particular pieces of sedentary territory, to exploit but also, it was hoped, to protect and promote. Nomads and sedentarists were forced to coexist on a local basis. With the *tumen* self-supporting, the khan could reduce taxes on both nomads and sedentarists. In this way, by the beginning of the fourteenth century a certain stability was achieved in the Chaghatai khanate. Yet it was precarious. The *inju* state was not deeply rooted in either the sedentary or the nomadic sectors. This was made clear in 1334 when Kebek's brother and successor Tarmashirin became a Muslim, thus indicating a preference for the sedentarists. A new and more serious secession of the pure nomads took place, leading to the permanent division of the khanate between east and west. East of the T'ien-shan, a state called Moghulistan was established in Zungharia and the Tarim basin under the khan Chankshi, who was a Christian. Here the khans retained some real power, though from 1345 they became Muslim. West of the T'ien-shan, the khans increasingly became the puppets of the now half sedentarized *tumen*. These in turn became identified with their dominant *oboghs*, while the cities were falling under the control of urban mafias and dervish organizations, that Folk Islam which was becoming a major force in Central Asia.

By the middle of the fourteenth century, the effective power of the Chaghatai state was confined to Eastern Turkestan and even there it was crumbling. In Western Turkestan, it had come to an end. For all its military and political power, the *inju* state had not been able to resist the corrosive forces of society and ecology. Nomad secession and urban rejection had subverted the unity imposed by the Mongolian explosion. Yet out of the resulting anarchy, Tamerlane was surprisingly to appear and recreate unity for a century and a half. In the meantime, events in Central Asia had not been without impact both in the homelands and in the nascent world order.

THE CHAGHATAI KHANATE AND THE HOMELANDS

The Chaghatai khanate contributed different things to different homelands. All the contributions, however, should be seen in the context of the set of changes affecting all the homelands generally in the post conquest situation.

First, the political situation had changed. The original Mongol empire resembled a business. There was the main board: the Great Khan, his secretariat and general staff. There were the shareholders: the original Mongol *oboghs* and their Turkish auxiliaries. There was the common enterprise in the sedentary lands. By 1300 the structure was different. The executive main board had disappeared and its functions had been transferred to the subsidiaries. The Great Khanate was now hereditary in the house of Tolui, and in a branch of it that was based, not in eastern Mongolia, but in north China. The original *ulus* of Tolui disappeared with the unsuccessful candidacy of Arigh Böke against Khubilai. So too did the *ulus* of Ögödei in the unsuccessful candidacy of the sons of Güyüg against Möngke despite the long and at times nearly successful attempt of his grandson Qaidu to revive it. After Qaidu's death *c.*1302 most of the *ulus* of Ögödei fell to Chaghatai. So two of the four original *ulus* had disappeared by 1300. In their place were two new *ulus* both derived from the house of Tolui: the Il-khanate in Persia and the khanate of Cathay in China. Together with Chaghatai and the Golden Horde, they constituted the executive subsidiary boards which managed their respective sedentary areas.

Nevertheless, the Mongol empire had not dissolved into four independent states. A number of bonds remained.[9] First, the authority of the Great Khan continued to be recognized as something more than a head of the commonwealth. Imperial princesses were sent from Peking, embassies came to instal new local khans and Khubilai's grandson Temür (Ch'eng-tsung (1294–1307)) consciously promoted peace among his relatives. High commissioners played a role in local politics. Second, all four Mongol successors retained a family likeness in institutions, ways of doing business, and concepts of international relations. In all there reigned the *altan urugh*, or golden lineage of Chinggis; in all there was an *inju* core of nomads or ex-nomads; in all a council of four *qaraci* or guardian beys tended to take active charge of the government; all distinguished between zones of direct and indirect rule, empire and satellites. Third the international clans, elements of which might be found in all the *ulus*, formed an ongoing element of unity. These multi-*ulus* oboghs, the component syndicates of the Mongol regulated company, included clans like the Qunggirat, the

Jalayir, the Barlas and the Arlat. Fourth, down to the middle of the fourteenth century, there was considerable interchange of personnel, particularly at the level of the *se-mu* or assistant conquerors. These included Turks such as the Kipchak, Qanli and Qarluk, but also Indo-Europeans like the Russians and the Alans. All these people constituted *tumen* in the Yüan army in the time of the Kipchak prime minister El Temür who died in 1333.[10] Unity had changed rather than disappeared.

Second, the military situation had changed. There was a shift from light cavalry to heavy. There were four reasons for this. First, the further the Mongols went from the pastures of Central Eurasia into the deserts and oases of the Middle East, the forest agriculture of Europe and the wetland horticulture of China, the greater became the difficulty of conducting war with light cavalry supplied by mobile civilian pastoralists. Second, even if it had been convenient, the *inju* state could no longer rely on the nomads. Nomad secessions forced a change in military style. Third, enemy heavy cavalry had improved. In particular, the Mamluk sultan al-Nasir, (1288–1340), who checked the last offensives of the Il-khanate, began the systematic breeding of large horses in his studs outside Cairo, a move which led eventually to the development of the English thoroughbred. Immediately, it led to more and better chargers for Islamic heavy cavalrymen. In combination with his existing advantages of a faster, longer winded mount, better weapons and greater professionalism, this gave the sedentary heavy horseman the edge over the steppe light horseman. In Hungary and Lithuania too the heavy horseman improved. Mongol *inju* states began to adopt the arm of their enemies. Finally, the core of Chinggis' army, 101 chiliarchies out of 129, passed on his death to the *ulus* of Tolui, which in effect dissolved itself in the usurpation of Arigh Böke and the revolt of Qaidu. By 1300, the Mongolian steppe had ceased to be a source of military horsepower. While the Golden Horde and the Chaghatai khanate had alternative sources of supply in the steppes of Kipchak, Central Kazakhstan and Semirechie, the Yüan dynasty and the Il-khanate had perforce to turn to heavy cavalry. It was in the organization of heavy cavalry that the Alans became important in China.

Third, the economic situation had changed. The period of the early Chaghatai khanate saw a post war recovery. The damage done by the Mongols was repaired remarkably quickly. As early as 1238 and the Tarabi rebellion, Mahmud Yalavach, in addressing the Mongol authorities, referred to the restored prosperity of Bokhara. Marco Polo described Bokhara as 'the finest city in all Persia' and Samarkand as 'very large and splendid'.[11] The Mongolian explosion stimulated as well as destroyed. Traditional economies suffered from thesaurization and under use of capacity. Looting and the extravagance associated with conquest could stimulate. Juvaini lays stress on the generosity and high spending of both Ögödei and Möngke. Where damage was not repaired, new centres took up the slack. Eastern Turkestan may have benefited from the devastation of Western Turkestan. In his account, Marco Polo says: 'The biggest city, and the most splendid is Kashgar. The inhabitants live by trade and industry'.[12] This revival of trade was both a source of revenue for the *inju* states, the more necessary in view of their higher military costs, and a field for their continued cooperation. An example of this was the ill-starred scheme of the Il-khan Geikhatu to introduce the Chinese system of paper currency to Iran on the advice of the Yüan high commissioner Bolad Ching-sang.[13] In general economic revival promoted political stability.

Fourth, the religious situation had changed. In the century before Chinggis, Nestorianism, originally a sedentary mercantile religion, had come to predominate on the steppes of central and western Mongolia. Both the little invasion of Yeh-lü Ta-shih and the great invasion of Chinggis had appeared in the guise of a Nestorian eschatology. Yet, as the Mongolian explosion cooled, it was not Nestorianism that triumphed, but, in three out of four of the *inju* states, Islam, and in the fourth there was an increase in the number of Muslims. This development is not explained by sedentarization. In that case, while Chaghatai and the Il-khanate might have turned Muslim, the Golden Horde should have become Eastern Orthodox and the Yüan dynasty, Confucian. Sedentarization, anyway, is not the best description for the crystallization of the *inju* state out of both nomads and sedentarists.

The true reason for the religious developments must be sought in the intellectual needs of the leaders of *inju* states. Chinggis had created a universal empire which his successors modified into a Eurasian commonwealth headed by a Chinese emperor. The Yüan emperor had no need of a new ideology. His bureaucratic empire provided itself with one, which could only be some form of Confucianism. Personally then he could please himself. In the case of Khubilai what pleased him was Tibetan Tantrism, picked up in the Sino-Tibetan borderlands in his younger days as would-be khan of Southeast Asia. For the regional khans, however, the choice of religion was a serious one with political implications. Nestorianism, their initial choice, was too provincial for a universal empire. It lacked the culture with which to animate a court, attract personnel and conduct international relations. Eastern Orthodoxy or Catholicism might have appealed, but the first was too hostile to Nestorianism and the second too distant. Buddhism was seriously considered by the Il-khanate, which was in touch with Tibet via its territories in Kashmir, but its appeal was too esoteric. Islam, however, was to hand, universal and exoteric. It had, moreover, already established itself as a religion of Turkish-speaking aristocrats and armoured knights. Yet the choice of Islam was unfortunate. Islam participated least in the basic information circuit. Islamic states lacked legitimacy in an Islamic society increasingly dominated by dervish orders. An Islamic commonwealth headed by a Confucian emperor was really a nonsense. By adopting Islam, in its then form, the *inju* states condemned themselves to provinciality, illegitimacy and vulnerability to rejection by society. Islam attracted but it was fatal attraction.

In the evolving environment of the post conquest homelands, the Chaghatai khanate played a variety of roles. Its impact was primarily political in China, military in Islam and India, economic in Europe. In religion, the Chaghatai khanate was not yet active. That was to come later.

China

The Chaghatai khanate played a considerable part in the political changes of the Yüan dynasty in the first third of the fourteenth century.[14] These changes involved a double movement. On the one hand, the *se-mu*, the assistant conquerors from Central and Western Asia, gained at the expense of the old Mongol clans. This was largely through the shift from light to heavy cavalry, which the *se-mu*, and in particular the Alans, provided. On the other hand, the central government, which increasingly sought legitimacy in Confucian terms, gained at the expense of the frontier armies, whether *se-mu* or Mongol in one direction, and of the provincial administration, dominated by non-Confucian clerks and Muslim financiers, in another. The outcome of this double movement, the Chinese version of the crystallization of the inju state, was the rule of Toghto, Yüan prime minister form 1340 to 1354. Toghto was a Merkit, a Forest Mongol from outside the oligarchy. He was a patron of *se-mu*, taking over the clientele of the earlier Kipchak prime minister El Temür. Unlike his immediate predecessor, his uncle Bayan, Toghto was a civilian and pro Confucian. He sought to increase support for the consortium by giving bonus shares to *se-mu* generals and Chinese bureaucrats and by getting the firm, under the slogan *kung-li* 'merit and profit', to undertake welfare functions for everyone. He built up a huge patronage empire, expanded money supply, developed agricultural settlements in the north to avoid expensive grain transport from the south, and carried out a major reconstruction of the Yellow river. In the event, these policies did not work. Toghto made enemies faster than friends and over-extended the resources of the regime. His government, nevertheless, offered the best hope of stabilizing the Yüan *inju* state, and his failure was accidental rather than essential.

Central Asia's role in these developments went back to the early fourteenth century. The revolt of Qaidu had cut the Yüan dynasty off from its source of light cavalry. To counter Qaidu and his would be successors, Khubilai's grandson and successor Temur organized a new style heavy cavalry army, based on *se-mu* and alliance with the Chaghatai khanate, then under Tuva and Kebek, two of its most constructive rulers. The commander of this army was Temur's nephew Qaishan, who built up a patronage empire on its basis. He succeeded his uncle in 1307 and is known in history as Wu-tsung, the martial ancestor. He died in 1311 and the throne was taken by his brother, backed by a civilian clique, who was later given the name of Jen-tsung, the humane ancestor. The Qaishan clique, which had saved the *ulus* from Qaidu, thus felt cheated of power. In 1316, its leader, Qaishan's son Qosila, who might have hoped to follow his father on the throne, fled to the court of the Chaghatai khan, where he married a Qarluk princess. The Qaishan clique could not prevent the succession of Jen-tsung's son Ying-tsung in

1320. He was murdered, however, in 1323 by the Chief Censor
Tegsi with the aid of the Alan guard and, no doubt, the conniv-
ance of Qosila. But again the throne escaped him and went to
a cousin, Yesun Temür, who represented a conservative alliance
of Old Mongols and financial officials. Qosila had to content
himself with recognition as a quasi-independent ruler between
Chaghatai and the territories of the Yüan.

In 1328 another opportunity occurred. Yesun Temür died
and his ministers could not secure enough support for the
succession of his son. The Qaishan clique, supported energeti-
cally by the Chaghatai khan Eljigitei, Kebek's successor, seized
power at Peking. But it was not Qosila who benefited. Although
welcomed as emperor on his return from long exile, he was
soon murdered by a more civilian *se-mu* group led by the Kipchak
El Temür, being replaced by his brother Tugh Temür and
under increasingly Confucian and civilian ministers, notably
the great Toghto. With the support of its Chaghatai allies, the
Qaishan clique finally did triumph at Peking, but only at the
price of civilizing itself and basing its power, not on the
frontier armies, but on the central government. Chaghatai,
both before and after the split of 1334, continued to be a factor
in Yüan politics, especially through the Christian Alans who
received via Central Asia the large horses they could not breed
in China. The prominence given to Bishbalik, Derbend, and
possibly Sarai, on the Korean world map of 1402 may be explained in terms of this Chaghatai connection.[15]

Islam

On the Il-khanate, the impact of the Chaghatai khanate was
primarily military. It furthered the shift from light to heavy
cavalry, but in this case as an enemy rather than an ally, and
with more negative political results. In China, the failure of
Toghto was accidental. In Persia, the failure of the successors of
Abu Said was essential.

Of the Mongol successor states, the Il-khanate was least well
placed to maintain its army on the basis of light cavalry. Persia
did contain nomads, but they were mountain transhumants, no
great horse breeders, and the Il-khanate never enlisted them as
partners. The early Il-khans tried to remain nomads. They
spent the summer on the plains of Karabagh, the winter on

those of northern Iraq. Their failure to win a decisive victory over the Golden Horde in the Caucasus both made this policy impossible and removed the option of using the Alans as the basis of heavy cavalry. Against the light cavalry which the Chaghatai khans sent against them, to give their nomadic subjects the kind of wide-ranging, freebooting war they liked, the Il-khans had to rely on their own Persian heavy cavalry, the traditional weapon of Iran against Turan. This was effective militarily. The battle of Herat in July 1270, when Abaqa defeated Barak, confirmed the verdict of Ayn Jalut that sedentary heavy cavalry, properly organized, could defeat steppe light cavalry. Yet politically the costs were high. The Il-khans became dependent on the local aristocracy. From this followed conversion to Islam, the generalization of military fiefs, *iqta*, their extension from pasture to arable to support large horses, and the making of fiefs hereditary. Ghazan, who did all these things, is usually regarded as the greatest of the Il-khans, but it is arguable that he took the easy way out. In effect, he abdicated the *inju* state to Muslim culture on the one hand and to Persian society on the other. Where Toghto concentrated power and over-extended it, Ghazan fragmented power and under-extended it. As a result, the Il-khanate became unstable and collapsed the first of the four *inju* states. Relations with Chaghatai had contributed to this outcome.

India

Here, too, the impact of the Chaghatai khanate was primarily military, but with different results. If Chaghatai attacks initially strengthened but ultimately weakened the Il-khanate, it was the other way round with the Delhi sultanate. Mongol penetration of India was more significant than is sometimes supposed. Initially, it was checked more by the situation in the Chaghatai khanate than by Indian climate or resistance. The need for centralized defence against the Mongols, however, became a basis for the revival of the Delhi sultanate under Muhammed Shah Tughlak (1325–1351) and Firoz Shah (1351–1388). Muhammed Tughlak was one of the most ambitious rulers of India. He planned to invade China, did invade Tibet, and introduced a token currency on the Chinese model. The Chaghatai invasions pushed the Muslims of India further to the south. They stimulated the growth there of two rival centres of state power: the Muslim Bahmani sultanate of the Deccan and the Hindu kingdom of Vijayanagar. In Persia, the military changes prompted by the Chaghatai invasions strengthened society and culture at the expense of the state. In India, especially via the development of bigger elephant corps, they strengthened the state at the expense of society and culture.

Europe

In the Golden Horde, the European Mongol successor state, the impact of the Chaghatai khanate was primarily economic. In the revival of international trade which followed the Mongolian explosion, the lion's share went to the northern land route. The southern sea route was as yet too underdeveloped, and the central land route was too often interrupted by the wars of the Mamluks, the Il-khanate and the Chaghatai khanate, though Tabriz was prosperous. Under Uzbek (1311–1340) and Janibeg (1342–57) the Golden Horde provided peace. It was in contact in the Crimea with the Genoese treaty port of Caffa which enjoyed its maximum prosperity in the first two-thirds of the fourteenth century.[16] Its possession of Khiva was of more advantage to it than was Herat to the Il-khanate. Khiva was both a supplier and an entrepot. It supplied its own silks: *organium* (Urgench) and *corusmisna* (Khwarazm); and forwarded those of China, much purchased by the Genoese at Tana at the head of the sea of Azov in Alan country. The Genoese travelled far into the interior: Antonio Sarmone made his will in Peking in 1330; an Adorno bought seven camel loads of goods in Mazar-i-sharif in 1372. Khiva handled balas rubies from Badakhshan, indigo from Hindustan, rhubarb from Tangut, Chinese porcelain and ginger. It produced ceramics, including majolica, which it supplied to the cities of the Golden Horde.

The Golden Horde was the most successful of the *inju* states.[17] Thanks to its position on the Kipchak steppe, it was able to preserve its nomadic character longer than the Il-khanate and to avoid nomad secession and urban rejection better than the Chaghatai khanate. The khans continued to nomadize, spending the winter in one of the Sarais, the summer in the Volga Bulgaria lowlands or the plain north of the sea of Azov. Till the fifteenth century, divisions were within the *inju* consortium, generally on east–west lines, rather than between it and other social groups, The khans, therefore, were able to make their capitals, first Old Sarai founded near Astrakhan in 1254 by Batu and then New Sarai founded near Volgograd in 1332 by Uzbek into headquarters, arsenals and rest places for spending the profits of the *inju* state. Excavations at Selikyonnoye (Old Sarai) and Tsareva (New Sarai) have revealed, via weapons, glass, ceramics and building, the hothouse Baroque urban culture enjoyed by the Turkish nobility of the Horde. In the reign of Uzbek, most of this nobility converted to Islam, to align itself not, as in the Il-khanate, with its heavy cavalry, but with its by-appointment merchants. The conversion gave the Horde oligarchy a more pronouncedly urban character and increased its tension with the still nomadic Nogais to the west and the Kazakhs to the east. On these nomads, however, it was still militarily dependent, since the shift from light cavalry to heavy went least far in the Golden Horde. The development of trade, therefore prepared the way first for the Great Trouble, a period of succession disputes after the death of Janibeg based on rival nomad groups, and then, after the revival under Mamai and Toktamish had been aborted by Tamerlane, for the permanent secessions and rejections of the fifteenth century. Long before these deconstructive results were arrived at, however, the northern land route had carried something much more deadly than political and social friction.

THE MICROBIAN COMMON MARKET

A first consequence of the Mongolian explosion had been the conceptual unification of the world in the basic information circuit. A second consequence, with its origins in the Chaghatai khanate, was a biological unification. From the middle of the fourteenth century, there began to develop a single, uniform disease structure for the whole of humanity. It is this interchange of bacteria and viruses which Le Roy Ladurie has termed the microbian common market. Of course, even today, some diseases are more prevalent in one place than another. Thus bilharzia or schistosomiasis, a snail born parasitic disease, is more widespread in Egypt than elsewhere. River blindness, onchocerciasis, haunts Nigeria. Sleeping sickness, carried by the tsetse fly, is a disease of Central Africa. Kala-azar is a disease of North China. Malaria and leprosy have their habitats. Generally however, twentieth century man lives in a single disease world. Cancer and heart disease, increasingly the major killers, are known everywhere. In the modern world, dying is standardized.

It was not always so.[18] It was not so as between Europe and Asia until the fourteenth century: not so between Eurasia and America, Eurasia and Africa until the sixteenth century: not between the rest of the world and Australasia until the eighteenth and nineteenth centuries. Until then, death was compartmentalized, folkloric almost. Some diseases, it is true, were widespread, such as malaria and tuberculosis, because of their association with neolithic agriculture and pastoralism. Many, however, were localized. Thus before the interchanges of the microbian common market, syphilis was confined to America, cholera to India, plague to Upper Asia, yellow fever to America or West Africa. Smallpox and measles were unknown in America or Australasia. The microbian common market, therefore, commenced with epidemics: sudden decompartmentalization of diseases. In itself this was something new. In antiquity and prehistory, disease structure was dominated less by epidemics than by endemics: infantile dysentery, malaria, tuberculosis, and parasitism – hookworms, Ascarid worms, filariae, Guinea worms.[19] Against the parasites, mankind could only respond with its first addiction: excess consumption of salt. The new epidemics produced a worsening of human biological conditions, an aggravation of death, as in the neolithic revolution. Thus in sixteenth century America, a high percentage of the Indian population was destroyed in an involuntary genocide by the new diseases of smallpox, measles and influenza brought by the Spaniards. Similar destruction was done to the Aboriginal population of Australia in the early nineteenth century, while at the same time Indian cholera posed a deadly threat to the early industrial population of Europe. Gradually, as epidemics turned into endemics, or were marginalized by quarantine, innoculation and sanitation, the counter offensive of the basic information circuit, the microbian common market changed its character. While remaining international, it became an exchange, not of death, but of weapons against death. Eventually the exogenic causes of death by bacteria and viruses were driven back, leaving only the endogenic causes: cancer, heart disease, and old age.

In the history of epidemics Central Asia played a crucial role. It was the diffusion point for the first, greatest and most deadly of the new epidemics, plague. It was the leading transmitter of the last, the one which prompted the establishment of modern sanitary institutions, cholera. It was the worst sufferer on the steppe at least, from the most psychologically demoralizing, syphilis. Earlier, in the period of the Islamic conquest, Central Asia had played a part in the diffusion of what by the fourteenth century had become the worst of the Eurasian endemics: smallpox. Of Indus valley origin, smallpox, the red death of children, claimed twice the number of victims as the Black Death, but it made less impact psychologically, because its assaults were regular, its lethality was comparatively low (in the West, on average, 10 per cent) and, as Darmon says, it could be banalized and domesticated in the nursery.[20] The Black Death was never domesticated. Its lethality was high: 70 per cent in the case of bubonic plague, 95 per cent in the case of pneumonic and septicaemic. It struck adults and adolescents rather than children, especially females. Till its final assaults: in the west as Marseille in 1720, in Moscow in 1770, and in the east in Manchuria in 1920, it remained savage and unanticipated though in fact following a periodicity related to the sun spot cycle.[21]

That the European Black Death of 1349 was plague, *Yersinia pestis*; that it was the same disease, imported from the same place, as the plague of Justinian which infected Europe from 540 to 750; and that it was transmitted again to Europe from northern Central Asia via the northern land route, as a result of Janibeg's catapulting of bodies over the walls of Caffa during the siege of 1347; is highly probable but not certain.[22] It has been suggested that the Black Death was not plague, but anthrax, or alternatively, that it was a form of food poisoning caused by microfungi in rye bread.[23] In favour of the anthrax hypothesis is the fact that medieval chroniclers refer to the deaths of cows and sheep as well as humans, while in modern outbreaks of plague, as in Manchuria, though rabbits are susceptible to the bacteria, pigs, oxen and poultry are not. However, the immunity of domestic animals is not universal. In the Chinese plague area of Yunnan, it was reported in the nineteenth century that: 'The rats fell dead, and then comes the turn of the poultry; after the poultry have succumbed, pigs, goats, ponies and oxen successively die off'.[24] While Procopius' description of the plague of Justinian makes the diagnosis of bubonic plague almost certain, its origin was attributed by him and by Arab authors to Egypt and Ethiopia. To this it may be replied that Thucydides had attributed the pestilence of Athens (certainly not plague: typhus is still the best candidate) to Egypt, and for both Christians and Muslims, Egypt was the land of plagues. Finally, it may be doubted if the episode at Caffa was the sole source of the infection. In 1346 plague was already in Astrakhan and Tabriz, and once in those emporia, was bound to spread west even without Janibeg's early essay in bacteriological warfare. Nevertheless, the episode was significant for both Italy and Egypt, its epicentres in Europe and Islam. The theory of *Yersinia pestis* from Central Asia via the northern land route remains the most convincing to date.

Where had the plague been before Astrakhan and Tabriz? In 1341 it had been in Samarkand according to the concordant testimony of the Andalusian Ibn Khatimah and the Englishman Baker de Swynbroke. Before that, from 1338, it had been in the Chaghatir khanate: Semirechie and lowland Kirghizia. For this there is archeological evidence. In the 1920s, the Russian archaeologist D. A. Chwolson examined two Nestorian cemeteries near Lake Issyk-kul, not far from the Chaghatai capital of Almalik. He found an unusually large number of deaths relating to the 1330s and in particular three headstones, dated 1338–9 which described what their owners died of in terms highly suggestive of plague. Issyk-kul is in marmot country, the basic animal reservoir of *Yersinia pestis*. It was a minor trade centre in salt, so a line to Almalik, or Samarkand, and thence along the northern land route to Astrakhan (Old Sarai), or the central land route to Tabriz, is plausible, especially as fleas do well in textiles. At this time, since the last effective Il-khan Abu Said died in 1338 and trade was disrupted on the central land route, the northern land route was probably indeed the carrier. Tabriz will have imported from Sarai. In Central Asia, the background was the split in 1334 between nomadizers and sedentarizers which followed the conversion of Tarmashirin to Islam. The split caused movement of population, especially among the Nestorian bourgeoisie of a Semirechie then more urbanized, who were pulled both ways. The Nestorians were the earliest victims of the new epidemic and their decline as an element in the Chaghatai polity may partly be attributed to it.

Plague was carried to Islam and Europe. Did it also spread at this time to India and China? Ibn Battuta claims to have seen plague in India during his stay in the reign of Muhammed Tughlak, but Dols is sceptical about this as it seems too early. Probably it came later, not directly from Central Asia, but indirectly from Iraq via the Persian gulf or from Egypt via the Red sea. There is little sign of early plague in Persia or in Arabia where it was introduced later by a Yemeni prince returning from exile in Cairo.

As regards China too, the evidence is not clear until the late sixteenth century. The Chinese population experienced a calamitous fall between 1200 and 1370, from 120 million to 60 million, worse than Europe's. The causes, though, may have been war – China was actually conquered by the Mongols; famine – a bad one in 1323; or diseases other than plague – cholera, of which Möngke may have died. There are signs of plague in 1346: Peking specifically in 1354, and serious, unspecified epidemics around the turn of the fourteenth and fifteenth centuries. A new interest in foreign drugs has been suggested as a motive for Cheng Ho's voyages. Might not new drugs mean new diseases mean plague? China certainly was in touch with Central Asia through its embassies to the Timurids. Against these arguments is the consensus of early European travellers – Mendoza, de Rhodes, Rodriguez – that there was no plague in China. Possibly, however, their evidence relates to South China, where plague has never been a problem, or they caught North China between episodes. Chinese sources, studied by Helen Dunstan, do indicate both bubonic and pneumonic plague in the 1640s, and possibly in the 1580s, at a time of increased contact with Manchuria.[25] Yet China had been in contact with marmot areas before, notably in the early fifteenth century during the campaigns of the Yung-lo emperor in Mongolia and Manchuria. China, therefore, had probably been touched by the empire of *Yersinia pestis* before it was extended to America by the Europeans. China, however, protected by the Gobi and the reluctance of camel fleas to move to humans, was less affected than Europe, Islam or India. No secondary animal reservoir, like that of Kurdistan in the west, is found in China, except in Yunnan which was too marginal to affect the mass of the population. Japan, still more isolated, escaped plague altogether.[26]

Plague was the foundation of the microbian common market. It was the first of the new diseases to be generalized to all four primary civilizations. In demographic terms, however, it functioned more as an apex than a foundation. Its impact was greatest in Europe and Islam. At no time, however, was it responsible for more than 10 per cent of deaths in a century, generally 5 per cent. This was less than smallpox at over 10 per cent, and much less than infantile dysentery at 20 per cent. What made plague demographically significant was not its absolute death totals, but its marginal effect and particular incidence. First, to a death rate of 35 per thousand, it could add a further 6 per thousand, which put the death rate ahead of the maximum birth rate of 40 per thousand. Population growth became impossible. Second, plague affected particularly adolescents and young adults, especially women, because they were inside more. It reduced the working and reproducing population, depressed the economy and choked off earlier demographic pressure. Third, the incidence of the plague was heavily urban. Two-thirds of all who died of plague were in cities. Biraben calculated that, for three hundred years, plague raised the long term urban death rate in Christianity and Islam from 40 per thousand to 60 per thousand. Elites, particularly clerical elites, were severely hit. Cities became places of death, inured to periodic catastrophes which reduced their population by a quarter. Yet, by the same token, they became places of immigration, youth, reproduction, renewal, and in appropriate circumstances, dynamism. In 1667 Pepys recorded a conversation with Lord Robartes on this subject:

> I observed therein, to the honour of this City, that I have not heard of one citizen of London broke in all this war, this plague, this fire, and this coming up of the enemy among us; which he owned to be very considerable.[27]

In institutional terms, plague was a brake in Islam but an accelerator in Christendom. In Islam, the general demographic undertow and the particular periodic hecatombs, especially of elites, in the major centres of society and culture, was a depressant. It was an important ingredient in that prevailing sense of 'bad times' which Basim Musallam sees as shaping Islamic demography until the twentieth century.[28] Muslim attitudes to plague were more fatalistic than those in Christendom. Scapegoats were less sought, sins were less blamed or expiated, medical orthodoxy on miasmic origins less questioned. Those who died of plague would have died anyway.

In Christendom, late medieval culture might be obsessed with sin and death, but it was a constructive obsession, a therapeutic catharsis, which dissipated fear by constantly reliving it. Macabre sensibility lay on the interface of the microbian common market and the basic information circuit.[29] Remarkably quickly, first in municipalities, then in principalities, finally in kingdoms, Europe rejected the immobilism of medical theorists, committed as in Islam to miasmism, and on the basis of the observed facts of contagion and infection, established institutions of quarantine and isolation. It was these which first lowered the deaths in epidemics, then reduced the number and frequency of epidemics, and finally allowed the virtual elimination of plague through the development of immunity: possibly, as Biraben thinks, through inoculation from cats with *Yersinia pseudotuberculosis* which gives 100 per cent protection from *Yersinia pestis*; or, as others think, through the natural development of antibodies, or a spontaneous decrease in the virulence of the bacteria.

The gradual success of quarantine and its containment of plague to the eastern Mediterranean gave Europeans confidence in reason, in theories. Directly, success was celebrated in religious monuments: Santa Maria della Salute in Venice, the Plague Column and the Karlskirche in Vienna. Indirectly, it promoted the scientific revolution, the Enlightenment, and belief in progress. The retreat of plague, followed not long after by the headlong flight of smallpox before variolation and vaccination, was one of the earliest and most convincing manifestations of progress. It made Europeans believe in themselves and in their attitude to the world. The microbian common market was transformed by the basic information circuit into a world sanatorium. In this reversal, too, Central Asia played a role. For variolation, the prototype of all inoculation, spread more or less simultaneously to Constantinople in one direction, and to Tibet and China in the other in the eighteenth century. It probably originated, not in Caucasia, as the Europeans thought, but in Transcaspia, one of the Turkestans. This is the view put forward by Père D'Entrecolles in a letter to du Halde from Peking in July 1726.[30] He suggests that the transmission was effected by the Armenian merchants who travelled the Central Asia trade routes with colonies in all the main centres. If this view is correct, Central Asia supplied healing as well as hurt, the weapons of peace as well as those of war.

5 Tamerlane and the Global Arsenal 1370–1405

Tamerlane was the greatest political Central Asian. His reign from 1370 to 1405, initiated the most active period of Central Asian history. This period, thanks to the impetus imparted by him, was to last to the beginning of the sixteenth century. The name Tamerlane is the sixteenth century European form of the Turkish Timur or Temür-i-link, Temür the lame, a name given him because of a slight limp, variously explained by injury in an early battle or a tubercular infection. Tamerlane was a politician turned soldier. Inside Central Asia, he created a new kind of composite army, his impact on the surrounding homelands was that of an enemy, and his contribution to world history was to what may be called the global arsenal: a new pool of military technology on which all states increasingly drew. This pool remained in much the form left by Tamerlane till the transformations produced by the industrialized warfare of the nineteenth century. Tamerlane and Napoleon were essentially contemporaries.

Tamerlane was primarily a conqueror. Except for Alexander he conquered more than anyone else, more than Chinggis, and did a horrifying amount of destruction. Living in a harsh and grim century, the worst for civilization since the Dark Ages, he was himself perforce harsh and grim. Yet, unlike Chinggis, there was a gleam of enlightenment about him. Although illiterate, he promoted a form of culture which dominated the Islamic world for three centuries and influenced the European Renaissance. Although a nomad, who preferred to live in a tent, and be on the move, he was a Muslim (of a kind), spoke two if not three languages, played chess, liked to be read history at mealtimes, loved buildings, appreciated porcelain, and carried round a portable bath. Although beginning with light cavalry, he ended the supremacy of the steppe horseman initiated by Chinggis. Tamerlane was a second Chinggis but also an anti-

Chinggis. Eclecticism and intellectual curiosity were his hall-
marks. It is these, rather than his conquests, which make him
interesting. Ibn Khaldun, who met him outside Damascus in
1401 wrote:

> This king Timur is one of the greatest and mightiest kings
> ... he is highly intelligent and very perspicacious, addicted to
> debate and argument about what he knows and also about
> what he does not know.[1]

TAMERLANE IN CENTRAL ASIA

Between 1360 and 1370 Tamerlane created a political machine
and a new kind of army. Both were rooted in the political
background of the Chaghatai khanate and the circumstances of
their creation, but in the grand design which guided Tamerlane's
efforts to make them permanent, they went beyond past and
present toward a different future.

The Chaghatai khanate lacked stability. The *inju* state satis-
fied neither the nomads nor the sedentarists. *Oboghs* (nomadic
tribes) and *sarbadars* (urban mafias: the word literally meant
a head on a gibbet) pulled in different directions. Even when
the khanate was divided in 1334 into nomadic and sedentary
halves, stability was not achieved. On the contrary volatility
increased. In the east, in Semirechie, Zungharia and the Tarim
basin, the khans of Moghulistan could maintain a nomadic
state only for a generation, but then converted to Islam, and fell
under the control of the half sedentarized *oboghs* of the southwest, notably the Dughlat of Kashgaria. In the west, in
Transoxania and Afghan Turkestan, the Muslim khans failed to
establish a normal Islamic state based on bureaucrats, slave
soldiers and the *ulema* (law doctors). Instead, they fell under
the control of semi-nomadic *oboghs*: the Arlat in the west, the
Barlas in the centre, and the Jalayir in the north; and two non-
tribal military groups, the Qaraunas and the Qa-uchin. Moreover, despite their increasing institutional similarity, Moghulistan
and Transoxania remained ideological enemies. The westerners
referred to the easterners as Jats, or robbers. The easterners
referred to the westerners as Qaraunas, literally mongrels.

It was in this unstable world that Temür Barlas built up his political machine. He was born in 1336, not far from Samarkand, the son of a lesser chief of the Barlas *obogh*. The Barlas were one of a group of five or six ex-Mongol, now Turkish, *oboghs* or pseudo *oboghs* which provided the four *qaraci* beys or regents who constituted an informal council of state with or against the khans.[2] The Barlas held the area between the Oxus and the Jaxartes around Samarkand. The Qaraunas and the Arlat held the middle Oxus and points south into Khorasan and Afghan Turkestan. The Jalayir held the Jaxartes and Ferghana. The Qauchin, military professionals rather than a tribe, held scattered positions all over the *ulus*. By 'hold' was meant, in the oases, the exercise of taxing rights for the tribe in accordance with Kebek's assignment of *tumen* to particular pieces of sedentary territory, and for the chiefs, ownership of some agricultural or meadow land. In 1346 Qazan, the last even minimally effective khan, was assassinated by Qazaghan, amir of the Qaraunas, supported by the Arlat *obogh*. Strictly, the Qaraunas were not an *obogh*. The name meant mixed or mongrel. It referred originally to Mongol task forces or garrisons, drawn from more than one *obogh* or even *ulus*, or from Turkish auxiliaries outside the Mongol tribal system altogether, but whose descendants, hereditary soldiers, had by the middle of the fourteenth century become the main fighting force of the khanate. Qazan, in other words was eliminated by his own commander in chief who, under a puppet Chaghatid, established a federation under the ascendancy of the Qaraunas. Of this federation the Barlas were members. In 1358, however, Qazaghan was assassinated, his son was less forceful, the Barlas, the Jalayir, the more aristocratic *oboghs*, seceded, and the federation collapsed.

In 1360, the weakness of Western Chaghatai attracted invasion from the khan of Moghulistan, Tughluq Temür, who, despite his nomad background, was a recent convert to Islam. A strong ruler, he aimed to give his nomads booty, acquire more sedentary subjects and reunite the *ulus*. With the Moghul invasion, the Qarauna ascendancy failed and Temür Barlas, who since 1356 had been an officer in the amir's army, went over to the khan. But Moghul rule proved unpopular. The Jats seemed barbarians and resistance was continued by Qaraunas from northern Afghanistan led by Qazaghan's grandson, Husayn. In 1362 Tamerlane changed sides again and rejoined the Qaraunas. But the move was premature. The main Moghul army returned and Husayn and Tamerlane had to flee to Khorasan. In 1363, however, Tughluq Temür died, the next khan was less able, and the amirs of Kashgar were taking over Moghulistan, so the freedom fighters returned to Transoxania, with Husayn becoming chief amir like his grandfather. It looked like a resurrection of Qarauna ascendancy with the Barlas as their deputies. But in 1365 the Moghuls invaded again. The Qarauna and Barlas forces were defeated at the battle of the mire, fought during a thunderstorm when the ground was bad for big, shod, sedentary horses, but good for small, unshod, steppe ponies.

The Moghuls, no doubt, expected an easy conquest now, but again something unexpected happened. The *sarbadars* of Samarkand closed the gates and refused to surrender. Moreover they organized ambushes and withstood a siege until epidemic broke out among the Moghul horses. The Moghuls retreated not only from Samarkand but from all Transoxania, since they now had nomad versus sedentarist troubles back home. Husayn returned from Afghanistan, but his prestige was weak. The Moghuls had been defeated, not by the warriors, the *oboghs*, but by the artisans, the *sarbadars*. To reestablish himself, Husayn therefore seized control of Samarkand and put the *sarbadar* leaders to death, except for one whose life was pleaded for by his right hand man Temür Barlas, who also paid the fine he imposed on the city. Now that the Moghuls had gone, a struggle for power between Husayn and Tamerlane was inherently probable in accordance with the rules of blood tanistry. To court the *sarbadars*, therefore, was good policy, though Tamerlane seems to have been the first nomad politician sufficiently unsnobbish to do so.

As Tamerlane may have calculated, Husayn replied with a countermove which cost him the support of the other element in politics, the nomads, particularly non-territorial military professionals such as the Qa-uchin. Husayn decided to build himself a permanent capital and urban base on the site of Balkh in Afghan Turkestan, ruined since the time of Chinggis, but now to be developed as an anti Samarkand. The move to a fixed capital annoyed the nomads in general, while the economies which the building of the new capital entailed, made Husayn appear stingy to the army officers – a bad image for a nomad ruler. Tamerlane played on this, spent freely himself, and suggested that Husayn had behaved in a cowardly fashion in the battle of the mire. Soon he was the hero, not only of city guilds and dervishes, but also of the swordsmen, the young blades of the army, the *bahadurs*. At the same time, he kept the support of the non Qarauna *obogh* chiefs, especially the Barlas and the Jalayir, obtaining some support even from the Arlat, Husayn had to do all the unpleasant post-war things: Tamerlane did his best to do all the pleasant ones. When he finally revolted in 1370 at the head of his coalition, Husayn had little support left and he was easily defeated and killed.

Tamerlane now had the task of constructing a regime which should be more than a Barlas ascendancy. What he constructed was both a political machine and an army, an army resting upon a political machine. For war was not only the means by which power had been acquired, but also one of the ends for which it was to be exercised.

The political machine has been analyzed by Beatrice Forbes Manz.[3] It may be seen as consisting of six concentric circles. First, at its core, was Tamerlane himself, his wives, his children, their spouses, grandchildren, closest supporters, and personal retinue. After 1370, some of the latter became Tamerlane's marshals. They were placed in charge of *tumen*, military units of a nominal 10,000 or, in the conquered territories, of major garrisons drawn from a number of *tumen* or *oboghs*: in effect new mixed units or Qaraunas. At this level, Tamerlane's regime was a more personal one than had existed before. There were no ex-officio *qaranci* beys or council of state. Next, there were the loyal tribes, particularly the Barlas and Jalayir *oboghs*. Tamerlane, however, had no wish to be the prisoner of his natural supporters. The *obogh* chiefs therefore were either taken out of their tribal context or replaced by the marshals or people taken from the third circle. Politics were substantially detribalized under Tamerlane. Third, there were the Qaraunas, the defeated supporters of Amir Husayn, whom Tamerlane inherited and was careful not to dissolve. Instead he put them under his closest associate and high constable Chekü Barlas and used them as a counterweight against his own tribal supporters. Fourth, Tamerlane was consistently supported by the Qa-uchin, the extra-tribal, non-territorial, hereditary professionals who, after 1370, provided reliable servitors in garrisons and acted as a military provostcorps. Fifth, Tamerlane and his marshals recruited soldiers from the nomadic population of the empire

outside Transoxania: in the east from the Moghuls, in the north
from the Kipchaks and Golden Horde, in the west from the
Azeris and Turks of eastern Anatolia.[4] Finally, sedentarists, generally Persian speaking, were incorporated as infantry auxiliaries, sometimes under local dynasties, or in the siege train,
which the army came to require. Thus politically the Chaghatai
ulus was restructured by Tamerlane on more personal, dynastic
and meritocratic lines.

The army resting upon this political machine was increasingly a composite force of horse, foot and artillery rather than
a nomad people in arms. Its centrepiece was the heavy cavalry
of armoured knights so frequently portrayed in Timurid art.
This was provided by Tamerlane's personal supporters and
retinue to whom he made grants of sedentary land for the
upkeep of their chargers. Tamerlane, however, continued to
use nomadic light cavalry from the Chaghatai *oboghs* and went
to war accompanied by a vast tent city. Sedentary infantry formed
part of the expedition against Toktamish in 1391 and fought in
the great battle of Kanduzcha on June 18, though this was
primarily a victory of heavy cavalry over light.[5] Following his
campaign in India, Tamerlane acquired an elephant corps.
They led the attack on the Ottoman army in the battle of
Ankara on July 28 1402, though this too was primarily a heavy
cavalry victory, this time over Janissary infantry.[6] Tamerlane
made use of sophisticated artillery weapons in the sieges of
Aleppo and Smyrna and even evinced some interest in seapower.
In military technology, as in state building, Tamerlane was
eclectic and effective.

There remained the problem of permanence. In 1370
Tamerlane had come to power as the candidate of both the
swordsmen and the *sarbadars*, though the fundamental interests
of the two, as nomads and sedentarists, were still opposed.
Both, however, were demoralized after ten years of war and
needed leadership. Tamerlane became Great Amir, but kept a
tame Chinggisid as khan to reassure the nomads and secure
Mongolian legitimation. He married Husayn's widow, Sarai
Khanum, a daughter of the Chaghatai khan Qazan, to gratify
the Qaraunas and to consolidate his position as imperial son-in-
law, *güregen*, the highest title to which a non-Chinggisid and
Turk could aspire. But it was all temporary and precarious.
Tamerlane's basis of support would split, crumble and desert

him, as Husayn's had done, unless he could find some way not just of juxtaposing but of uniting nomads and sedentarists. This was the problem which had baffled all governments in the *inju* states, and particularly in the Chaghatai khanate, since the death of Chinggis.

Tamerlane's originality lay in going beyond improvisations, such as those of Tuva and Kebek, to the construction of a system which would give both halves of the population what they wanted, not just temporarily, but permanently in institutional arrangements. At its simplest, this system can be described as peace at home and war abroad, peace for the oases, war for the steppe. Specifically, it meant externalizing the violence of the *oboghs* and swordsmen and making it serve the interests of the townspeople and merchants. A key element in this scheme was a conscious design to reactivate the silk road, the central land route, and make it the monopoly link between Europe and China. Monopolization was to be achieved by war: primarily, against the Golden Horde, the master of the principal rival, the northern land route; secondarily, against the states of western Persia and against the Moghuls to the east in order to place the silk road under unified control politically; and finally, against India, Egypt and China in order to cripple the second rival, the southern sea route, as far as this was possible without a navy.

Tamerlane's grand design and the campaigns which put it into effect were an illustration of what Sir Halford Mackinder called the power of the heartland: Central Asia dominating the homeland peninsulas of Europe, Arabia, India and China. Such a dominance, Tamerlane believed, would satisfy the contradictory demands of his subjects for peace and war. The sedentary population would get peace at home, trade and the capacity to pay the *tamgha* or capital levy on business. The nomads, especially the rank and file outside the tribal oligarchies, would get war beyond the frontier: the kind of mobile, destructive, booty gathering war they liked. For Tamerlane, unlike Chinggis' successors, did not aim at permanent occupation or the creation of new *inju* states, but simply at devastation. The programme was not entirely new. Khubilai had been a Confucian emperor at home, while sending Mongol armadas against Japan and Southeast Asia. Tuva had invaded India and Kebek had developed Andijan on the central land route. The Il-khans had been promoters of trade, and it was their route resting on Tabriz and Sultaniya that Tamerlane sought to unify and reactivate. Admittedly too, Tamerlane probably partly stumbled on his policy because of its immediate political advantages.

Yet it is likely that Tamerlane grasped the problem as a whole and worked out its general answer, though obviously not in modern terms. Early in his career, he took the title or epithet *Sahib Qiran* symbolized by three circlets forming a triangle. It was an astrological term which meant 'Lord of the Fortunate Conjuncture'. It expressed his sense not just of balancing or juggling ruler, nomads and sedentarists, as his predecessors had done, but of integrating them into a dynamic institutional system. The Castilian ambassador Clavijo who was in Samarkand in 1404 noted the conqueror's unusual interest in trade: 'Thus trade has always been fostered by Timur with the view of making his capital the noblest of cities', and stressed the immense revenue he received from it.[7] It was an immensely destructive system for those outside it. Bishop Jewel in his *Apology* compared the Pope, the forerunner of Antichrist, to 'Tamerlane the king of Scythia, a wild and barbarous creature.'[8] Similarly, Botero in *The Greatness of Cities* compared Tamerlane to Attila and Chinggis as scourges of God in Asia, 'where like a horrible tempest or deadly raging flood he threw down to the ground the most ancient and worthiest cities and carried from thence their wealth and riches'[9]. Yet, as Botero saw, in the eye of the storm, in Samarkand itself, there was a possibility of civilization, which Tamerlane sought to realize. For his grand design included, not only conquest and commerce, but also culture to serve as the lingua franca of the top elite. This culture was both Islamic and secular.

Within the spectrum of Islam, Tamerlane was eclectic, but with a bias to modernism rather than fundamentalism. Among sedentarists and most nomads, Islam could now be taken for granted. Tamerlane coexisted with an *ulema* of the Hanafite law school. On his return from India, possibly inspired by what he had seen in Delhi, he built the colossal Friday mosque known as Bibi Khanum, a structure the size of Milan cathedral, whose dome imitated that of the Ommayad mosque in Damascus. Yet Tamerlane founded no *madrasa*, or higher Islamic college in his own name, and did not incorporate the *ulema* into his machinery of government. With the folk Islam of the dervish orders, who now dominated the oases and were making progress on the steppe, Tamerlane's relations were likewise ambivalent. He avowed himself the disciple of Sayyid Baraka, the holy man of the commercial city of Tirmidh, and on his death buried him in the tomb he had built for himself and the imperial family, the Gur Amir. He constructed one of his finest buildings at the tomb of Ahmad Yassawi, whose order, the Yassawiya, was doing most to spread Folk Islam among the nomads. In Samarkand, Tamerlane developed the cemetery complex of Shah Zindeh north of the walls, a centre of popular religion focused on the shrine of the legendary Kusam ibn Abbas, cousin of Muhammed. Yet Tamerlane kept his distance from Baha ad-Din Naqshband, the founder of the most traditionalist, popular and later most powerful order, the Naqshbandiyya. His leading theological adviser, the Hanafite cadi Abd al-Jabbar Khwarazmi, was reputed to be a Mutazilite or modernist while he himself, at one time at least, was regarded as a Shiite. Some scholars have queried this but it makes sense in that Shiite authoritarianism was frequently allied with Mutazilite modernism against Koranic fundamentalism and *sharia* traditionalism. Tamerlane's Islam was eclectic but consistent.

Tamerlane's secular culture was aesthetic rather than literary or scientific. He loved buildings, gardens, *bibelots*, displays, *objets d'art*. Indeed, it has been said of Tamerlane, as of Goering, that he loved art so much that he could not help stealing it![10] Thus foreign buildings, such as the Ommayad mosque at Damascus, were sketched by official artists even as they went up in flames. The Byzantine palace gates of the Ottoman capital of Brusa were carried off to Samarkand, where they were much admired by Clavijo.[11] Thousands of craftsmen and artisans were deported to Samarkand from Sultaniya, Shiraz, Baghdad and Damascus to new industrial suburbs named after those cities. Yet Tamerlane also established a *kitabkhana* for the copying, illustration, binding and storage of books. He employed historians to chronicle his deeds and his questions to Ibn Khaldun about the Maghreb suggest scientific as well as strategic interest. Moreover, his secular culture was couched in terms of the *Shah-nama*, the prompt-book of a heroic but cultivated military aristocracy. In the war against the Golden Horde, Tamerlane saw himself as Rustum defeating the hosts of Turan and coming to the aid of his son in the heat of battle. Against western enemies, he figured as an eastern Alexander, of Alid and Fatimid descent as in the *Shah-nama* Alexander had been of Achaemenid descent, revivifying Iran at the same time as purging its leadership. Yet Tamerlane was also the successor of Chinggis who died on his way to China to prove himself his equal by restoring the Yüan to Peking. Alternatively, he was again Rustum who fought the Khaqan of China in Khotan or Alexander who built the Great Wall of Gog and Magog. In culture, as in religion, politics and war, Tamerlane was eclectic. Like Chinggis he died on campaign, but his body, like Alexander's, rested in a splendid tomb in an imperial city.

TAMERLANE IN THE HOMELANDS

In the light of his grand design, Tamerlane's campaigns, bewildering at first sight and apparently purely reactive, became coherent. First between 1370 and 1385, following a period of internal reform to complete his restructuring of the political system, there were campaigns east to overawe Moghulistan, north to recover Khiva, and west against the successor states of the Il-khanate in Persia and Iran. All these had the implied aim of asserting Chaghatai control of the central land route from Tabriz to Turfan. In these campaigns, Tamerlane did not display striking military genius or achieve signal political success, especially against the Moghuls whose light cavalry retained a tactical edge. Second, between 1385 and 1395, campaigns were directed north against the Golden Horde, the master of the currently predominant northern land route, an operation explicitly destructive in its aims. This was the most difficult of Tamerlane's campaigns and the only one in which, his combination of strike power and logistics, he showed strategic genius. It produced the victories of Kanduzcha in June 1391 and of the Terek river in April 1395 and led to the destruction of the trading cities of the Horde, Astrakhan, Tana and Sarai. Third, in 1398–9, Tamerlane raided India. This was a looting expedition primarily, but also a blow against the southern sea route, and ideological display: a *jihad*, an imitation of Alexander, and doing what even Chinggis had not done. Fourth, between 1400 and 1404, there was the campaign against the Islamic Far West, the Mamluks and the Ottomans, and to some extent Christendom in the guise of Eastern heterodoxy and the Knights of St. John. This too had both commercial and ideological dimensions: to secure the Western terminus of the central land route in Aleppo, to hit the southern sea route in its Egyptian outlet, to conquer infidels and to repress heretics. Finally, in 1405, there was the unfinished campaign against China: to secure the silk road's eastern terminus in Peking, to equal Chinggis, and to outdo even the legendary Alexander by going beyond the Wall. Through these campaigns Tamerlane became part of the history of the homelands.

The Golden Horde and the Russias

In the period following Tamerlane, the Golden Horde fragmented. From the main body in Sarai, there seceded to the west, three Turkish city states, Astrakhan, Kazan and the Crimea, and to the east, three Turkish nomadic hordes, Nogai, Sibir and Uzbek. As a result, it is said, the princes of Russia in Lithuania, Novgorod and Moscow were able to assert their full independence, and Moscow, by its annexation of Novgorod in 1482, could claim the succession to the khans. It is tempting to ascribe these developments to Tamerlane's defeat of Toktamish, and in particular to his devastation of the central Horde cities and the northern land route on which their prosperity and its stability depended. While Tamerlane's impact was real, this view requires nuancing.

The Golden Horde was an *inju* state with a difference. Its relations to its sedentarists, the Russians, were less close than those of the Il-khanate to the Persians, Chaghatai to the Iranians of Central Asia, or the Yüan to the Chinese. The cities in which its oligarchies had their arsenals and turned Muslim were either its own creation, as with the two Sarais, or were the creation of non-Russians: the Genoese and the Venetians in the Crimea and Tana, the Bulgar Turks and Finno-Ugrians in Kazan. The conflicts which afflicted the Horde, during the co-reign of Nogai in the thirteenth century, during the Great Trouble before Tamerlane in the fourteenth century, and in the city and nomad secessions in fifteenth century after him, were political rather than social or ecological, violence within the *inju* consortium rather than against it. Though Tamerlane exacerbated these conflicts by his blows against the northern land route, which reduced the dividend to be distributed, it is arguable that the *ulus* of Jochi died by its own hand rather than by that of Tamerlane.

The immediate result of Tamerlane's intervention, indeed, was a strengthening of the Horde, at least externally. On the defeat of Toktamish, Tamerlane replaced him with Timur-Kutlugh, grandson of Urus Khan, a former ruler of the Blue Horde or eastern half of the *ulus* of Jochi. He partnered him (perhaps in imitation of his own position as Great Amir) with the amir Edigei, a member of the Manghit *obogh* from Magyshlak in the Nogai confederation, as co-ruler. This move represented a strengthening of the nomadic element in the now partly deurbanized Horde. Timur-Kutlugh and Edigei proved anything but puppets. In August 1399 they defeated Vytautas of Lithuania, Belorussia and the Ukraine, the strongest prince in Russia of his day, at the battle of the Vorskla river near Poltava. By 1405 they were sufficiently independent of and threatening to Tamerlane for him to receive an embassy at Otrar from Toktamish, in exile in Siberia but still hoping to regain power in the Horde. Edigei recovered Khiva from the Timurids in 1406, raided Muscovy in 1408, and renewed the traditional alliance with the Mamluks in 1409. He was unable to maintain his position, however, against the Khan and the house of Toktamish, and was driven from power in 1411. Yet his career suggests that Tamerlane was not the only, or the chief, factor in decline of the Golden Horde.

Similarly, it is not clear that Tamerlane made the fortune of Moscow. Though Vytautas lost the battle of the Vorskla river, he remained the strongest ruler in Russia till his death in 1430. If Lithuania did not retain its leading position among the principalities of Rus, it was less because of the Vorskla than because of the union of Krevo with Poland in 1386 which re-oriented Lithuania west rather than east, and the subsequent conversion of the pagan Lithuanians – the last Europeans to Christianize – to Catholicism rather than Orthodoxy. The grand dukes thereby made it more difficult to rule Belorussia and the Ukraine. They gave Moscow the chance to assert its claim to be, not so much the Third Rome, as the Second Kiev, the centre of all-Rus Orthodoxy. This claim was reinforced by the acquisition of Novgorod and the new Russia of the northeast in 1482. Yet the Vorskla may have made a difference. If it had gone the other way, Vytautas might have separated from his cousin Wradyslaw of Poland, undone the union of Krevo, and reunited the Russians round Vilnius or Kiev rather than round Moscow. Tamerlane was not the only factor in the development of fifteenth century Russia, but his impact cannot be ignored.

India

Tamerlane's campaign in India is usually regarded as a mere looting expedition like those of Tuva or a pure mission of destruction. In fact, it was more than this in both intention and impact. In intent, it may be associated ideologically with Tamerlane's desire to imitate Alexander and surpass Chinggis. Historically, it looked back to Mahmud of Ghazna, the patron of Firdausi, on whose Turco-Iranian court Tamerlane modelled his own, and who was best known in Islam as a conqueror of India. Politically, it looked forward to the conflict with the Ottomans. The Ottoman sultan had defeated the Serbs in 1389 at Kossovo, the combined princes of Christendom under Sigismund of Hungary and John of Burgundy in 1396 at Nikopolis. He was a *gazi*, a warrior for the faith and conqueror of infidels. Except marginally in the Caucasus, all Tamerlane's victories to date had been over Muslim princes. A campaign in India, where the Tughluq dynasty could be represented as falling down on the *jihad* was a convenient way of acquiring Islamic prestige. It was also a way for acquiring appanages and military experience for Tamerlane's grandsons, Muhammed Sultan and Pir Muhammed, the children of his eldest son (at least by a free-born Muslim) Jahangir. Jahangir had died in 1375 and the ageing Tamerlane envisaged his sons as his heirs.

The impact of the campaign was considerable. Where Tuva's raids had strengthened the Tughluq dynasty by forcing it to centralization and firearms, Tamerlane's expedition fatally weakened it by the sack of Delhi. Moreover, it re-opened India to the Pushtun hill people of what was to become Afghanistan, as formerly in the days of the Ghorids. India was not to be closed again till Tamerlane's descendants, Babur, Humayun and Akbar, took charge of it and reconfined the Afghans to their hills. The Afghan Lodi dynasty, which had succeeded the Tughluq, had not been effective rulers of India. They brought too many of their tribal conflicts with them, so that the Muslim drive to the south against Vijayanagar lacked leadership and cutting edge. Paradoxically, Tamerlane the *gazi* contributed to the survival of the Hindu community, and hence, in the long run, to its resurgence in the days of the *raj*. A similar paradox has sometimes been suggested in Tamerlane's relations with Western Islam and Christendom, though here with less justification.

Western Islam and Christendom

Tamerlane's campaign in the west was directed against two enemies: the Ottomans and the Mamluks. In Tamerlane's eyes, which of the two was the more significant? Here a distinction must be made between military and political priorities. In military terms, Tamerlane will have recognized that the Ottoman composite army was, potentially at least, the more dangerous opponent. Though Tamerlane had a high regard for its quality, the Mamluk army had not developed beyond the heavy cavalry, which had frustrated the Il-khanate, whereas the Ottomans, since Kossovo, combined Janissary infantry, Serbian knights, Anatolian *spahis*, and Turcoman light cavalry. Moreover, the Mamluk command was divided and irresolute, whereas the Ottoman leadership was centralized and Tamerlane regarded Bayezit as an excellent general. His first moves west therefore were directed against the Ottomans: the securing of his own rear area at Tabriz and in the winter pastures of Karabagh, the closing of the door to Bayezit through the occupation of Konia, Sivas and Samsun. In political terms, however, the Mamluks had the higher priority. For Tamerlane's grand design, Aleppo, the Western terminus of the central land route, was an essential part of his empire. So too was the land corridor from the Tigris to the sea, the old classical route from one Seleucia to the other. It was along this route that Tamerlane marched to take Aleppo in 1400, Damascus in January 1401 from the Mamluks, Baghdad in July from the Jalayir sultans, before returning to the Anatolian front to defeat Bayezit at the battle of Ankara in July 1402.[12] After Kanduzcha, Ankara was Tamerlane's greatest victory, but it was really won by manoeuvre before being won on the battlefield, when Tamerlane placed himself between the Ottomans and their base. Bayezit was an excellent general, but an essentially European one, and neither he nor his troops were used to the Asiatic war of movement conducted by

Tamerlane. Clavijo reports that after Ankara, Tamerlane was expected to return to the attack on the Mamluks, but in fact, his main objectives accomplished, after a brief stay on the plains of Karabagh, he returned to the east to prepare the final campaign against China.[13]

The impact of the campaign needs careful assessment. It is sometimes argued that the battle of Ankara deferred the fall of Constantinople for fifty years and saved Christendom from deeper penetration by an earlier and more dynamic Ottoman empire. The first argument may be accepted, though the loss of Anatolia might have led to more interest in Rumelia, but not the second. Ankara was a serious defeat for the Ottoman army and produced a leadership crisis, but nothing more. The strength of the Ottoman state lay not in any particular army or sultan, but in its institutions: the dynasty, the *kapikullari* meritocracy, the *devsirme* career open to the talents, the Janissary infantry, the associated *timariots*. These were consolidated rather than subverted by Ankara. Moreover neither Constantinople nor Christendom generally, absorbed in schism and the Hundred Years War, used the respite from the Ottomans to strengthen themselves. From the Ottoman perspective, Ankara was a *défaite sans lendemain*. Tamerlane would not have had it otherwise. He had no wish to to destroy the Ottoman state, and were it not for its threat to his flank in eastern Anatolia might not have fought it. In 1395 Tamerlane wrote to Bayezit, whom he addressed as the Sultan of Edirne, proposing a partition of the Golden Horde along the line of the Dnieper, i.e. a deflection of Ottoman interest to the north rather than to the east.[14] In this the Great Amir may have perceived Ottoman interests more clearly than the sultan.

If Orthodox and Catholic Christendom gained little from Tamerlane, Eastern heterodoxy lost much. Tamerlane planned to restore the North Syrian corridor, long a military frontier between north and south, as an east–west commercial thoroughfare. But it was to be a Muslim thoroughfare and he systematically destroyed Christian institutions in the area, monastic, episcopal and mercantile.[15] Clavijo reports demolition of Armenian churches in eastern Anatolia.[16] The Jacobites were not able to elect a *maphrian* between 1379 and 1404. Though the Eastern Christian communities had been under increasing pressure from their Muslim neighbours ever since the Il-khans threatened a Christian *revanche*, Atiya argues that it was Tamerlane who destroyed the Nestorians as a national and international organization in northern Iraq and gravely weakened the Jacobites in Kurdistan and northern Syria. The long survival of these rival Christian communities has been largely forgotten because Tamerlane so thoroughly suppressed them. Tamerlane might be polite to the Castilian ambassador Clavijo and give him precedence over the representatives of the Ming emperor, but his Islamic commitment, whether Mutazilite or Shiite, was real.

If Eastern heterodoxy lost much through Tamerlane, the Mamluks, his other Muslim enemy in the west, lost something. The Mamluk state was a foreign military oligarchy of slaves without masters, the culmination of the Islamic tradition of slave soldiers and an adaptation of the Mongols' *ordo* the better to resist them.[17] As foreign, as needing constant immigration, the Mamluks lived in alliance and symbiosis with the Golden Horde. Tamerlane's weakening of the Horde, therefore, weakened the Mamluks, and consolidated the transition from Kipchak to Circassia as their recruiting area. Circassia, neither Indo-European nor Turkish in language, was a highly provincial background for a successful ruling class. Though the Mamluks recovered Damascus and Aleppo after 1405, and retained them till their defeat by the Ottomans in 1516, their power was less. Ayn Jalut had been avenged.

China

Tamerlane never invaded Ming China, but this threat to do so had a profound impact there. The first Ming ruler, the Hung-wu emperor (1368–1398), was not particularly interested in foreign policy. He was primarily an internal revolutionary and though he allowed his generals to fight campaigns against the Mongols or their associates, his purposes were basically defensive. He contented himself with sending embassies to former Yüan tributaries asking that the Ming be recognized as the new overlords. One of these reached Samarkand in 1395 and was promptly imprisoned by Tamerlane who was already planning his campaign to control the trade route, restore the Yüan, equal Chinggis and surpass Alexander.

Hung-wu died in 1398. After a period of civil war, in 1402 he was succeeded by his son the Yung-lo emperor (1402–1424), who had been concerned with China's Inner Asian frontier and in particular with its shortage of good cavalry horses. He at once began a crash programme of horse breeding and buying, no doubt in anticipation of an invasion from Tamerlane, and in the meantime sent another embassy to Samarkand. This was the embassy encountered by Clavijo. Its terms of reference annoyed Tamerlane and it too was imprisoned, though probably some word of what was going on reached Peking. Yung-lo took no immediate action, but in 1405 the first of his great naval expeditions to the west under the eunuch admiral Cheng Ho set sail, paralleled by a flurry of diplomatic activity by land. The primary purpose of these missions was to end China's isolation in the face of an attack from Tamerlane. Unlike his father, Yung-lo was interested in foreign policy. Indeed, unique among Chinese emperors, he made it a top priority. He was an external revolutionary. He planned to restructure China's place in the world by giving it a new oceanic dimension. Yüng-lo was promoted to this remarkable innovation by Tamerlane, though this could not be admitted in the record. He saw that the answer to the power of the heartland was seapower, the power of the circumference as represented by Cheng Ho's fleet. Here Yung-lo was reacting not just to Tamerlane's threat but to his contribution to the world order in the institution of the global arsenal.

THE GLOBAL ARSENAL

Down to the Mongolian explosion, styles of warfare were disparate. The steppe with its innumerable ponies, mobile rear-area, people in arms, projectile preference, *guerre à l'outrance* contrasted with Iran with its big horses, armoured knights, support services, professionalism, impact preference, chivalrous welfare. Iran contrasted with an earlier, 'democratic' tradition of massed heavy industry and brutal, enslaving war, dormant in Europe since Classical antiquity, but in China revived by the Sung. In 1200 gunpowder was confined to China, war galleys to the Mediterranean, paddle wheelers to the Yangtze lakes, war elephants to India, the horse to the Old World. Everywhere generals and admirals acted within traditions and operations were less competition between equals than trials between different systems. From the Mongolian explosion, however, there began a process of osmosis which produced a standardized global arsenal in cavalry, artillery and seapower. Military intelligence travels fast and enemies are quick to imitate. Like the microbian common market, the global arsenal was rooted in the basic information circuit, but as a voluntary, not an involuntary part of this process. Tamerlane was both effect and cause, expression and agent.

Cavalry

The Mongolian explosion was based on the temporary superiority of light cavalry. From the middle of the thirteenth century, beginning with the battle of Ayn Jalut, heavy cavalry began to regain the advantage. To reduce inferiority in numbers, more big horses were bred in studs. Professionalism, where the Iranian knight had always had the advantage over the Turco-Mongolian herdsman, was promoted. Advantages with armour, bows and equipment were extended. Knights were better coordinated with other units – infantry, light cavalry, and artillery – in what became for the first time composite armies. Organization, the factor which had surcharged the steppe, was brought up to Chinggisid standards. The Ottoman party state, the Mamluk military brotherhood, Tamerlane's political machine, all borrowed from the *ordo*. Defeats, like Ankara, no longer caused states to dissolve, as the tribal and city polity of the Khwarazmshah had dissolved. Ayn Jalut was followed by the success of the Il-khanate against the Golden Horde, the defeat of first Arigh Böke and then Qaidu by the Alan heavy cavalry of Khubilai, the ascendancy within the Golden Horde of Nogai, again in association with the Alans, and the inability of the Moghuls to reunite the Chaghatai khanate. Historians have been quick to document the superiority of the steppe. They have been much less so to document its reversal.

Of this reversal, Tamerlane's campaigns against the Golden Horde, culminating in the battles of Kanduzcha and the Terek river, were the climax. It is clear from contemporary illustrations that the core of Tamerlane's army consisted of armoured knights, taken out of their tribal structure, attached to the Timurid courts, and provided with grants of sedentary land known as *soyurghal* on which to maintain their large horses. From literary sources, especially Clavijo who was interested in nomads, it is also clear that Tamerlane continued to make use of steppe light cavalry accompanied on campaign by its civilian population. To this mixture of heavy and light cavalry, Tamerlane later added the super-heavy cavalry of his elephants. His army, indeed was the most composite of the fourteenth century. The Golden Horde, on the other hand, never made the transition from a simple to a composite force. The failure of Nogai to consolidate, the subsequent dominance within his horde of the Manghit *obogh* of Magyshlak, and the ascendancy of the eastern Blue Horde over the western White Horde, all spelt the continued preponderance of light cavalry. It was this which was defeated in the campaigns against Tamerlane. Here he was a true anti Chinggis. By contrast, the Ottomans made their way increasingly composite. In the Balkans they combined Janissary infantry and artillery with their own *timariot* heavy horse and with light cavalry supplied by their satellite the Crimean khanate. It was in the Balkan-Ukraine region too that there developed the intermediate horseman: the hussar, Cossack or Uhlan, mounted on a big horse, but with the saddle, short stirrups, weapons and absence of body armour of the light horseman.[18]

Artillery

Tamerlane's role in the rise of artillery and firearms, as an essential part of composite armies, has not been sufficiently appreciated. One reason for this is that their history is too completely identified with that of gunpowder and the gun.[19]

The earliest successful firearm was based not on gunpowder, but on naphtha. This was the famous Greek fire, essentially a flame thrower operated by bellows, supposedly invented by Callinicus of Heliopolis (Egypt or Syria, it is not clear) *c.*650 AD. It was certainly used against the Muslim sieges between 671 and 678, against the Rus in 941, and against the Pisans off Rhodes in 1103. Greek fire came to China *c.*900, probably via the southern sea route. It is first mentioned in 917 as a gift from Ch'ien Liu, king of the Hangchow city state of Wu-yüeh, to A-pao-chi, founder of the northern Khitan kingdom of Liao, doubtless with a view to common defence against the expanding empire of the Five Dynasties in Honan, Hopei and Shansi. A reference for 919 specifies that the *meng-huo yü* (fiercely-burning oil) and its siphon-like projector pump came from the Arab world, *Ta-Shih kuo*. Gunpowder, the formula for which is first mentioned in a Taoist text *c.*850 AD, found its first military use, in a low nitrate form, as ignition for naphtha based flame throwers. Its use in this way is first mentioned in the *Wu-ching tsung-yao* (complete essentials of military science) of 1044, but as an already established practice, which probably went back to the tenth century. Naphtha, however, was never wholly satisfactory. In 975, for example, the Southern T'ang admiral Chu Ling-pin was defeated by the Northern Sung, when the wind turned his flame throwers back on his own ships. It was therefore increasingly replaced by gunpowder. Indeed in Arabic, *naft*, which had originally referred to Greek fire, came to denote first deflagrating low nitrate gunpowder and then explosive high nitrate gunpowder. Nevertheless, naphtha continued in use, especially in Middle Eastern armies to whom oil was readily available, and in the form of napalm still does. There are a number of indications that Tamerlane used such weapons: against elephants in India, mounted on elephants against Aleppo, and against ships in the siege of Smyrna.

When gunpowder replaced naphtha it did so first in the form of the back-firing rocket rather than the forward-firing gun. The military rocket, or fire arrow *huo-chien* originated in the civilian firecrackers known as 'ground rats' *ti lao-shu* which made their appearance in China in the twelfth century. Around 1200, 'ground rats' were used to power incendiary arrows instead of the crossbow and in 1245 rocket-propelled fire arrows were being used in units of the Sung navy exercising in the Ch'ien-t'ang estuary. These rockets were propelled by middle nitrate, 'whoosh', gunpowder. Rockets, however, did not long retain their predominance. Though they continued to be used in the Chinese navy down to the Opium War, in the army, from the late thirteenth century, that is under the Yüan dynasty, they were increasingly replaced by hand guns and cannon using explosive, high nitrate and forward-firing gunpowder. These were developed out of the metal barrels employed when coviative projectiles were added to naphtha-based and gunpowder-ignited flame throwers. The earliest representation of a hand gun is in a Buddhist cave temple, dated 1250–80, Ta-tsu in Szechwan, first recognized as such by Robin Yates in June 1983.[20]

An actual gun dated to 1288 is in the Heilungkiang museum and several cannon survive from the mid-fourteenth century. Cannon first played a decisive role in naval actions on the Yangtze during the interregnum between Yüan and Ming.

In the West, references to gunpowder rockets appear in the late thirteenth century, especially in works ascribed to St. Albert Magnus, and they were in military use at Ghent in 1314. They were soon, however, superseded by gunpowder cannon. The earliest European picture of a cannon is in a manuscript of Walter Demilametés' *De Nobilitatis . . . Regum* of 1327 and they were employed at Crécy in 1346. Where rockets had their longest ascendancy was India and India was the inspiration for their revival in Europe initiated by William Congreve.[21] According to Alam Khan, gunpowder weapons, presumably rockets, were introduced to India by the Chaghatai invasions of the early fourteenth century. Here they led to modifications in military architecture and were adopted by governments, Muslim and Hindu, in both north and south. In the north, the cost of firearms was a factor in the development of the more centralized regimes of the Khalji and Tughluq Delhi sultanates, which was one result of the Chaghatai invasions.

Flame throwers and rockets formed part of Tamerlane's military inheritance. He also took steps to acquire hand guns and cannon. Clavijo noted that, 'From Turkey he had brought their gun-smiths who made the arquebus . . . Again he had gathered here in Samarqand artillery men, both engineers and bombardiers, besides those who make the ropes by which these engines work.'[22] While Clavijo does not give details and various translations are possible, the true arquebus is the *Hackenbüchse*, the German hand gun with steadying rests, the immediate ancestor of the musket, while bombardiers and tow suggest some kind of cannon which the Ottomans had used at Kossovo in 1389. Hand guns and cannon were thus probably introduced to Central Asia from the west by Tamerlane. The Chinese already had cannon, but it was from Central Asia, most likely from the Moghul khanate of Turfan, that matchlock muskets were introduced to China, possibly in the time of Yung-lo, certainly by 1520. The Chinese account of the war with Turfan between 1505 and 1524 states that the Moghuls had learnt the use of firearms from Rum, i.e. the Ottoman empire. Tamerlane, therefore, by his commitment to a composite army, contributed to the diffusion of artillery technology as part of a single global arsenal. Subsequently, his descendants, the Mughals, were to make hand guns and cannon more widely used in India, just as his predecessors, the Chaghatai khans, had introduced rockets.

Seapower

Tamerlane and seapower appear a paradox. Most likely Tamerlane never saw the sea. He was the incarnation of the heartland – Braudel's *fortune monstrueuse des terres*, Bernard Shaw's war god of Turania – and seapower, and more specifically oceanic power, is its antithesis.[23] Yet Tamerlane did play a role in the genesis of seapower as an ingredient in the global arsenal. First, by his threatening accumulation of military power in the heartland, he provoked the first manifestation of oceanic power in Cheng Ho's voyages. Second, although Tamerlane did not live to see these voyages, he may have heard of the preparations for them, and even before, showed interest in the oceanic margins of his world. Third, Tamerlane's interest in the Far West, his invitation to the Castilian king, the information acquired by Clavijo, came closely upon the beginnings of Iberian seapower: the Castilian expeditions to Tetuan in 1400, to the Canary islands in 1402, the Portuguese expedition to Ceuta in 1415. Tamerlane both contributed to global consciousness and provided a further input to the basic information circuit.

Historians, like contemporaries, have been puzzled by the purpose of the six Chinese maritime expeditions between 1405 and 1433. The official explanation, a search among the Chinese communities of Southeast Asia for Yung-lo's predecessor the Chien-wen emperor, who was supposed to have survived the storming of Nanking by his uncle in 1402, seems among the least plausible. Other explanations: immediatization of relations with new states like Malacca, recanalization of private Chinese overseas trade into official, non-Chinese tributary channels, exotica to ornament and legitimize an usurped throne, scientific curiosity and a search for drugs in a time of new diseases, apply to some of the voyages, but not to all of them in detail. In Ma Huan's account, the climax of the voyages was Mecca.[24] It may be inferred, therefore, that their primary purpose was to make contact with the Muslim world beyond

Tamerlane as a potential ally for China in case the great invasion eventuated. This would explain the voyages as far as Ormuz and Aden, but not, it might be supposed, the tentatives southward toward the Madagascar channel and perhaps the Cape of Good Hope. But here too a strategic purpose may be conjectured. Yung-lo will have heard of the precedence given over his ambassadors to Samarkand to those of Henry III of Castile. If the Franks of the Far West were so significant, should not China have direct contact with them? Yung-lo's death in 1424 interrupted the series of voyages, so that the last in 1431 was only a reprise to compensate the military for the withdrawal from Vietnam, but if they had been pursued, Cheng Ho's armada might have appeared in the Tagus or the Guadalquivir. Such a thing was not inconceivable to contemporaries. Cheng Ho was a Muslim and Joanot Martorell has a Muslim fleet from the Canaries invade the England of Henry VI.[25] Tamerlane provoked a new awareness of sea, indeed, oceanic, power.

Tamerlane himself was not without some perception of seapower. He may never have seen the sea, but he will most likely have seen the Caspian, whose trade in salt, sturgeon and caviare was a significant link between the Golden Horde and the Il-khanate. Moreover its strategic role on the flank of the central land route will not have escaped him. In his meeting with Ibn Khaldun outside Damascus in 1401, Tamerlane asked the historian for a report – within 24 hours – on 'the whole country of the Maghrib.'[26] In particular, Tamerlane asked about the exact locations of Tangier and Ceuta, i.e. the keys to the straits of Gilbraltar and the Atlantic. It is difficult to believe that Tamerlane's interest was purely academic. Indeed, Ibn Khaldun was sufficiently worried by Tamerlane's interest to write a letter to the authorities in the Maghreb telling them what had transpired between him and the conqueror. Conquests in the Far West would not have formed part of Tamerlane's grand design, but it should be remembered that Alexander the Great in his famous last plans had envisaged a circumnavigation of Africa. At the lowest, Tamerlane's question indicates an awareness of the oceanic periphery of his world and hence of seapower. It may have been the conversation with Ibn Khaldun too which gave Tamerlane an interest in Castile and led to the invitation to Clavijo.

Clavijo returned to Seville in March 1406. Henry III died in

1407, but his interest in the basic information circuit did not die with him. His nephew by marriage was Henry the Navigator and his grandaughter was Isabella the Catholic. Clavijo's report was not printed till 1582, but it was widely copied in Spain and will have had its subterranean effect. In it he noted the difficulties of land communication with China.

> Now from the city of Samarqand it is six months' march to the capital of China, which is called Cambaluc . . . and of this six months' journey two are passed going across a desert country entirely uninhabited, except by nomad herdsmen.

However, there was another possibility. In Samarkand, Clavijo talked to a Central Asian merchant, 'who had been allowed to reside in Cambaluc during six whole months. He described that great city as lying not far from the sea coast, and for its size he said it was certainly twenty times larger than Tabriz.' Clavijo commented:

> If so it must indeed be the greatest city in all the world, for Tabriz measures a great league and more across and therefore this city of Cambaluc must extend to twenty leagues from one side to the other.[27]

Tabriz was the easternmost outlet for Western, especially Genoese, trade and on his visit Clavijo had noted 'There is indeed an immense concourse of merchants and merchandise here.'[28] If Peking was a bigger mart than Tabriz and close to the sea, it would not be difficult for someone in Seville, especially if they were Genoese and had read Peter d'Ailly's *Imago Mundi* and the Latin version of Ptolemy's *Geography*, both published in 1410, to conceive an even bolder voyage than those of Cheng Ho.

6 The Timurids and the Republic of Letters

The Timurids were the successors of Tamerlane. They maintained his empire, that amalgam of conquest, commerce and culture, from his death in 1405 to the fall of Herat to the Uzbeks in 1507. That empire had been created by force. It was maintained by diplomacy, especially cultural diplomacy. What the Timurids created was a Renaissance monarchy, one of the first and to that date the largest. Like other Renaissance monarchies, it both rested on and promoted a set of intellectual values and institutions. These, when linked to other such sets, eventually became a new world institution, the republic of letters. The Timurids – Shah Rukh, Ulugh Beg, Abu Said and Husayn Bayqara – should therefore be seen as one of its fountain heads, like their contemporaries the Hsüan-te emperor in China, the Medici in Florence, Pope Nicholas V and the Valois Dukes of Burgundy.

The Timurids differed from Tamerlane. He had been the Lord of the Favourable Conjuncture, the nomad with the portable bath, who straddled two worlds, living alternately in tents and palaces. They were sedentary aristocrats, civilians, seldom on campaign and then generally defeated, men of a world now dividing again between oasis and steppe. For just as the thirteenth and fourteenth centuries had seen a fusion of nomads and sedentarists, so the fifteenth and sixteenth centuries saw a repolarization. In this polarization, the Timurids fell on the sedentary side, but it too was increasingly polarized between upper class, cultured princely courts and the lower class philistine dervish orders. This second contest, within the sedentary world, the Timurids were eventually to lose. After 1510 therefore, they had, under Babur, to find a new country in India as the Mughals. For a century after Tamerlane's death, however, they continued, with considerable political skill, his empire based on the central trade route. At the same time, they carried to new heights, both as end and means, his other legacy of cultural patronage. As conquest ceased to be possible, commerce and culture received additional emphasis, especially, in regard to the latter, its secular component: books, paintings, carpets, workshops and colleges.

THE TIMURIDS IN CENTRAL ASIA

The succession dispute which erupted on Tamerlane's death showed how much the political scene had been changed by the conqueror. It was not traditional nomadic blood tanistry. The *oboghs* and their chiefs: the Barlas, the Arlat, the Jalayir, Qaraunas and Qa-uchin, who had dominated politics in the mid fourteenth century; were now of diminished significance.[1] The conflict was now between functional parts of the dynastic political machine, arrayed under different Timurid princes. Tamerlane died at Otrar on February 18 1405. Although nearly 70, and, as Clavijo reports, with failing eyesight and frequently having to be carried, he had not yet decided the succession unambiguously, whether because of vestigial adherence to blood tanistry or reluctance to confront the prospect of his own death.[2] Of his four sons, Jahangir, the eldest by a free mother, had died in 1375; Omar Shaikh, governor of Fars and a good soldier, in 1394; Miran Shah, nominal viceroy of the Il-khanate, was an alcoholic; leaving only the youngest, Shah Rukh, governor of Khorasan, as an active contender. There were, however, plenty of grandsons to contend.

There are signs that Tamerlane intended the succession to go by primogeniture. In that case, the heir was Pir Muhammed, governor of Kandahar, and second son of Jahangir, the eldest son, Muhammed Sultan, who had been highly favoured by Tamerlane, having died as a result of wounds sustained in the battle of Ankara. Clavijo was presented to Pir Muhammed when they were both in Samarkand. The ambassador tells us that, 'The people whom we found in attendance on him all paid him the utmost deference' and that he wore a great ruby like that of Tamerlane himself.[3] Pir Muhammed, however, had returned to India before the China campaign, so the army at Otrar proclaimed Khalil son of Miran Shah, like his father in his better days, a good fighting man, pro nomad and popular with the troops. An additional asset he possessed was his mother the Khivan princess Khan-zade, Tamerlane's favourite daughter in law, who had been married successively to Jahangir and Miran Shah. Clavijo describes her ungraciously as fair, fat and forty, but clearly she was a person of importance in Timurid high society. Next, the Persian civil servants and army reserves lent their support to Shah Rukh in Herat, who was married to Gawhar Shad, the daughter of one of Tamerlane's old colleagues and a political force in her own right. Finally, the regional government in the west at Tabriz, nominally under Miran Shah, in fact under his sons Umar and Abu Bakr, was another claimant, but it was soon eliminated by the rise, within its own bailiwick, of the Turcoman chief Qara Yusuf of the Black Sheep dynasty based on Azerbaijan.

Tamerlane's political machine divided itself along the lines of legitimacy, army, bureaucracy and provinces. Bureaucracy won out largely through its ability to raise funds to pay troops. In 1406, Shah Rukh and Pir Muhammed combined against Khalil. They lost but were saved as Khalil had to go north against the Golden Horde reviving under Edigei. In 1407, Pir Muhammed was murdered and Afghan Turkestan was partitioned between Khalil and Shah Rukh. Khalil, however, was losing the support of the army because once Tamerlane's treasure, which he had distributed lavishly, was gone, he had no money, while Shah Rukh with the bureaucracy could tax the resources of Herat. In 1409, Shah Rukh was strong enough to take Samarkand, thereby extending his resources. Khalil's state dissolved, though he remained a force in politics till 1411 and his family survived in the establishment. Shah Rukh did not remain in Samarkand. He returned to Herat, leaving his son Ulugh Beg as viceroy of Transoxania. Herat was becoming the better capital. It was more defensible militarily, it was more centrally situated in relation to trade routes both north–south and east–west, and it was less dominated by dervishes hostile to the Timurid courts. Above all, it was more Persian and bureaucratic. Where Tamerlane's bureaucracy at Samarkand wrote, according to Clavijo, in Chaghatai Turkish in Uighur script, Shah Rukh's bureaucracy at Herat wrote in Persian in Arabic script.[4] It was important therefore to be close to sources of recruitment. Samarkand, however, remained as a second capital. From 1410, the empire was effectively binuclear.

Between 1410 and 1449, Central Asia was dominated, if not completely controlled, by the joint rule of Shah Rukh and

Ulugh Beg. In this unusual partnership, the relations of father and son have been a matter of controversy. Barthold regarded Ulugh Beg as the driving force, as more Turkish, secular and military, while Shah Rukh was more Iranian, religious and civilian and ruled by his wife, Gawhar Shad. Denis Sinor reverses this. He sees Ulugh Beg as an otherworldly scholar and starwatcher, where Shah Rukh was the skillful politician and diplomat. In fact, father and son were equally matched. They agreed on principles but divided functions. Shah Rukh was in charge of revenue, religion, diplomacy and art; Ulugh Beg was in charge of expenditure for the army and science. Together they developed a new basis for, and a new technique of, empire which lasted for forty years, as long as Tamerlane's original empire, and met the new circumstances they faced.

Tamerlane's death released forces of change created by his success. In theory his empire was a balance between nomads and sedentarists. In fact, that balance was increasingly tilted against the nomads. Only nobility with *soyurghal*, professional soldiers, those associated with one of the Timurid courts, benefited from the wars and the empire they sustained. The ordinary herdsman was left out. Because he was left out, he began to secede and return to the steppe. The fifteenth century saw the reemergence of purely nomadic societies: in western Turkestan, the Uzbeks, Kazakhs and Turcomans; in eastern Turkestan, the Kirghiz and the Oirats. The loss of these nomads weakened the military force of the empire. Lacking steppe ponies and supporting light cavalry, its rulers had to rely exclusively on oasis-bred large horses and heavy cavalry. Ulugh Beg's wars against the Uzbeks to the north and the Moghuls to the east were unsuccessful, so were Shah Rukh's wars against the Turcomans to the west. Unlike Chinggis' successors, Tamerlane's successors attempted no further conquests. Instead a policy of limiting and civilizing the empire was adopted. The campaign against China was called off. Azerbaijan and western Persia, including Tabriz, the western exit of the central land route, was abandoned to the Black Sheep Turcomans after 1420. Khiva was relinquished to the Golden Horde. Moghulistan was allowed to resume its independence under its Chaghatai khans with the justification that they increasingly followed Timurid policies. The Timurid empire contracted to western, sedentary central Asia (Transoxania and Khorasan), with subsidiaries in southwest Persia around Shiraz and outworks in Afghanistan around Kabul and Kandahar. Tamerlane's basic policy, the enrichment of Herat and Samarkand by promotion of the central trade route, was maintained, but it was now pursued by means other than aggressive war, namely by cultural prestige and international diplomacy.

Under Tamerlane, culture had been an accidental decoration, an idiosyncrasy of the ruler who might have preferred wine, women and song, or cruelty, as many nomads did. Under his successors, however, culture became an essential instrument of government. It was consciously designed to attract, recruit and reward men of ability to make government more acceptable, rational and efficient in diplomacy, jurisprudence and finance. Today we tend to underestimate both the rarity and utility of brain power in pre-modern circumstances and the consequent need to entice and foster it by conspicuous high culture. High culture in religion, art and science was not always available. It needed deliberate promotion by someone who commanded resources, in practice the secular prince. Equally, to the prince, literacy, objectivity, the ability to distinguish facts and values, words and things, means and ends, and the training to express these things verbally and on paper, paid big dividends in the intelligence of government. Timurid culture, therefore, was more than decoration. It aimed to produce a brain drain, to give the Timurids a quasi-monopoly of high I.Q.'s in Inner Asia, and to establish a government uniquely intelligent and secular. Like much in Timurid culture, this idea was perhaps ultimately derived from China, reflecting the literate meritocracy of the Chinese examination system. In turn, Timurid practice illustrated and transmitted the notion of meritocracy first to the Ottoman state and then to Renaissance Europe.

International diplomacy, the other new technique, also owed something to Tamerlane. He had written to Charles VI of France, received a letter from Henry IV of England, invited a mission from Henry III of Castile, as well as receiving embassies in Samarkand from the Mamluks and the Ming. But his successors carried it much further. Shah Rukh aimed to keep open the central land route, and also the increasingly important north–south land routes, by means of contacts with other rulers. These contacts would, in addition be culturally prestigious. He sent missions to Egypt, West Persia, South India and China, and received embassies from the Golden Horde and Tibet. He made Herat the most internationalist centre of the day.

Of this diplomatic activity, we are best informed about relations with China.[5] Relations had started badly. Tamerlane had imprisoned Hung-wu's ambassadors and insulted Yung-lo's. Between 1408 and 1415, however, further embassies passed between Peking and Herat. Yung-lo began to see that with the death of Tamerlane things had changed in Central Asia. Nonetheless, with the situation confused during the interregnum and the possibility of the militaristic Khalil gaining the upper hand, he still insisted on the full rigours of Chinese protocol, with the acceptance of satellite status by the Timurids. Shah Rukh felt obliged to reject relations on these terms. Then from 1416, the atmosphere changed. Using a new eunuch ambassador, Li Ta, Yung-lo began to adopt Central Asian diplomatic language. He addressed Shah Rukh as an equal and admitted, contrary to Confucian usage, the mutual advantages of trade. Shah Rukh at once responded. He allowed his ambassadors to perform the kowtow in Peking, though his chief of mission claimed that he never let his forehead actually touch the ground! With these bilateral ideological concessions, a modus vivendi was arrived at. Shah Rukh obtained the right to trade at Peking in order to enrich Herat and Samarkand. Yung-lo obtained security: the withdrawal of any threat of invasion, an implicit promise not to support the Oirats with whom he was fighting, and the opportunity to import large horses to build up his heavy cavalry. Both obtained too an agreed framework for coexistence.

Shah Rukh died in 1447, leaving the secular Ulugh Beg, hated by the dervishes, politically isolated in Samarkand. In 1449, he was forced to abdicate by his son Abd-al Latif, based on Herat and supported by the religious party in Samarkand, and was subsequently murdered. In 1450, Abd-al Latif was removed by Ulugh Beg's generals, but his replacement, Abdullah, another grandson of Shah Rukh, could make no headway. In 1457, he too was eliminated by a coalition of the urban Naqshbandi dervishes under Khoja Ahrar and the nomad Uzbeks under Khan Abul Khayr. They acted in the name of Abu Said, a grandson of Miran Shah and nephew of Khalil, a representative of the military component of the Timurid machine, the losers of 1405–10. It was a social as well as a political revolution.

Radical townspeople and recidivists to nomadism were combined against the Timurid court by Khoja Ahrar who was extending the Naqshbandi organization from the oasis to the steppe.

Abu Said was at first very weak and had to make concessions to his backers. The Uzbeks were allowed to ravage the sedentary areas, they were paid a huge indemnity levied on the upper classes, and their khan's name was put in the Friday prayers as co-ruler. Khoja Ahrar was named Shaikh ul-Islam, i.e. chief theologian and jurisconsult, and the dervishes began to control the *ulema*, the council of canon law doctors, hitherto under royal control. At Khoja Ahrar's instance, the non-Koranic *tamgha* tax on trade, much objected to by the craft guilds, was lifted in Samarkand and Bokhara. Meanwhile Herat revolted under a more liberal Timurid and in 1458 it was temporarily occupied by the Black Sheep Turcomans. Gradually, however, things improved for Abu Said. The Uzbeks were distracted by Kazakh revolt and Oirat invasion. Khoja Ahrar was checked by the appointment of a second Shaikh ul-Islam. Herat was retaken in 1456 and the capital transferred there to escape Uzbeks and dervishes. In 1462, Abu Said was able to instal a friendly and pro sedentarist khan in Moghulistan, Yunus (1462–87), so that trade routes east were reopened. At Herat, once the Turcomans withdrew, Abu Said was able to restore the Timurid court system. In 1469, however, he went on campaign against the White Sheep Turcomans now dominant in Western Persia. He hoped both to re-open the trade routes and, by building up his army, to put himself in a position once more to challenge his enemies in Transoxania. In fact, however, he was defeated and killed by the Turcomans. Abu Said was not a successful ruler, but he fought back against dervishes and nomads and thus made possible the last flowering of the Timurids in Central Asia under Husayn Bayqara between 1469 and 1506.

The death of Abu Said left a power vacuum. In Samarkand, Khoja Ahrar filled it by putting a son of Abu Said, Sultan-Ahmed, on the throne from 1454 to 94, but he was a complete puppet of the dervishes. In Herat, power was seized by Husayn Bayqara, a great grandson of Tamerlane's son Omar Shaikh, whose family had become identified with the civilized anti-dervish party, especially through Iskandar, governor of Shiraz between 1409 and 1414. Thanks to the temporary eclipse of the

Uzbeks whose khan Abul Khayr died in 1468, Husayn Bayqara, in his youth a competent soldier, was able to extend his rule to Khiva. As he also ruled in Merv, he controlled a considerable segment of the north–south route from Russia via the Volga and Caspian to India, which, in the growing chaos, was becoming more important than the east–west route. Husayn Bayqara revived Shah Rukh's techniques of international diplomacy and cultural prestige. In 1490 he sent a mission to Ivan III in Moscow to encourage commercial contacts, especially the fur trade. Herat was also in touch with India and the spice trade and functioned as a major Eurasian entrepot and source of silks, ceramics and spices for the west.

Husayn Bayqara's chief interest, however, was cultural patronage. He made Herat for a time the greatest centre of art and letters in Asia. In his patronage, he was seconded by his prime minister Mir Ali Shir Navai, the founder of Chaghatai Turkish as a literary language, and by his chief spiritual adviser, the Persian mystical poet Jami, who tried to introduce into eastern dervishism the liberal illuminism associated with the western dervishism of Jalal ad-Din Rumi's Mevleviyya. There is a famous description of Husayn Bayqara and his court by his cousin Babur, the founder of the Mughals of India. Babur spent some time in Herat in his youth and never forgot it. The sultan, he says, was tall and athletic, 'being slant-eyed and lion-bodied, slender from the waist down'. He continued:

> His was a wonderful age. In it, Khorasan, and Herat above all, was full of learned and matchless men. Whatever the work a man took up, he aimed and aspired at bringing that work to perfection . . . the whole habitable world has not seen such a town as Herat had become under Sultan Husayn Mirza.[6]

It was a true Renaissance community of merit, excellence and *virtu*, which attracted people from all over Asia. Consequently Husayn Bayqara never lacked for knights and counsellors. By a mixture of firmness, conciliation and personal prestige, he kept control of the local dervishes and out of major foreign war for thirty years. Khoja Ahrar died in 1490 which helped, Sultan-Ahmed, puppet ruler of Transoxania, in 1494 which did not, because it produced a prolonged and damaging succession dispute among the local Timurid princes, chronicled by Babur. This conflict drew in the Moghuls and opened the way to a revival of the Uzbeks. In 1500 the Uzbeks took Samarkand. They were expelled by Babur, the heir now of the military house of Miran Shah, but they returned in 1501. In 1505 they took Khiva from Husayn Bayqara and in effect reduced him to Herat and Khorasan alone. In 1506 Husayn Bayqara died, and in 1507, the Uzbeks, who were simply waiting for the great sultan to die, took Herat.

The death of Husayn Bayqara was followed by a four cornered struggle between the Uzbeks, the Moghuls, the Timurid princes and the new Safavid dynasty of Persia. None of the parties won convincingly, but the Timurids did least well and under Babur took the road for India. The greatest civilized age in Central Asia was over, subverted by nomads and dervishes. Tamerlane's attempted amalgamation of the two ecologies had failed. But it had had a long run, and it left as its legacy the Timurid culture, which, surviving its origins, was now diffused to the homelands.

TIMURID CULTURE IN THE HOMELANDS

After 1510 circumstances in Central Asia ceased to be propitious for Timurid culture. As we shall see, it was not completely extinguished there, but things were never the same again because the Timurid courts had gone. The scholars, artists, craftsmen and scientists who had lived under their protection had to look for other patrons. The result was a wide diffusion of Timurid culture within the Islamic world and even beyond it. To understand the diffusion, something more must be said about first the institutional basis for Timurid culture in Central Asia and then about its actual content.

First, it was based on the court, in the sense of the households of the ruler and his associates in politics. The rulers were the entrepreneurs of Timurid culture. It was they who commissioned the buildings and books, gave pensions to artists and scholars, and set the tone for the rest of the upper classes. Tamerlane's court, as described by Clavijo, was a place of lavish entertainment. Clavijo arrived early in September 1404 and over the next seven weeks, he attended at least ten parties, given variously by the Amir, his empress or daughter in law. These functions were occasions not only for eating and drinking, but also for display of clothes, furnishings, *objets de vertu*, buildings and gardens.[7] The princes imitated the rulers. Notable patrons included Iskandar b. Omar Shaikh at Shiraz, a friend of lyric poets and painters; Ibrahim b. Shah Rukh, also at Shiraz, similar and a famous calligrapher; and Baysunghur b. Shah Rukh at Herat – calligrapher, bibliophile, patron of painters, vizier (1415–33) until he drank himself to death at the age of 38. These men more or less withdrew from politics to devote themselves to culture. Both rulers and princes were supported by ministers. Mir Ali Shir Navai was not only Husayn Bayqara's prime minister, but also his paymaster. He formed the customs at the Caspian part of Astarabad and his munificence to caravanserais (52) and bridges (14) suggest a partnership with business. Navai financed the restoration of the Friday mosque at Herat between 1498 and 1500 and endowed a religious complex to the north of the city.

Second, the aristocracy took up the initiative of the top leadership. Timurid culture was not simply for the glory of the ruler. Rather, his glory reflected that of the elite, as well as vice versa. Lentz and Lowry in their recent monograph argue that in Timurid art a 'new and highly refined visual language emerged that celebrated the elite and articulated its vision of might and grandeur.'[8] Again, they explain: 'the Timurid elite developed a sophisticated visual vocabulary that projected a carefully crafted princely vision.'[9] This elite consisted of courtiers, higher civil servants, knights and the more liberal religious leaders: a meritocracy as much as an aristocracy, financed through *soyurghals*, tax-free estates or benefices, granted originally for life, but increasingly on a hereditary basis. The products of Timurid culture: the books, paintings and carpets; all reflect an aristocratic or meritocratic background. After the Koran, the number one book was the *Shah-nama*, that casebook of cultivated chivalry, a secular ideal for the present in the guise of nostalgia for the past. No doubt people did not live up to the ideal, but Babur's memoirs show them trying, and an ideal deprives brutality and philistinism of ideological support.

Third, though highly aristocratic, Timurid culture was not exclusive. There was some popular outreach. The principal institution here was what may be called the welfare mosque. Mosques, whether founded by the dynasty or the elite, frequently included not just the *masjid* for daily and Friday worship, but also the *madrasa* or college of higher education, the *mektab* or primary school for boys, the *imaret* or soup kitchen for the poor, care centres for the physically or mentally sick, *haman* or public baths, *khan-aqah* or dervish hostels, *serai* or hospices for travellers, especially merchants and pilgrims. Islam had always been a social religion, but solidarity was given new emphasis by the Timurids, who wanted to show that their political machine benefited everyone. The emphasis was part of the defensive counter *sarbadar* strategy, but in the background there was a genuine desire to create, through the mosque complexes, a humane Islamic welfare state. Mir Ali Shir Navai, with his promotion of Chaghatai Turkish as a literary language alongside Persian and Arabic, may not have been the advocate of mass literacy Soviet propaganda later portrayed, but his intention was inclusive as Turkish moved down the social scale and became the vernacular.

Court, aristocracy and welfare mosque were the matrix of Timurid culture in Central Asia. Its subsequent diffusion therefore depended on finding, if not identical, then functionally similar institutions, elsewhere. Similarly its content must find an intellectual resonance. That content may be understood as consisting of four layers, like the skin of an onion.

First, because most visible, was architecture. As Lentz and Lowry say, besides small precious objects for a limited audience, 'on a more public level the dynasty's ideology was conveyed through a spectacular building programme.'[10] Of this programme, there are considerable remains at Samarkand, Herat, Meshed and Mazar-i-Sharif. At Samarkand, in addition to Tamerlane's Friday mosque (Bibi Khanum), his imperial mausoleum, the Gur-i Amir, and his Shah Zindeh cemetery complex beyond the walls, there is Ulugh Beg's *madrasa*, the earliest of the buildings on the Registan. That central square, the first of its kind in Islam, is essentially Ulugh Beg's conception, though he intended its four sides to be occupied by a *madrasa*, a mosque, a *khanaqah*, and a caravanserai, a more secular arrangement than what currently exists.[11] At Herat, time, assisted by British demolition in the 1880s and Soviet in the 1980s, has taken a harder toll.[12] The citadel, rebuilt by Shah Rukh, survives despite becoming a Soviet bastion, as does the Friday mosque restored by Mir Ali Shir Navai. But of what was Herat's greatest glory, the so-called *musalla* ('smithfield'): Gawhar Shad's Friday mosque, *madrasa*, and mausoleum, plus Husayn Bayqara's *madrasa*; only four minarets of the last, the tomb itself with one lopsided minaret, and the stump of one of the once splendidly tiled minarets of the Friday mosque, survive. In Meshed, however Gawhar Shad's Friday mosque for the tomb of Iman Reza remains, as at Mazar-i-Sharif does the so-called tomb of Ali constituted by Husayn Bayqara.

Most of the architects of the Timurids remain anonymous. One who does not is Qavam al-Din of Shiraz, a contemporary of Brunelleschi, who worked in the reign of Shah Rukh. He is credited with Shah Rukh's *madrasa* and *khanaqah* outside Herat (now lost); Gawhar Shad's Friday mosque at Meshed, and, greatest work of all in the eyes of contemporaries, Shad's Friday mosque, *madrasa* and tomb in the *musalla*.[13] Like Alberti and Brunelleschi, Qavam al-Din drew part of his inspiration from Platonic notions of geometrical, cosmic and human proportions and harmony. Ghiyath al-Din Jamshid al-Kashi, chief mathematician and astronomer to Ulugh Beg, wrote a *Key to Arithmetic*, which contained an influential chapter on the geometry of architecture. Starting from this theory, Timurid architecture, as a style, developed five leading characteristics: monumentality and an intention to impress; free standing position, the outside as important as the inside; the dome, copied from the Great Mosque of Damascus, but raised to give an impression of floating above the surrounding buildings; massive use of coloured, especially blue, tiles both within and without, the local imitation of Chinese porcelain, if not the real thing; and the presence throughout of what may be called a Sino-Byzantine aesthetic, the first conscious synthesis of east and west, to express universality, princely munificence and social concern. It was a secular Mannerism.

Second, inside the buildings, there were books and book illustrations. Here the chief name is that of Bihzad the miniaturist, court painter to Husayn Bayqara. Islam was rather hostile to representational art, which was seen as an impious imitation of the activity of the Creator. What was allowed was abstract art: geometrical patterns, arabesque and decorative calligraphy, as much prized in Islam as in China. Out of such decoration used on book covers, page headings, colophons etc., there developed the idea of book illustration in the ordinary sense: not for the Koran of course, but for scientific works, especially herbals, and eventually secular literature such as the *Shah-nama* and the *Yusuf and Zuleika* of Firdausi and the various *Khamsa* (quintets) of the classical Persian poets. Such illustration began at the court of the Il-khans, not yet completely Muslim, possibly under influence from China. It was taken up by Iskander and Ibrahim at Shiraz, transmitted to Herat and Baysunghur who imported a number of Tabriz masters, and extensively patronized by Husayn Bayqara. As Lentz and Lowry say: 'illustrated poetry became the supreme expression of Timurid taste.'[14] Bihzad was the most famous of the Herat School. Much is ascribed to him, so it is difficult to know what is authentic. One work, dated and signed by him, illustrates a poem by Jami on the theme of Yusuf and Zuleika. The story could be read, despite its biblical antecedents, simply as secular romance, but it could also be taken, like the *Song of Songs*, as a paradigm of mystical insight. Bihzad's interpretation oscillates between these two levels of meaning. Its merits, like those of Timurid painting generally, are not the tactile values favoured by the Florentines, but rather colour, detail and dreamlike atmosphere. This last was achieved in part by the use of motifs from Southern Sung landscape. It is difficult not to think that the whole miniaturist movement in Islam was set off by the westward transmission of Chinese art. Timurid painting defines itself by Sassanian or secular themes, Chinese techniques in a Turco-Persian Rococo synthesis.

Third, inside the books and illustrated by the miniatures, was literature. Renaissances consist in a shift from philosophy and new, specialist, scholastic writing to philology and old, generalist, creative writing: fiction, *belles-lettres*, poetry both epic and lyric, literary criticism and comparison of languages. Under the Timurids new luxury editions of the Persian classics were put out: the *Shah-nama* of course, but also the *Humay and Humayun* of Khwaja Kirmani, the *Khamsa* of Nizami, the *Gulistan* of Sadi. An important role was played here by Shah Rukh's brother Baysunghur who established a new *kitabkhana* in Herat. The Herat *kitabkhana* was a design centre with sections for different crafts and albums of stock drafts for motifs. Baysunghur himself edited the *Shah-nama*, collected an immense number of Islamic manuscripts, and kept 40 copyists constantly at work in the scriptorium, some of them using the new *nastaliq* calligraphy. There were echoes of Ptolemy Soter's library at Alexandria, but of course it was also very Chinese. All Baysunghur did not do, but it was fatal in the long run, was to imitate the Franks and introduce the Chinese invention of printing. Mir Ali Shir Navai might argue for vernacular literacy, but without printing and more effort to educate girls as well as boys, it was hopeless. Islam had no iconography of the fifteenth century Virgin Mary sitting reading her book of hours.

Fourth, there was science: the innermost, most secretive and fugitive component of Timurid culture. Naturalism might be a better term. Renaissances appeal not only from philosophy to philology, but also from learning to nature. This is one root of science, but without new theory it may be sterile. The Islamic world had always been interested in astronomy. It was part of the Babylonian and Greek traditions it inherited, but it was contaminated with astrology and often religiously suspect. It was then radical when Ulugh Beg set up an observatory outside Samarkand to the north, supplied it with a team of scholars, and set them to construct astronomical tables, i.e. a gazetteer of stars. The observatory had a huge sextant for measuring celestial angles and the tables remained the most accurate and complete in the world until the seventeenth century. However, Ulugh Beg's naturalism did not lead anywhere, at least in Islam. His work was essentially encylopaedic. There was no new theory, no discovery of discovery, nothing which Aristotle could not have done. Nevertheless, the Timurid naturalist renaissance was one current flowing into the scientific revolution. Intellectual revolutions are the result of giants standing on the shoulders of dwarfs, or at least ordinary mortals. Not the least of these was the scientist sultan of Samarkand. The Islamic star map and the Chinese clock were necessary preconditions of Newton.

Timurid culture was transplantable. It was not tied to the bases provided by the Timurid political machine. But it had institutional and contextual prerequisites, and the presence or absence of these among the heirs of the Timurids determined what could be and was inherited.

The most direct heirs of the Timurids were the Ottomans. True, the Ottoman empire was a party state rather than a political machine and the personality of the ruler had less scope than in the Timurid empire. Moreover, the problem of nomads and sedentarists was peripheral rather than central. Nevertheless, Timurid culture found considerable resonance at

Bursa, Edirne and Constantinople. The early Ottoman empire was a relatively liberal party state. It needed cultural glamour and intellectual *glasnost* to recruit among Slavs as well as Turks. It only gradually became a conservative party state with an exclusive orthodoxy. Contact with the Timurids began before the death of Tamerlane. Bayezit I was a cultural as well as political rival. Crusaders taken prisoner at the battle of Nikopolis were impressed by his court in the same way as Clavijo was by that of Tamerlane. Interaction continued after 1405. Ulugh Beg's first chief astronomer was Musa Pasha Kadizade Rumi from Anatolia. After Ulugh Beg's death, his last chief astronomer Ali Kushchi sought refuge from the dervishes with Mehmet II. Subsequently Mehmet II sent presents of books to Jami and return gifts from Herat went to him and Bayezit II. The Ottoman context had both advantages and disadvantages for Timurid culture. The dervish orders, the Mevleviyya and the Bektashiyya were more liberal, but the canon lawyers, the *ulema*, were correspondingly illiberal. In the long run, the canon lawyers won out, but for 150 years the Ottomans were receptive to Timurid influences.

Architecture was particularly influenced. At Bursa, the dome of the Yesil Camii, built by Mehmet I and Murad II as the Ottomans recovered from Ankara, was originally covered with green tiles. At Constantinople, the first mosque of Fatih, built by Mehmet II, had a dome raised on a drum. His garden pavilion the Cinili Kiosk (tiled pavilion) was modelled on Ulugh Beg's Chini Khaneh (China house). Godfrey Goodwin writes: 'Built in 877/1473, the building is Timurid in appearance and the exterior glazed bricks are very much in the tradition of Central Asia.'[15] The mosque of Bayezit II is Timurid in its layout. It included an imperial tomb, a large *madrasa*, a massive bath house, a caravanserai plus fountain, all designed to serve the adjacent covered market which itself owed something to the *chahar su* in Herat. Sinan, the greatest Ottoman architect, shows Timurid influences. It is these which make him meta-Byzantine, so that the Suleimaniye is not just a replica of Santa Sophia. His masterpiece, the Selimiye in Edirne, is Timurid in the dominance of its floating dome, its external colour (though by stone rather than by tile), and its handling of space. Similarly, the Sultan Ahmet mosque of his conservative successor Mehmet Aga is Timurid in its return to brilliant blue tile.

Architecture was not the only art form which showed Timurid influence. Miniatures in the Herat style continued to be produced in sixteenth century Istanbul. The Ottomans maintained Timurid interest in geography and even briefly had an astronomical observatory until it was closed by *ulema* hostility, especially that of the law students, the *softas*. In their country houses on the Bosporus, the *yali*, the Ottomans had excellent gardens in the Timurid manner, and in the Seraglio, the gardeners, the *bostanci*, even briefly became an echelon of state. Beyond these details, the Ottoman empire, at the height of its power, had a world scope reminiscent of Tamerlane. It operated in three continents, thought about the conquest of China as well as the capture of Vienna, tried to reactivate the central land route by both military and naval means, fought religious social revolution, while at first sitting close to Islamic orthodoxy. Like the Timurids, the Ottomans recruited talent wherever they could find it. Beneath Turkish names one finds Italians, Bosnians, Greeks, Russians and Tatars. Renegation, another name for brain drain, was so successful that it threatened to become a substitute for creativity in the Ottoman empire. Indeed, one might say that as long as the Ottoman empire was Timurid, it was successful, expansive and healthy.

An alternative to going west to the Ottomans was going to ground in Persia and hoping for better times. Among those who did this was Bihzad who died at Tabriz in 1536, having left Herat in 1510. Those who went to Persia came under the rule of the Safavids. The Safavid empire under Shah Ismail was a radical Shiite revolutionary movement. It was a cultural revolution directed against conventional or conservative Sunni orthodoxy. It was not, therefore, initially very favourable to Timurid values, though some Timurid princes of Miran Shah's line supported Ismail against the White Sheep Turcomans. Ismail's successor, however, Shah Tahmasp (1524–1576), who had been governor of Herat (1516–22), took up the Timurid tradition of patronage. But the better times the refugees had hoped for only really came in the reign of Shah Abbas the Great (1587–1629). He institutionalized the Shiite revolutionary movement and made the Safavid regime more like the Ottoman party state through the introduction of Georgian-Circassian Janissaries. He also promoted trade actively through the conscript Armenian community of New Julfa in a way reminiscent of Tamerlane.

His capital, Isfahan, 'the greatest opera set in Asia', gives a Timurid appearance as a royal city of mosque complexes, coloured tiles, gardens and caravanserais, set round the Maidan-i Shah, an obvious derivate of the Registan in Samarkand.[16] Like the Timurid empire too, the Safavid was bilingual. It had originated in Turkish-speaking Azerbaijan and Turkish remained the language of the court even in Persian Isfahan. Nevertheless, though Isfahan looks more Timurid than Istanbul, because the outward form of the buildings has not undergone the influence of Santa Sophia, the Safavid context was less suitable for Timurid culture than the Ottoman. While Ottoman Timuridism was pursued for several generations and put down institutional roots, the reign of Shah Abbas was something of a personal interlude. Despite Shah Abbas, the Safavid movement was too nationalist, too exclusively Shiite, too socially divisive to be sympathetic to Timurid ecumenism, secularity and social solidarity. Timuridism declined slowly in seventeenth century Iran and vanished completely in the eighteenth century when the Safavids were overthrown by the Afghans.

Third, if one did not care to go west or to ground one could follow the Timurids south to India where they became the Mughals. There were many Timurid features in Mughal culture. The Taj Mahal is a late Timurid building, Akbar's new universal religion had antecedents in Central Asian ecumenism. Persian was the language of the bureaucracy, miniature painting flourished as far south as the Deccan. Yet even more than in the Ottoman empire and Persia, the context was different. Despite the continuity in dynasty and political form, in time everything suffered a sea change. The Taj Mahal is not merely Timurid; one would not mistake a miniature from the Deccan for one from Herat; Akbar's *Din Ilahi* was not just the Timurid house religion. South of the Hindu Kush, there were neither nomads nor oases. India was chronically short of horses, so both the pony and the charger gave way to another military tradition based on elephants and a huge travelling circus of semi-armed batmen. The Mughals were the heirs of Tamerlane, but the context was so different that even the political machine functioned differently. What could be maintained of Timurid culture was only bits and pieces, essentially decoration.

Finally, Timurid culture continued in the east, in Moghulistan, especially in the reigns of the Chaghatai princes[17] Said of Yarkand

(1504–1533) and Mansur of Turfan (1504–1544). Said was a soldier and mini-Tamerlane. He fought campaigns in the west against Badakhshan, north against the Kirghiz, south against Ladakh, Baltistan and Kashmir, and died on the march east on *jihad* against Tibet. It is hard not to see these campaigns as an attempt to turn Altishahr into a Trans-Himalayan hill state based on trade routes east–west, north–south, with Yarkand as a mini-Herat. Said, the hero of Mirza Haidar Dughlat's *Tarikh-i-Rashidi*, was the most ambitious of the rulers of Kashgaria. He was a liberal, extravagant prince in the Timurid style: literary, musician, poet; but his achievements were personal and precarious and his goals were not pursued by his successors. Mansur, on the other hand, was less flamboyant, and cannier. He concentrated on taking control of Hami from its Chinese satellites and then on establishing good trading relations with Peking. In both these aims Mansur succeeded. Hami became the capital, the khanate continued to 1930, and Timurid traditions of hospitality, melons and garden palaces were maintained.[18] By the seventeenth century, however, the power of the dervishes was on the increase in Moghulistan, though less in Turfan and Hami than in Kashgaria. Everywhere Timurid culture was in retreat. It left only its impressive ruins in Central Asia, its witness to the possibility of an Islamic renaissance, and legacy to the republic of letters.

THE REPUBLIC OF LETTERS

The term 'the republic of letters' first appeared in Europe in the early seventeenth century in that interlude of peace between the wars of Philip II and those of Richelieu and Olivares which Voltaire saw as the seedbed of the Enlightenment. It was only in the eighteenth century, however, that it became fully a reality as a set of interlocking institutions and individuals with common secular interests in the arts and sciences and to some extent a shared methodology. The republic of letters was a specialized differentiation of the basic information circuit. It was the civilian counterpart of the military global arsenal: a new international nucleation of information, intelligence and criticism. For although the republic of letters was centered in Europe, specifically northwest Europe, it spread itself to greater or less depth to southern and eastern Europe; to Islam, India and to China. A man like the Jesuit father Antoine Gaubil, who resided at Peking from 1722 to 1759 and attempted to build up a unified picture of Eurasian history, geography and astronomical information, was in touch not only with Chinese scholars, but also with correspondents in Paris, London and St. Petersburg, as well as making use of Arabic and Persian sources.[19] Although only a thin, unevenly spread and discontinuous veneer, the republic of letters already in the eighteenth century was the precursor of the modern university world, with its research institutes, specialized journals, international conferences, scholarly correspondence, data banks and information exchange. It was a first manifestation of what Teilhard de Chardin was to call the convergence of the noosphere, the involution of human thought upon itself.

Unlike the basic information circuit, the microbian common market and the global arsenal which were the result of diffusion, the republic of letters was the result of convergence. It was, so to speak, a federal republic of *Lände*. It was the product of the convergence of local and regional republics of letters, though it was eventually to find a first centre in the Paris–London–Berlin triangle. Enough has been said about the Islamic republic of letters, and the Timurid contribution to it. Something needs to be said about the European and Chinese republics and about the context of renaissance in general prior to their federation.

The European renaissance, the shift in interest from the specialist, scientific writing of antiquity to its generalist, non-scientific writing, the move from scholasticism to *literae humaniores*, followed earlier and smaller renaissances, under the Carolingians and in the twelfth century which did not generalise themselves or were eclipsed by the needs of the technostructure in law, medicine and theology. It was in origin simply an intellectual fashion and self-regarding sub-culture. That it suddenly became first an Italian and then a European movement, has usually been attributed to the needs of princely diplomacy for rhetoricians and of the laity generally for a less professional and vocation-oriented education, though one which would in fact lead to employment at court. Courts, bureaucracy and letters went together. The revival of ancient letters prompted the appearance of literary criticism and this in turn led to the development of philology as practised by Lorenzo Valla and Erasmus. Although an anti-technical movement, against the specialized language of the schools, humanism was itself a technique rather than a philosophy. Or rather, it was a technique before, in the hands of Erasmus, becoming the *philosophia Christi.* It was the new learning before being the new religion.

In China, on the other hand, the development of philology and the techniques of textual criticism in the *k'ao-cheng hsüeh* (school of empirical research), whose achievements paralleled those of Valla and Erasmus, as has been shown by Benjamin Elman, had a different background.[20] In China, bureaucracy was earlier and better developed than in Europe. Without a multi-state system within, the need for diplomacy was correspondingly less. Thanks to the early invention of printing and the presence of the examination system, much less of the literature of antiquity had been lost or fallen into abeyance. With the expulsion of the Mongols and the fading of the Buddhist or Manichaean millenarism which had inspired the early Ming, Confucianism, in the sense of the study of a canon of ancient texts, could resume its place in Chinese society and culture. It was, however, a scholastic Confucianism dominated by the needs of the examination system and the rationalist philosophy of Chu Hsi. In the sixteenth century, this dominance was challenged by the intuitional philosophy of Wang Yang-ming, who promoted a more interiorist and moralized 'Protestant' Confucianism. The challenge was only half successful: a heart transplant which the body in part rejected. It generated, not renewal, but intellectual sectarianism which heightened the growing factionalism in the Chinese bureaucracy toward the end of the sixteenth century. It was against these philosophical factions, the Sung learning, that some scholars, in a spirit of a plague on both your houses, developed exact philosophy, the *k'ao-cheng hsüeh*, sometimes called the school of Han learning because its went back to the Han texts and scholarship, on which all the Confucianisms claimed to be based, yet in practice ignored. In China, therefore, the new learning came after the new religion.

The approximate contemporaneity of the renaissances in Islam, Europe and China is striking and calls for explanation. Bureaucracy and lay education are certainly relevant, but they account better for the differences than the similarities. From the time of Burckhardt, renaissances have been presented as taking place in a context of optimism and hope: the revival of classical light after medieval darkness. Jean Delumeau, however, has argued that the European renaissance, and the same view could be taken of the Islamic and Chinese renaissances, took place in a context of pessimism and despair: centuries of plague, war, foreign invasion, social disruption, political breakdown, and, above all, fear.[21] Renaissances, therefore, were initially retreats rather than advances, a search for quiet corners rather than vantage points, pleasures which it was recognized could only be ephemeral. In this sense, they may be seen as a response to the disasters of the Mongolian explosion, the microbian common market and the gunpowder warfare of the global arsenal. Yet the retreats always contained an element of *reculer pour mieux sauter*. As the various disasters were mastered or attenuated, they increasingly took on this character, both psychologically and intellectually. Within cultures, renaissances became republics of letters and republics of letters set out to federate between cultures.

Federation was at first tangential. Central Asian science played a role here. In China, Islamic astronomy had been introduced during the Yüan period. The early Ming were careful to preserve the contact. In 1382 the Hung-wu emperor received a work on astronomy, translated into Chinese from either Arabic or Persian by a team of Muslim and Chinese scholars. In 1482, another work, on the planetary ephemerides calculated according to Muslim methods, was published.[22] When the Jesuits arrived in Peking, the board of astronomy, an imperial department in a system where calendrical issues were a matter of state, was still in the hands of Muslims from Central Asia. Most likely, they will have made use of Ulugh Beg's tables in their calculations. In Europe, too, Ulugh Beg's tables were one of the earliest borrowings. They were translated into Latin by John Greaves, a protégé of Archbishop Laud, and published in London in 1652, after he had been expelled from the wardenship of Merton by the parliamentary commissioners. Merton, of course, had been a centre of mathematics since the beginning of the fourteenth century and it was appropriate that this cultural connection should be made under its auspices. Greaves had obtained a manuscript during his tour to the east in 1635–40, either at

Constantinople, or more likely, given the state of astronomy on the Golden Horn, at Cairo. Greaves was interested in Central Asia. He wrote an *Elementa Linguae Persicae* and to his work on chronology in 1650 added a *Chorasmiae et Mawaralnahrae, hoc est regnum extra fluvium Oxum, descriptio,* out of various Muslim authors. A third area where intercultural astronomical contact was made was Northern India. Here the Hindu Maharajah Jai Singh of Jaipur (1686–1743) set up observatories on the Samarkand model in Delhi, Jaipur, Ujjain and Benares. He regarded himself as the successor of Ulugh Beg, while at the same time using European material both ancient and modern: Ptolemy, Flamsteed, La Hire.[23]

Another unexpected liaison area in the republic of letters was the Crimea.[24] An Ottoman satellite from 1475 to its transference to Russia by the treaty of Kucuk Kainarca in 1774 and annexation in 1783, Crim Tartary was in some ways the last Timurid state. It had a dynasty, the Giray; abundant nomadic cavalry, also Alan or Nogay heavy cavalry; and a civilized capital, Baghce saray. In the eighteenth century, the Khans, threatened by both the Sultan and the Tsar, tried to modernize both their society and culture by the introduction of European elements. In addition to promotion of wheat export through a free port, and the opening of gold and silver mines in Circassia, the measures included translations of plays by Molière and correspondence with Frederick the Great.[25]

In the Ottoman empire itself, cultural elements from the west, began to be introduced during the so-called tulip period. In the reign of Ahmet III (1703–1730), the grand vizier Nevsehirli Damat Ibrahim Pasha introduced European type town planning, resident embassies abroad, and the printing press. In Timurid mode, he also revived the manufacture of coloured tiles at Tekfursaray and founded a *darul hadis,* or college for advanced studies in the *sharia,* on a lavish scale. It included a readership in the *Mathnavi* of Jalal ad-Din Rumi, which would have pleased Jami. Under Abdulhamit I (1774–89), foreign advisers began to be used without even formal conversion to Islam. His successor, Selim III (1789–1807), brought European actors and works of art to Constantinople for the first time.[26]

In addition to details like Ulugh Beg's astronomical tables, Central Asia also supplied the republic of letters with prototypes of some of its leading institutions. Ulugh Beg's *madrasa* was one of the first of the King's colleges, contemporary with that of Cambridge and preceding that of Louvain. Ulugh Beg's scientific group was a precursor of the Royal Society while Mir Ali Shir Navai's three hundred and sixty poets anticipated Richelieu's forty immortals. Gawhar Shad presided over something like a salon, while Jami's *Kreis* foreshadowed many other literary coteries. It is not suggested that any other republics of letters, except those in the Islamic world, copied directly from the Timurids. There is only similarity, not continuity. Nevertheless, like situations give rise to like institutions, and similarity was a condition for the convergence of cultures. Once the cultural shock of different ideological integuments had worn off or been relaxed from within, the common elements in secular art and science would naturally come together.

One of the most bizarre buildings in England is Brighton Pavilion, built by Nash for the Prince Regent between 1815 and 1820. Nash is best known as a classicist in his Regent's Park buildings and All Souls, Langham Place. He was also capable of neo-Gothic and in Brighton of what is variously called Hindu or Oriental. While the immediate inspiration of Brighton pavilion was Indian, its remoter origins surely were Timurid. The concept of a pavilion, residential, yet flimsy in appearance and vacational in function, harks back to the tents and garden palaces in which Clavijo was entertained. George IV had something in common with Husayn Bayqara. Both were cultured, the first gentlemen of their societies, self indulgent, disapproved of by the godly, yet skilful in the projection of images to political ends. George IV's visit to Scotland in 1822, with its conciliation of clans, Kirk and Freemasons, carefully stage-managed by Sir Walter Scott, has only to be translated into terms of *oboghs*, *ulema* and dervishes to become Timurid.[27] George IV the last of the Timurids? Maybe, but 1822 was only half a century or so before his niece was given the Timurid title of Kaiser-i Hind by an even greater showman than Scott, England's first Jewish prime minister, and undoubted member of the republic of letters.

7 Uzbeks, Zunghars and the Religious Internationals

From the beginning of the sixteenth century to the end of the eighteenth, the state in Central Asia lost the initiative to society and culture. This had begun with the Timurids' substitution of civility for force as the bond of empire, but now it went further. Initiative passed specifically to religious culture and institutions, whose clerical organizations intimidated the state and dominated society, both sedentary and steppe. The rise of clericalism was not necessarily a symptom of decline. On the contrary, it represented the final stage of the active phase of Central Asia's involvement in world history. It contributed powerfully to the formation of a further world institution: the religious internationals. Buddhism, Christianity and Islam had always been world religions in theory, unlike Western paganism, Hinduism or the indigenous Chinese religion ('Sinism') which never had a universal vocation, or Zoroastrianism and Judaism which refused it. Until the sixteenth century, however, none of the three possessed internationals, in the sense of institutions, capable of acting world-wide in a variety of social circumstances and intellectual milieus. With the emergence of the Jesuits, the Naqshbandiyya and the Gelugspa, out of their original habitats and earliest functions as reformations, the world religions acquired religious internationals. The co-existence of these bodies, their interaction, their bonding by conflict and emulation, their common commitment to militancy and mission at home and abroad, constituted a new world institution. Of these first religious internationals, for to their number one might later add Evangelical, Shiite and Masonic internationals, two, the Naqshbandiyya and the Gelugspa, were Central Asian. In the period of clericalism, therefore, Central Asia made a major contribution to a set of institutions whose vitality, though often pronounced extinguished, is not yet dead. Unlike the nomadic empires, the *inju* states or the Timurid courts, the Jesuits, the Naqshbandiyya and the Gelugspa are still with us.

THE RELIGIOUS INTERNATIONALS IN CENTRAL ASIA

The rise of the Central Asian religious internationals was shaped by the political background. The departure of the Timurids for India in 1519 left Central Asia divided. First, there was again a division between steppe and sown: between the nomadic states of the Kazakhs and Zunghars in Central Kazakhstan, Semirechie and Zungharia, and the oasis states of the Safavids, Afghans, Uzbeks and Moghuls in Afghan, Western and Eastern Turkestan. This division resulted from the failure of the *inju* state, the phenomenon of nomad secession, and the external repolarization of ecologies. Second, within each of the ecologies, there were sharp ideological divisions: between Muslim Kazakhs and Buddhist Zunghars on the steppe: between Shiite and Sunni, dervishes and *ulema*, Khafiyya and Jahriyya in the town. These divisions too resulted from the failure of the *inju* state, the phenomenon of urban rejection and the internal repolarization between notables and populace. In these fragmented political circumstances, religious organizations alone could provide a minimum of cross-class, cross-ecology unity.

Naqshbandiyya

Here the relevant background was the rise of the Uzbek polity: the loose political structure through which princes of the house of Jochi, whose followers took the name of Uzbek, conquered Transoxania in the first decade of the sixteenth century. Uzbek history may be divided into three phases: pre-conquest and renomadization, conquest and endo-nomadization, post-conquest and clericalism.

First, pre-conquest and renomadization.. The Uzbeks began as a nomad secession, not from the Chaghatai khanate like the Turkmen and the Kirghiz, but from the Golden Horde. It formed part of a set of urban rejections (Kazan, Astrakhan and the Crimea) and nomad secessions (Sibir, Uzbek, Nogai) which, by the close of the fifteenth century, had brought the Golden Horde effectively to an end as a state. In 1422, a group of nomad clans east of the Lower Volga, which included such famous Turco-Mongol names as Qangli, Qunggirat, Manghit, seceded from the central authority of the khan at Sarai. They called themselves Uzbeks, the name being variously interpreted as 'free men' or a reference to the successful Golden Horde khan in the early fourteenth century. Their first leader, Barak, ravaged the lower Volga area between Sarai and Astrakhan, but he was murdered in 1428.

Barak was succeeded by Abul Khayr, a descendant of Batu's brother Shiban (Stephen, probably a Nestorian), who had had an appanage east of the Volga. The ruling house was therefore henceforward known as the Shibanids. Unlike Barak, Abul Khayr abandoned the sedentary world altogether. In 1431 he moved eastward into the Central Kazakh steppe. Here, between 1431 and 1446, he used the traditional north–south migration routes to build an autarkic nomadic community. For, in addition to renomadization, he established in suitable areas patches of agriculture alongside the primary activity of herding to make the nomads independent of the sedentarists even for grain. Such exo-sedentarization, as it may be called, was to be characteristic of subsequent nomad empires such as those of the Altan khan, Zunghars and Kalmuks, but it was begun by Abul Khayr. In 1446, however, Abul Khayr changed policy. He moved south towards the Aral and the Syr. He resumed contacts with the sedentarists and established links with Khoja Ahrar and the Naqshbandi opponents of the Timurids in Transoxania. Probably he sought further elements of trade and culture to consolidate his state. It proved a mistake. The new policy was too much for some clan chiefs who revolted and in 1456 formed a new nomad secession, including Qangli, Qunggirat and Jalayir, calling themselves the Kazakhs. This again meant something like the 'free men'. Abul Khayr might have crushed this revolt if he had not been attacked in 1457 by yet another nomad secession, the Oirats, who were non-Muslims, Shamanists, though some of their rulers had Muslim names. Under all these blows the Uzbek state broke up. Most of the *oboghs* went over to the Kazakhs, leaving only a nucleus to Abul Khayr who died in 1469. Clearly Abul Khayr was an able man. He ruled nomad peoples for forty years and, despite disasters, died in his bed. Equally clearly, he fell between the two stools of too little sedentarization for viability and too much for the prejudices of his followers. Abul Khayr identified these contradictory imperatives but he could not reconcile them.

Second, conquest and endo-nomadization. The conquest of

Transoxania was achieved by Abul Khayr's grandson, Muhammed Shibani who led the Uzbeks from 1496 to 1510. For twenty years after the death of Abul Khayr, we hear and know little about them. After establishing leadership, Muhammed Shibani moved the remaining loyalists, probably rather upper class in composition, to the steppe north of Yasi in the middle Syr. In 1487 he was appointed governor of the town by the Moghul khan Mahmud. Yasi was a commercial centre on a north–south trade route, but more importantly, it contained the tomb, rebuilt by Tamerlane, of the famous twelfth century dervish, Ahmad Yasawi. It was the headquarters of the Yasawiyya, the other big dervish border in Central Asia beside the Naqshbandiyya, which specialized in missions to nomads. Here Shibani reconstructed the Uzbek state as the secular arm of the Yasawiyya. Beyond Yasi, he established good relations with Khoja Ahrar, spent some time himself as a theological student in Bokhara, and kept his clans trim by hiring them as *condottieri* to the Moghuls of Moghulistan who were asserting themselves against the last Timurids. In this way, while retaining a light horse steppe army based on the pastoral fringes of oases, what may be called endo-nomadization, Shibani switched from the nomad secession of his grandfather to being the sword arm of dervish urban rejection directed against the Timurid courts.

Shibani's chance came in the long succession mêlée among the Timurid princes which followed the death of Sultan-Ahmad, Khoja Ahrar's puppet khan, in 1491. Both Shibani and the khans of Moghulistan fished in troubled waters, selling their services to rival claimants and gradually superseding their employers. By 1500 Shibani could throw off the mask and campaign openly for himself. In 1501 he captured Samarkand from a Timurid claimant, in 1505 Khiva from Husayn Bayqara, and in 1507, after Husayn's death, Herat itself. The war, however, went on and became a four-cornered struggle between the Uzbeks in Transoxania, the Moghuls in Semirechie, Babur – the leading Timurid claimant now – in Afghanistan, and the Safavids under the Shiite messiah Shah Ismail in Khorasan. In this war, which is described in Babur's memoirs, no one won a clear victory. In 1503 and again in 1510, Shibani defeated the Moghul khans Mahmud and Ahmad and eliminated them from Transoxania. He went on to defeat Babur, who, as a last resort, was forced into alliance with the Shah and the Shiite revolution. Ismail and

Shibani met in battle at Merv on December 2 1510. The Uzbek
light calvary was crushed by the Shah's Turkish artillery and
Shibani was killed. But Merv was inconclusive. Although the
Shah occupied Herat and Balkh and Babur reoccupied
Samarkand and Bokhara, neither could maintain themselves.
Babur's alliance with the Shiites drove the Naqshbandiyya, hitherto uncommitted, definitely over to the Uzbeks, and he had to
evacuate Transoxania. When the Shah sent another army to
support him, it was defeated by Shibani's nephew Ubaydullah,
who now had urban backing, at the battle of Ghajdavan on
November 12, 1512. Ghajdavan did not cancel Merv. The Uzbeks
were never to rule in Herat and Merv and always had an enemy
to the west. But it left them in possession of Transoxania. Here
they constructed a regime on the bases of their nomad clans,
now naturalized on the margins of the town, and the Naqshbandi
dervishes, now, like the Yasawiyya, projecting their influence
into the steppe.

Third, post-conquest and clericalism. Most of what we know
about the Uzbeks in the sixteenth century comes from Ottoman sources, especially a state paper dateable to 1530–3, concerned with the possibility of alliance between the two Sunni
powers against the Safavids.[1] It is clear that the Uzbek state, at
any rate until the latter part of the sixteenth century, was a
polity rather than an empire. It was a loose confederation of
aristocratic-led nomad *oboghs* quartered on the various city states,
in a manner reminiscent of the system introduced by the
Chaghatai khan Kebek. The whole Uzbek people, or military
machine, was divided into *tumen* or myriads, i.e. notional units
of 10,000 with pasturing rights in the immediate environs of the
oasis and taxing rights over the oasis as a whole. Nomadic,
pastoral values thus coexisted with agricultural and commercial
infrastructure in an system of endo-nomadization. In the cities
themselves, the Uzbek chiefs worked closely with the dervish
orders, especially the Naqshbandiyya, who, in this period produced a second outstanding leader in Ahmad Kwajagi Kasani
(1461–1542), known as the Makhdum-i Azam or Grand Master.
He was originally from Kasan in Ferghana, but, after extensive
travels outside Central Asia, based himself on Bokhara through
alliance with Khoja Ahrar's former deputy there, Khoja Islam.
As a result, Bokhara became the effective capital of the Uzbek
polity rather than Samarkand. Uzbek government was not uni-

fied. The oldest suitable descendant of Abul Khayr was elected
as khan, but real power rested with the *tumen* commanders and
a council of four regent beys on the model of the later Golden
Horde and its successor states. The Uzbek polity was militarized. In the first half of the sixteenth century, it employed its
strength in ceaseless but fruitless campaigns to recover Herat,
Merv and Khorasan from the Safavids. Battles were won, cities
captured and looted, especially when the Shah was fighting the
Ottomans in the west, but the campaigns led nowhere. The
only result was increased devastation of Khorasan, more disruption to the central land route, greater poverty at home, less
political stability because of military uncertainty and diminished taxable capacity.

To overcome division at home and isolation abroad, the
Uzbek leadership turned to the dervish orders, especially the
Naqshbandiyya. The result was clericalism. In 1558 Anthony
Jenkinson, the agent of the Muscovy Company and the first
Englishman to visit Central Asia, noted that in Bokhara the
Shaikh ul-Islam or metropolitan as he called him, was more
powerful than the king. Ubaydullah, the most effective of the
early Abul Khayrids, had been given Khoja Ahrar's personal
name and, based on Bokhara, lived up to it in his policy.
Abdullah II (active 1557–1598, khan from 1582) tried to build
up a more centralized type of regime. He did so in alliance with
the Naqshbandi Juybari shaikhs of Bokhara, led by Khoja Islam
who died in 1563. When he became khan in 1582, his election
was ratified, not by the four regent beys as in the past, but by
four leading dervishes. He achieved personal control and internal stability by alliance with the church against the dynasty, to
such an extent that, thanks to his purges, when he died in 1598,
there were no Abul-Khayrids left to succeed. The throne therefore passed to another branch of the Shibanids, the Janids,
descendants of the exiled khans of Astrakhan, one of whom
had married Abdullah's sister. The second Uzbek dynasty was
even more clerical than the first. Extensive grants of *waqf*,
inalienable, tax free grants of land as endowments were made
to the Naqshbandiyya. Imam Quli Khan (1608–1640), the most
effective of the Janids, added the new dervish-dominated Shirdar
madrasa to the Registan in Samarkand. At the same time, the
Janids relaxed Abdullah's control of the aristocracy. They allowed it to turn their life-time military benefices (*soyurghal* or

tankwah) into hereditary service and tax free *allodia* (*milk-i hurr-i khalis*). The Uzbek polity demilitarized itself and became a kind of Polish commonwealth: weak king, irresponsible aristocracy and dominant clericalism. The dervish orders became the leading institution in state, society and culture.

The Naqshbandiyya was the prime beneficiary. Other orders or *tariqats* (ways) existed.[2] The Kubrawiyya, founded by a man killed in the Mongol storming of Urgench, was dominant in Khiva where an Abul Khayrid survivor made himself independent of the Janids in the seventeenth century. The Yasawiyya remained strong along the Syr and among the nomads of Central Kazakhstan, but it acted as a partner rather than a rival of the Naqshbandis, despite their differences in devotion (*dhikr*). Then there were the Kalenderis of *Arabian Nights* fame: non-denominational, free mendicants, without specified devotion, who were introduced to Central Asia by Shaikh Safa of Samarkand at the turn of the sixteenth and seventeenth centuries. The Naqshbandis, however, were predominant in Samarkand and Bokhara (Herat was under the Shiite Safavids). They were reinforced by their international prolongations in which neither the Kubrawiyya nor the Yasawiyya shared.

Tariqats were a cross between a Catholic religious order and a Protestant denomination. Since they were not formally clerical, they also resembled the lay confraternities, which played so important a part in Christian devotion in the century before the Reformation and during the Counter Reformation.[3] *Tariqats* differed in their degree of organization: the Kalenderi least, the Mevleviyya – with its hereditary grand master or *celebi* at Konia – most, but in general they were loosely structured institutions, more like the pre-Cistercian Benedictines than the Dominicans or Jesuits, an extended family more than a monolith. The essence of a *tariqat* was a master (*murshid, pir, shaikh, ishan, khoja*), with a special doctrine, or more usually devotion, to add to the common stock of Islam, plus disciples (*murid*) and adherents who were organized into various levels of initiation and commitment. Orders which inclined to crypto-Shia, like the Bektashiyya, the spiritual home of the Janissaries, might produce doctrinal innovations, but most *tariqats* were orthodox prayer groups.[4] Dervish devotion was known as *dhikr* (praise) and it might go on for several hours. *Dhikr* took one of two forms: silent meditation or mental prayer, *dhikr-i khafi* (silent praise), which could nevertheless be highly emotional and lead to convulsions, raptures and Pentecostal phenomena; vocal recitation or intonation of texts, *dhikr-i jahri* (noisy praise), accompanied by music or dancing, which again could lead to autohypnotism, ecstasy and charismatic occurrences. The exponent groups were designated Khafiyya or Jahriyya, which may be loosely translated as contemplative-mystical and revivalist-evangelical. Initially, orders concentrated on one rather than the other: thus the Naqshbandiyya was Khafiyya, while the Yasawiyya was Jahriyya; but there was a tendency for the more international orders to combine both practices in different branches. This was the case with the Naqshbandiyya and had profound effects on its development, especially in China.

Dervish leaders based their authority not on inspiration, though their followers sometimes pushed them into claiming to be the Mahdi, but on lineage (*silsila*): either biological, a hereditary holiness in a line of *khojas*; or spiritual, an initianic chain stretching back either to the founder, one of the orthodox caliphs or the Prophet himself. Such lineages formed a devotional parallel to *hadith* (tradition): 'I heard A say that B said that C said . . . that the Prophet said'. In the case of the Naqshbandiyya, the first link was Abu Bakr, to whom the Prophet was supposed to have introduced the practice of *dhikr-i khafi*. This point was emphasized by the sixteenth century Naqshbandis to assert their rejection of the Shiites who did not accept Abu Bakr as a legitimate caliph. Whatever its remoter origins, dervishism as an *approfondissement* of Islamic devotion first came to Central Asia in the person of Khoja Abu Yaqub Yusuf Hamdani who died in 1140. It was his teachings that, in the darker days after the Mongol invasion, Baha ad-Din Naqshband (1318–1398) claimed to be reviving.

The new leader lived and died in the vicinity of Bokhara. His tomb at Boveddin just outside the city became a place of pilgrimage, three visits to it being regarded as equivalent to a *haj*.[5] Baha ad-Din was probably of humble origin. One account, indeed, makes him the public executioner. His *cognomen*, the painter or patterner, may indicate membership of a craft guild, though later it was taken to refer to the imprint of God as a result of *dhikr-i khafi*. Both as a potential *sarbadar* and as a Bokharan – Bokhara was always a counter Samarkand – Baha ad-Din and his disciples were held at arms' length by Tamerlane and his immediate successors. It was not until the reign of Abu Said that the Naqshbandi, now led by Khoja Nasir ad-Din Ubaydullah Ahrar, obtained court patronage. Khoja Ahrar came originally from Tashkent, and through his influence among the nomads he acted as broker in the alliance with the Uzbeks which gave Abu Said the throne in 1451. From Bokhara, Naqshbandi dominance was now extended to Samarkand. On several occasions Khoja Ahrar visited Herat, though here his influence was checked by another more liberal Naqshbandi line represented by Jami, the poet and philosopher of the court of Husayn Bayqara.

Khoja Ahrar died in 1490. Though the Naqshbandis gave their support to the Uzbek conquest of Transoxania, Muhammed Shibani distrusted theocracy and killed Khoja Ahrar's sons. His organization was reconstituted, however, by the Makhdum-i Azam. Initially, he favoured Babur against the Uzbeks, but following the victory of Ghajdavan in 1512, he remained in Central Asia and worked closely with them till his death in 1542. Under the Abul Khayrids and Janids, the Naqshbandiyya consolidated its position at every level. It received the patronage of the ruler, it was plenteously endowed with *waqf,* it controlled *mekteb* and *madrasa,* it maintained chaplaincies among the craft guilds, it established missions among the pastoralists, it participated in long distance trade and *haj* traffic, it opened new branches in the centres of Islam outside Central Asia. The variety of its portfolio and its indispensability in every relationship made the Naqshbandiyya the most powerful institution in Muslim Central Asia.

Gelugspa

Here the relevant background was the rise of the Zunghar empire, not a mere polity, but a real state, the last major nomadic political construct. Like the Uzbeks, the Zunghars began in renomadization, but they went on to exo-sedentarization, a naturalization of sedentary elements on the steppe, rather than to endo-nomadization, and if they too ended in clericalism, it was one which involved not just their relativization but their elimination.[6]

Zunghar means left or east wing. The Zunghars, who comprised the Khoshot, Derbet, Khoit and Choros *oboghs,* were the eastern half of the Oirats: the Uriad or alliance which had constituted itself in Western Mongolia in the first half of the eighteenth century, when the Yüan dynasty failed to maintain authority on the steppe after its expulsion from China by the Ming in 1368. The Oirats were a phenomenon of renomadization. The Western Mongols, the successors of the Naiman and Merkit, had only been conscripted, junior partners in the *Yeke Mongghol Ulus*. They had supported the nomadizing revolts of Arigh Böke and Qaidu against Khubilai. Their princes remained non-Chinggisid and took the title, of Chinese origin, transcribed by the Europeans as kontaisha (*hung-taiji, huang-t'ai-chi,* or imperial prince), rather than khan or qaghan. When their first great leader Esen took the title of khan following his capture of the Ming emperor at the battle of T'u-mu in August 1449, it gave offence to the other Mongols and contributed to the downfall of the first Oirat empire. This downfall was followed by a revival of Chinggisid authority first under Batu Möngke (1482–1532) and then his grandson Altan Khan, especially in eastern and southern Mongolia.

The second Oirat or Zunghar empire was a phenomenon of the seventeenth century general crisis. It was initiated around 1620 by the Choros chief Khotokhotsin, better known as Batur Kontaisha. From a base in Zungharia in the pastures of the Altai on the Upper Irtysh, he extended his power to Semirechie in 1643 and made Kuldja or Ili, the ancient Chaghatai capital of Almalik, his winter headquarters. The constellation of Zunghar and especially Choros power, led to the flight westward in the 1630s of the leading *obogh* of the Barunghar, the right or west wing of the Oirats, the Torghud, across Kazakhstan to become the Kalmuks of the south Volga and north Caucasus. Like Abul Khayr in his first phase, Batur Kontaisha (*c.*1620–*c.*1660) and his successors Galdan (1673–1697), Tsewang Araptan (1697–1727), Galdan Tseren (1727–1745) aimed at an autarkic nomad community of a new kind. The Western Mongols were more cohesive than the Eastern, less eroded in their social structure. Further from trade routes, they required discipline for raiding. Trade, however, was beginning to suffer the effects of the world wide depression. Animal numbers too may have been declining as a result of the onset of the climatic fluctuation meteorological historians call the little ice age.

Times were ripe for a new deal. Gelugspa Lamaism had been

introduced to the Oirats in the early seventeenth century by the great missionary Zaya Pandita Namkhai Jamtso (1599–1662) who came from Amdo and translated one hundred and seventy Tibetan books into Mongolian.[7] Many Zunghars went to Lhasa, including Galdan, one of Batur Kontaisha's younger sons, who became a lama there before returning home to contest the throne after the death of his elder brother. The Zunghar leaders used Gelugspa lamaism to acquire a nucleus of literate people for their government. Through its monasteries, they acquired a fixed, ranch-type pastoralism for their economy alongside nomadic pastoralism. Into selected areas of the steppe, notably the rich Ili valley, they imported Muslim farmers and artisans, Taranchis, to produce grain and metals. Russian and Chinese building workers were attracted for special temple building at Kuldja and Ablai Kit in the Irtysh valley.[8] The Zunghars also welcomed Swedish prisoners of war escaping Peter the Great's prison camps, in order to develop fire arms. Under the kontaishas, Kuldja became a real town with the beginnings of urban culture. In 1648 Zaya Pandita helped the Zunghars reform the Mongolian (Uighur, ultimately Syrian) script and they also issued a revised law code, the first since Chinggis. The Zunghars, it is clear, envisaged a more diversified and self-sufficient steppe economy, which would rationalize the repolarization of nomad and sedentarist developing since 1350. It was a programme of steppe autarky via exo-sedentarization.

The program of the kontaishas did not exclude expansion. On the contrary, they wanted to include the maximum number of nomads in their empire and to this end they made attacks on the Eastern Mongols, the Khalkhas, in one direction and on the Kazakhs in the other. The attacks on the Khalkhas ran the Zunghars into war with the Manchus, which they lost, Galdan being killed. The attacks on the Muslim Kazakhs, while they did immense damage to these people, did not bring recruits, but simply drove them over to Russian protection.[9] While the Zunghars attacked nomads and intervened briefly in Tibet between 1717 and 1720, they did not attempt to conquer sedentarists in China or Transoxania. The Zunghar empire was not a repeat of the Chinggisid. The most they did was to acquire a financial protectorate over Altishahr, via the local Naqshbandi leader, the Makhdumzada Khoja Afaq, who called them in to break down the last resistance of the khans of Moghulistan to dervish theocracy. This was despite the fact that the Zunghars were Buddhists and against the Kazakhs, persecuting Buddhists: a case of common enemies and sociology proving stronger than ideology. From 1675 to 1750, the Zunghars used two theoretically rival, but in fact allied, religious organizations to ground an autarkic empire from the Aral sea to Lake Baikal and south to the Himalayas.

Why did this empire not consolidate itself? First, the Manchus in Peking as the Ch'ing dynasty would not and could not tolerate it. Ch'ing power in China rested on Ch'ing power in Inner Asia. Successive emperors worked first to limit Zunghar power, then destroy it. Second, to have survived Manchu hostility, the Zunghars would have needed Russian support and firearms, but the Russians were more interested in trading with Peking than allying against it.[10] They were not sorry to see the Zunghars eliminated from Middle Asia to make room for themselves. Third, the Zunghars were too few. They could not assimilate the Kazakhs, because of the religious divide. They were prevented from assimilating the Khalkhas by the Manchus. Even their western cousins, the Buddhist Torghud on the Volga, were not interested in joining them, indeed welcomed a Ch'ing embassy in 1714. Fourth the Zunghars were really working against the then drift of nomad society to smaller more aristocratic units. The Ch'ing who accepted this drift, indeed encouraged it, were on a much better footing for rallying Mongol support.[11] Most Mongol princes preferred what they expected to be a loose Ch'ing protectorate to a tight Zunghar empire. Fifth, through a mixture of force and diplomacy, the Ch'ing made a successful take-over bid for the support of the Gelugspa. From 1720 the Dalai Lama lent his support to the Ch'ing against the Zunghars, as subsequently did the Jebstundamba Khutughtu among the Khalkhas and the Chang-chia Khutughtu in Inner Mongolia. Gelugspa support was a major factor in the counter empire which the Ch'ing constructed against the Zunghars.

Though clericalism eventually subverted the Zunghars, they had done much to foster it. Like the Naqshbandiyya, the Gelugspa, the virtuous order, originated in Central Asia. Its founder, Tsong-kha-pa (1357–1419) was a Tibetan, but he came from Amdo in the old Tangut kingdom of Hsi-Hsia, the Koko-nor region, the modern Chinese province of Chinghai. In this unique interface, elements of Muslim, Mongol, Chinese and Tibetan cultures lay side by side in what was for all a frontier situation.[12] This origin, which the Gelugspa never shed, gave it a militant, missionary yet pragmatic character, reminiscent of the Jesuits. There had always been two main tendencies in Tibetan monasticism. First, there was a Tantric tendency, interested in magic and yogic techniques of ecstasy, rather antinomian with respect to the monastic rule (celibacy not enforced), with a positive, almost theistic metaphysics. Second, there was a Vinaya (disciplinary) tendency, opposed to magic, more concerned with public than private devotion, rigorist with respect to the monastic rule (celibacy enforced), with a negative almost atheistic metaphysics. In modern times, these two tendencies were represented by the Brug-pa (Drukpa), the dominant order in Bhutan and Ladakh, and the Gelugspa, originally from Amdo, which became dominant in Central Tibet and part of Kham.[13] In the fifteenth century, the two orders were rival reformations, the Brug-pa from the southwest, the Gelugspa from the northeast, both trying to establish themselves in Lhasa against the unreformed regime left by the Mongol protectorate. In this three-cornered struggle the Gelugspa won, partly because of its superior organization, but more because of its ability to mobilize outside support.

Under Tsong-kha-pa's immediate successors, the First and Second Dalai Lamas (1419–1475 and 1475–1542), the Gelugspa remained purely Tibetan: based in Amdo, not yet dominant in Lhasa. Then in 1578, the third Dalai Lama (1543–1588) obtained the conversion of the Altan Khan, the strongest Mongol ruler of the day, who had extended his power from Inner Mongolia into Koko-nor. The Fourth Dalai Lama (1589–1617), though given a Tibetan name, was a Mongol: a great grandson of the Altan Khan, to indicate the new unity between the Gelugspa and the *Altan Uragh*, the golden descent from Chinggis. But, despite support from a Mongol army in 1607, he steadily lost ground in Lhasa to the unreformed Karma-pa order. Outside Central Tibet, however, the Gelugspa continued to make progress. The Altan Khan, like the Zunghars, believed in exosedentarization: Gelugspa monasteries were therefore founded in his camp capital of Koke-Khota. In 1586 the Khalkhas, not to be outdone, founded the Gelugspa monastery of Erdeni Juu at

Urga. This was followed by the recognition there of an important incarnation, the First Jebstundamba Khutughtu (1632–1723), son of a Khalkha prince, who came to be regarded as the third hierarch in the Gelugspa world after the Dalai and Panchen lamas. Around 1620 Zaya Pandita began the conversion of the Oirats. Finally in 1642, a grand alliance of the Gelugspa's converts (the Torghud of the far west, the Zunghars in Semirechie and the Khoshots of the Koko-nor, where between 1576 and 1582 the Gelugspa monastery of Kumbum close to Tsong-kha-pa's birthplace had been founded) intervened militarily at Lhasa. The allies established the Fifth Dalai Lama (1617–1682), as the spiritual and temporal ruler of Tibet. Central Asian force had made the Gelugspa the most powerful institution in non-Muslim Central Asia.

THE RELIGIOUS INTERNATIONALS IN THE HOMELANDS

Besides becoming dominant in their respective parts of Central Asia, the religious internationals also expanded beyond it into the homelands of Islam, Christendom, India and China. It was this expansion which differentiated them from simple reformations, local, regional or multinational, and which reinforced them in their original centres. Expansionary push was more characteristic of the loosely structured Naqshbandiyya, gravitational pull of the more centralized Gelugspa, but both orders possessed both capacities.

Naqshbandiyya

With the death of the Makhdum-i Azam in 1542, his organization both divided and expanded.[14] First, in Central Asia, predominance passed to the Juybari shaikhs, so named from a religious house outside Bokhara. They had been part of Khoja Ahrar's machine and they now resumed their independence. Their chief, Khoja Islam, was religious adviser to Abdullah II. He was also prominent in trade to Moscow and *haj* organization. Second, another group of Khoja Ahrar's disciples, associated with the name of Mawlana Khwajagi Amgangi, who had moved into India in the early sixteenth century, now extended their activities to the Ottoman empire in one direction and to

Southeast Asia in the other. Third and fourth were groups derived from the Makhdum-i Azam's two sons, the Makhdumzadas. The elder, Khoja Ishan, lacked ambition, though his descendants were to be different. He remained in Transoxania, accepted the dominance of the Juybari shaikhs, and remained loyal to the original Khafiyya devotion of the order. The younger, Khoja Ishaq Wali, however, challenged the Juybari shaikhs, was persecuted by them (one account says his tongue was cut off for heresy), moved to Eastern Turkestan and accepted ancillary Jahriyya devotion. This was probably to appeal more, like the Yasawiyya, to the nomads, for he found converts not only in the oases, but also among the Kirghiz of the mountains.

This move eastward was not without precedent. In the middle of the fifteenth century, a line of Naqshbandi Khojas descended from one Arshad ad-Din was established at Kucha and was encouraged by the Timuridizing Moghul khans. The new expansion was wider, both socially and geographically, and penetrated to the Chinese-speaking Muslims, the Tungans of Ninghsia and Kansu. Khoja Ishaq Wali went to Eastern Turkestan at the invitation of Abd al-Karim the Moghul ruler of Yarkand. Because of his theocratic propensities, the ruler turned against him, so the dervish withdrew to the T'ien-shan to direct the Kirghiz against him. The khan, to win some religious prestige, now went on *jihad* against the Buddhist Sari Uighurs in the Kansu panhandle. But, as the Khoja predicted, being unworthy, he was defeated, was succeeded by his brother Muhammed, who then, supported by the dervishes, brought the *jihad* to a successful conclusion. The Ishaqiyya, as it was called, was now dominant in Altishahr and the Kansu panhandle. The next ruler, Abdullah, sought to counterbalance it by inviting in the rival Khafiyya branch of the Makhdumzadas, descended from the Makhdum-i Azam's eldest son Ishan, in the person of his grandson Khoja Muhammed Yusuf who arrived in Eastern Turkestan in 1640. The move was successful in that the Ishaqiyya was checked and confined to Yarkand. But under Yusuf's son Khoja Afaq, who succeeded him in 1652, the old scenario reappeared: threat of theocracy, appeal to the Kirghiz, exploitation of dynastic rivalries, revival of the Ishaqiyya against the now overmighty Afaqiyya.

In 1670 Khoja Afaq was forced into exile by the Moghul khan Ismail. He went first to Samarkand, then to Tibet on his way to the Tungan communities of China. In Lhasa, the fifth Dalai Lama, who hoped to use Khoja Afaq to extend Tibetan rule in the Tarim basin, put him in touch with the Zunghars. In 1679, Galdan invaded Moghulistan, Kashgar opened its gates thanks to Khoja Afaq, and Ismail abdicated. The next ruler, Abdul Rashid II was little more than a Zunghar puppet put in to collect the capital levy they imposed. He gave his sister in marriage to Khoja Afaq, so that the Afaqiyya could now claim Chinggisid blood. Further intrigues followed. Galdan was aware that neither the khan or the khoja were loyal, but, about to go on campaign against the Khalkhas, when the two fell out, he had little choice but to eliminate the khan and make the khoja his viceroy. Khoja Afaq died in 1693, but the Afaqiyya continued and established Khafiyya bases among the Tungans of Kansu, especially at Ho-chou south of Lanchow.

The Naqshbandiyya also expanded south into India.[15] The major advance was in the reign of Akbar under first the Central Asian Muhammed Baqi-billah (1562–1603) and then his Indian disciple Ahmad Sirhindi (1564–1624). The Mughals, the direct heirs of the Timurids, were not sympathetic to the Naqshbandiyya, nor it to them. Akbar was faced by a protracted revolt in Afghanistan by the Rawshaniyya, a body subsequently taken over by the Naqshbandiyya, which has been seen as the headwaters of Afghan nationalism.[16] Even when Aurangzeb abandoned the Timurid house religion and returned to orthodoxy, he relied on an Erastianized *ulema* rather than any *tariqat*. Indeed, he declared the Naqshbandiyya heterodox. Nevertheless, the Naqshbandis prospered modestly. Their leadership was conciliatory and unpolitical. They carved out a role for themselves as chaplains and naturalizers to the stream of Central Asian immigrants on which Mughal India depended for soldiers, clerics and administrators. The most famous Indian Naqshbandis, Shah Wali Allah (1703–63) and his son Abd-al Aziz (d.1824), preached the symbiosis of sufi and *ulema*. The two indeed frequently made common cause, first against the basically un-Islamic Mughal state, and then against the new Wahhabite fundamentalism, which threatened all traditionalism. Nevertheless, thanks to the secularism of the Mughals, the depotentiation of the sufis by Akbar, of the *ulema* by Aurangzeb, neither had the articulation both possessed in the Ottoman empire.

To the Ottoman empire, the Naqshbandiyya came by two routes. First and earlier, it came directly from Central Asia, possibly in the time of Khoja Ahrar, certainly in the time of his immediate disciples. We know the name of an Anatolian Turk, Molla Abdullah Ilahi, who went to study with Khoja Ahrar, and of two Central Asians, Shaikh Ahmad Bukhari and Baba Haydar Samarqandi, who returned with him to Constantinople to found the Naqshbandi houses in the Fatih and Eyup districts. Second and later, it came indirectly from India via the Yemen and the Holy Places to Damascus, Baghdad and Constantinople. A product of this route was the Kurdish evangelist Maulana Khalid Baghdadi (1776–1827).

The growth of the Naqshbandiyya in the west was slow but massive. The Ottomans' first religious partners were the modernist Mevleviyya, with its famous Jahriyya dancing ritual, and the authoritarian semi Shiite Bektashiyya, at the opposite pole to the traditionalist Naqshbandiyya. However, as the empire evolved from a radical party state to a conservative party establishment, the Naqshbandiyya advanced. As Hamid Algar says:

> Sober and rigorous, devoted to the cultivation of God's law and the exemplary model of the companions, it was above all the order of the ulama: countless members of the learned institution gave it their allegiance.[17]

By the early nineteenth century, 6000 religious foundations, 75 per cent of them privately established, owned two-thirds of the land in the empire.[18] After the dissolution of the Bektashiyya in 1826, three of the five biggest religious houses in Constantinople were Naqshbandi, as were 30 per cent of two thousand-odd dervishes in the city in a total of sixty Naqshbandi foundations.[19] Some of these continued to be Uzbek immigrants. The Ottoman ruler was both sultan and caliph, where the Mughal emperor was only padishah. One of the secrets of the dynasty's longevity was that while the Mughals depotentiated both sufis and *ulema*, the Ottomans integrated both into their system.

Finally, the Naqshbandiyya expanded north. Three areas were significant. First there was Kazan, capital of an independent Khanate from *c.*1430 to 1552, and then headquarters of

Russia's trade to Central Asia. Scholarly interest in the intellectual history of the Volga Tatars has been directed to the Jadids, the nineteenth century modernists from whom contemporary nationalism, and supranationalism have developed. The conservative *ulema* and dervishes against whom they reacted have been relatively neglected. It is not clear when the Naqshbandi presence was implanted; whether under the independent khanate, or more likely, under Muscovite rule, when the Muslim community was under Christian pressure to convert, yet still strongly in contact with Central Asia through trade. Thus Abunnasir Kursavi (1776–1812), the first of the Volga Tatar Jadids, twice went to Bokhara where he studied with a dervish *ishan*, before returning to Kazan.[20] Second, there was Daghestan. This largely Caucasian, i.e. non Indo-European and non Turcic area, was missionized in the late eighteenth and early nineteenth centuries by Naqshbandi devotees from the Ottoman empire, especially Kurdistan, itself fairly new Naqshbandi territory. The background here was the desire of the Ottomans for a firm Sunni frontier against the Shiite Azerbaijanis and Iranians. The Naqshbandis, traditionalist, hostile to the Shia, loyal to the sultan-Caliph, fitted into this process of frontier stabilization. Third, there was Rumelia, the Ottoman Balkans, in particular Bosnia-Herzegovina. Here the Naqshbandiyya was not originally the most prominent order. That position belonged to the Bektashiyya. The Naqshbandiyya, however, ran it a close second and the Bektashiyya was dissolved in 1826. Nineteenth century Bosnia-Herzegovina had eight houses of which three were in Sarajevo.[21] Bosnia-Herzegovina, where the local aristocracy passed from Catharism to Islam, was one of the successes of the Ottoman *jihad*. It was a rear area for the unstabilized Christian frontier, just as Kurdistan and Daghestan were forward areas for the stabilized Shiite frontier.

Gelugspa

With a similar mixture of discipline and enthusiasm the Gelugspa was primarily a phenomenon of the Tibeto-Mongol world of steppe, plateau and high valley. At three points, however, the Gelugspa went beyond this terrain.

First, there was the Kalmuk extension to the west.[22] This was the result of the secession of the right or western wing of the

Oirats from the Zunghar empire. Led by Qo-örlög of the Torghud *obogh* the western Oirats founded what the Russians knew as the Kalmuk nomadic state of the Lower Volga. Although the Kalmuks rejected Zunghar leadership, they had already accepted the Gelugspa introduced by Zaya Pandita and they took it with them to the west. They remained in contact with Lhasa and subscribed to the building of the Potala. Under the greatest of the Kalmuk rulers, Ayuki (1672–1724), his nephew Arabjur went on a diplomatic mission to Lhasa and remained there for five years. His inability to return because of Kalmuk/Zunghar hostilities and his appeal to the K'ang-hsi emperor was the pretext for the Tulisen mission sent to Ayuki by the Ch'ing in 1712. In 1717, Ayuki's wife Darma-Bala, a cousin of Tsewang Araptan, proposed to make a pilgrimage to Lhasa to carry out rituals for her dead father. In 1718, Ayuki received an embassy from Lhasa, headed by Shakur-Lama, a Torghud who had gone to Tibet as a child, became a leading abbot there, and was now being sent home to become the ranking Kalmuk lama and a kind of apostolic delegate. Incarnations continued to play a part in Kalmuk politics, as may be seen from the activities of the regent of the exiled Karashahr Torghud in the twentieth century.[23]

Second, there was the Buriat extension to the north. The Buriats were the Mongols of the Lake Baikal region, but forest rather than steppe dwellers, who practised fishing and agriculture as well as nomadic pastoralism. Until the eighteenth century the Buriats were shamanists. In 1720, some Tibetan lamas arrived via the Zunghars and introduced the beginning of the Gelugspa. In the 1720s, a Buriat religious Dambadorji Caya-yin went first to Kumbum and then to Lhasa, where he was promoted to be the Pandida Khambo Lama and sent back to Buriatia as chief hierarch. He returned home in 1764, was recognized in his position by Catherine the Great, and founded the Goose Lake lamasery at Selenginsk as a centre for proselytization. It also became a centre of resistance to the activities of the London Missionary Society, which thanks to encouragement by Alexander I, Prince Golitsyn and the Russian Bible society, maintained a mission to the Buriats between 1816 and 1841. The lamas operated a printery and were more successful in making converts from the shamanists than the Christians, partly because they represented a locally prestigious, inclusive, international culture, where the L.M.S. seemed alien, exclusive, and provincial.

Finally, there was the extension eastward to China. The Ch'ing emperors early appreciated the growing importance of the Gelugspa. In this they followed Ming precedents. According to Tibetan sources, the Yung-lo emperor twice invited Tsong-kha-pa to visit him. This is possible because Halima, patriarch of the Karma-pa sect did visit Nanking and Yung-lo may have been interested in other Tibetan hierarchs as part of a policy of using Tibet to counterbalance the Timurids. In 1616, a mission was sent from Peking to pay respects to the Fourth Dalai Lama. As Inner Asians, however, the Ch'ing had more reason to be interested in the Gelugspa than the Ming, especially since the conversion of their rivals the Chinggisids and the Zunghars. In 1634, the Ch'ing took care to champion the cause of the reformed order in their war against Legdan Khan of the Chahar Mongols, who although a Chinggisid, supported the unreformed orders. In 1642, they were too busy fighting the Ming to participate actively in the Gelugspa crusade which installed the Dalai Lama in Lhasa, but they indicated their support. In 1651, a Ch'ing mission to Lhasa invited him to visit Peking, and in 1652 he came. The meeting was of sufficient importance for the Shun-chih emperor to treat the pontiff according to Inner Asian rather than Chinese protocol. This annoyed Shun-chih's Chinese subjects and even cast doubt on Ch'ing legitimacy in China. The Dalai Lama, moreover, was not impressed, and he and his son, the regent for his successor, leaned to the kontaisha's side in the Ch'ing-Zunghar conflict.

It became a cardinal object of Ch'ing policy to secure control of the Gelugspa. The foundation of monasteries was a means to this end.[24] In 1691, K'ang-hsi founded the Gelugspa monastery of Koko Sume at Kuei-hua. His son and successor Yung-cheng founded another at Dolon-nor out in the steppe, where the Khalkha princes had submitted to his father. Between 1753 and 1780, his son, the Ch'ien-lung emperor, developed a religious complex around his hunting lodge at Jehol, where he often received Tibetan and Mongol dignitaries. The Jehol complex, a mixture of Chinese palaces and Tibetan monasteries and temples, was a microcosm of the multinational Ch'ing empire. Descriptions were published in Manchu, Chinese, Mongol and Tibetan. The Gelugspa ingredient, however, was largest. The

most impressive building, erected in 1771 to commemorate the
return of the Torghud, was an imitation of the Potala. Another
major building was erected in 1781 on the occasion of the visit
to Ch'ien-lung of the Panchen Lama. In both these projects,
the Second Chang-chia Khutugtu, Rolpai (1737–1786), played
a prominent part. This incarnation had been created by the
Ch'ing to head the pilgrimage centre of Wu-t'ai-shan in northern Shansi, the shrine of Manjusri, the patron of the Manchus.
Rolpai, from Amdo, became Ch'ien-lung's chief adviser in
Gelugspa matters. He accompanied the emperor to Wu-t'ai-
shen, presided over the selection of a new Dalai Lama, took
charge of the translation of Tibetan books into Mongolian. Yet
Ch'ien-lung himself was never a Gelugspa convert. In one of his
inscriptions, he went out of his way to declare that his support
was political only: a condescending patronage of a necessary,
but still despised, ally in his empire. It was like George IV's
condescension to the Highlands, Presbyterianism and Freemasonry in Edinburgh. Consequently, in his Tibetan buildings,
there was, as Chayet indicates, no direct copying, but rather a
deliberate element of pastiche, just as there was with George
IV's orientalism at Brighton Pavilion.[25] Yet even this degree of
recognition by Chinese culture was a major achievement for
the Gelugspa.

THE RELIGIOUS INTERNATIONALS AS A WORLD INSTITUTION

Taken together, the religious internationals were more than a
set. At a deeper level of analysis they formed a single world
institution. To see in what sense this was so, it is desirable to
look at their Christian member, the Jesuits.

The Jesuits are often portrayed simply as part of what is variously analyzed as the anti-reformation, the counter reformation
or the Catholic reform. This viewpoint, however, was not that of
St. Ignatius, as has been shown by Dominique Bertrand.[26] St.
Ignatius thought from the beginning in global terms. His first
intention after his own conversion was to go to Jerusalem to
convert the Moors. He was friends for a time with Guillaume
Postel, who travelled extensively in the Levant, and preached a

Utopian polyglottism, leading to an ultimate Christian-Muslim reconciliation. More realistically, St. Ignatius in a letter of 1552 to the emperor, sketched out the future strategy of Lepanto: a great armada in the Mediterranean to protect the afflicted maritime regions, especially Naples, from the ravages of the Turkish fleet. For St. Ignatius, the crusade was the first form of universalism. Yet conversion was never wholly lost sight of. In his last years, St. Ignatius had plans to found Jesuit colleges in Malta, Cyprus, Constantinople, Lebanon and Tadjoura in Barbary. Again, St. Ignatius' well known sympathy for merchants, striking in view of his snobbish, declining military gentry background, is explained by his perception of trade as an international like his company of Jesuits. He early on made cosmopolitan Rome his headquarters rather than anywhere in imperial yet provincial Spain, just as it had been in the multinational university of Paris that he had sought his education. His fourth vow, of loyalty to the Pope, was to the most divine because most universal institution of the Church. St. Ignatius was global in means as well as ends. His cardinal principle of indifference gave him and his Jesuits an uncommitted, anti-ideological independence of particular circumstances, communities and classes. Indifference was liberty for personal development, universal service and omnimodality of action. The Jesuit could be all things to all men because he was at home everywhere and nowhere. What Bertrand calls St. Ignatius' sociodoxy and sociopraxis were rooted in a geodoxy and geopraxis: 'La Compagnie a eu avant même d'être fondée, une aire d'action internationale.'[27] St. Ignatius was a totalizer: everything for God everywhere by everyone, the *en pasi panta Theos* of Teilhard de Chardin.

The emergence of a world institution out of the religious internationals was only partly due to their direct interaction and mutual awareness. Society of Jesus, Naqshbandiyya and Gelugspa were reformations before they were internationals and in practice their immediate targets were internal to their own confessions. Nevertheless some interaction occurred and some awareness may be presumed. The conflicts between the Kalmuks and the Kazakhs in the early eighteenth century were religious wars in which each side may be supposed to have had an elementary knowledge of each other's institutions. Ayuki Khan, moreover, was in diplomatic contact with the courts of Constantinople and Bokhara where Naqshbandi influence was significant. Muslim merchants traded at Lhasa. The Jesuit lay brother Bento Gois passed through Yarkand, Turfan and Hami on his epic journey to China between 1602 and 1607 and would have had opportunities for observing the growth of the Naqshbandiyya. The Austrian Jesuit Johan Grueber, who returned from Peking to Europe overland between 1661 and 1664, stayed for a month in Lhasa. He provided a description of the Potala which passed into Athanasius Kircher's *China Illustrata* of 1667. Less superficial in his contact, was the Italian Jesuit Hippolyte Desideri, who, coming from India via Shigatse, spent five years, from 1716 to 1721, in Lhasa. He learnt the language, studied at the Gelugspa monastery of Sera, and wrote a large book in Tibetan. He identified the principal error of Gelugspa metaphysics as its refusal to admit a necessary being, *ens a se*, i.e. the existence of God. In 1728 Desideri returned to Rome where he died in 1733, the West's first Tibetologist.[28] A century later, up at Lake Baikal, the Pandida Khambo Lama was holding a ecumenical dialogue with the Evangelical International in the persons of the L.M.S. missionaries. Here he insisted that while 'Christianity was suitable for Europeans, lamaism was best for Buryats', and that 'Christianity and Buddhism are aspects of the same religion'.[29] A century and a half later his views would be echoed, with nuances, by a Benedictine.[30]

The world institution constituted by the religious internationals came about in four ways. First, their co-existence reinforced their own sense of global awareness. This was particularly evident among the Jesuits, who were the most self consciously planetary in their outlook. Thus the Portuguese Jesuit Joas Rodriguez, the great authority on Japan, when expelled from that country and forced to retreat to China, where there was also persecution, exulted in the cosmopolitan character of the Jesuit community he found at Macao: 'the glory of Our Lord here at the end of the world;' its mixture of Portuguese, Lithuanians and Chinese associates.[31]

Second, as a result of this new global awareness, there was a certain bonding between religions even by their mutual opposition. We live by our enemies, it has been said. Particularly was this so in the Naqshbandi houses of Zabid in the Yemen in the eighteenth century. Zabid was an important centre of studies for those who came on the *haj*. It was here that the global decline of Islamdom in the face of Christianity, Hinduism and the Ch'ing empire was first perceived and articulated. This perception was a major stimulus to the many forms of reactive Muslim neo-orthodoxy which developed in the late eighteenth century such as Wahhabism, the Senusiyya, and the Fulani *jihad*. Part of this movement was the Chinese *hsin-chiao* (new sect) of Ma Ming-hsin, which brought Jahriyya devotion and a more radical approach to politics to the Tungan Naqshbandi communities of Kansu and Ninghsia. Ma Ming-hsin was inspired by the Naqshbandi Misjaji Shaikhs of Zabid, themselves inspired by the earlier Jahriyya teaching of Ibrahim al-Kurani (1616–1690). Islam in danger was no longer local, the loss of this or that territory, but global, from Senegal to Ninghsia. *Jihad* therefore assumed a new significance as well as revival as its basis.

Third, as a result of this world wide confrontation, all three internationals possessed a special character of militancy and mission: a sense that the best defence was attack, that new territories must be won to compensate for the loss of old, and prevent further loss. Jose de Acosta, one of the founders of Jesuit missiology, wrote in 1604 of 'this new Christendom, which these last ages have planted in the farthest bounds of the earth'. He contrasted the position in America with that in Europe: 'Christianity, without doubt, augments and increaseth and brings forth daily more fruit among the Indian slaves: and contrariwise ruin is threatened in other parts where have been more happy beginnings.'[32]

Fourth, thanks to the militancy and mission, characteristic of the internationals was confessional innovation, despite their traditionalism. Theirs was a *traditio juvenescens*. Thus the Naqshbandiyya began to combine Khafiyya and Jahriyya which had formerly been opposed. Again its latest offshoot, the Nurju movement in contemporary Turkey, which looks back to the Kurdish Naqshbandi Said Nursi, uses audio cassette recordings of the master's teaching, allows women to play a more than passive role in the organization, and encourages the study of science and technology by its members.[33] In Tibet, the Fifth Dalai Lama, having achieved power in Lhasa, begin to patronize the highly Tantric Nying-ma-pa sects while the Sixth Dalai

Lama, a very equivocal figure, took up something which may
have been Manichaeism. In the same way, the Gelugspa monastery of Labrang, founded in 1709, sought a middle way between
the atheism of the Madhyamika and the semi-theism of the
Jo-nan-pa school. Finally, the Jesuits were innovators as well
as traditionalists. St. Francis Borgia and St. Peter Canisius encouraged the relatively new devotion to guardian angels, while
Jesuits were prominent too in promoting the new cult of St.
Joseph, the patron of a happy death. More radically, the Jesuit
theory of probabilism challenged moral absolutes in the name
of a personalized situational ethic, while in 1772 a Sicilian Jesuit
J. M. Gravina criticized the till then almost universally accepted
doctrine of *pauci electi*, that the damned outnumber the saved,
and asserted that God's mercy far outweighs His justice. With
these two innovations, the whole moralistic, theophobe universe of much traditional Christianity began to crack. In this
development, the problems of the good pagan and the committed member of a non-Christian religion, played a part. Globality,
therefore, prompted modernism even in those who rejected it.
It pointed forward to a de facto ecumenism, which the exceptionally farsighted or batty, like Guillaume Postel, had
already envisaged in the sixteenth century. The religious internationals even without meaning to, promoted new problems,
new answers, a new world institution.

Part III
Central Asia as Passive

8 The World Market and Early Modern Central Asia

From the middle of the seventeenth century, two developments took place in Central Asia which it is tempting to connect. First, to outward appearance, Central Asia declined: in military power, political stability and international independence; in population, cultivated acreage and urbanization; and in intellectual and artistic creativity. Decline was least deniable with regard to the state. In Transoxania and the oases, the unhopeful Janids lost the capacity to rule in the seventeenth century, were overrun by the ephemeral Persian conqueror Nadir Shah in 1740, and by 1800 had disappeared, with Western Turkestan partitioned between the three city states of Khiva, Bokhara and Kokand. In Semirechie and the steppe, the hopeful Zunghar empire was destroyed between 1750 and 1760 by its own internal dissensions and by the sustained intervention of the Ch'ienlung emperor, who went on to annex Eastern Turkestan from the Afaqi Makhdumzadas. Second, for the first time since the Mongolian explosion, Central Asia became more passive than active in the world order. From being a maker of world history, Central Asia became its recipient. The world institution to which Central Asia first became passive was the world market. Being based on a realignment of trade routes from continental interiors to oceanic peripheries, the world market, it is argued, put Central Asia at a disadvantage and led to its overall decline. When European travellers entered Central Asia in the nineteenth century, they found the fabled Timurid cities strangely shrunken. Arminius Vambéry gave Samarkand only 15–20,000 people, while British intelligence credited Herat with only 9000.[1]

Although the fact of Central Asia's decline has generally been accepted, its extent and mechanism have been disputed. Was the decline anything more than military and political? Vambéry saw merits in the dervishes with whom he travelled. He argued that while international Islam in its Naqshbandi form might set a ceiling to cultural progress, it also set a floor below which culture would not fall. Might not the political fragmentation in Western Turkestan have been only a change in the optimum size of political units, such as was taking place in other parts of the Islamic world?[2] Similarly, in Eastern Turkestan, it could be argued that membership of the Ch'ing commonwealth and economic community was preferable to many to Afaqi theocracy and Zunghar autarky. The dilemma of independent poverty or dependent co-prosperity was not confined to the twentieth century in Central Asia history.

Whether the decline of Central Asia was total or partial, the role of trade has been variously judged. On the one hand, there is the view stemming from Pritsak, that a decline in trade hit the Central Asian empires, the nomad states Uzbek and Zunghar, by depriving them of the taxable wealth which had been their fiscal base. Pritsak saw a mutual dependence, a symbiosis of *imperium* and *emporium*. Taxes on trade were the precondition for empire. The two declined simultaneously as the world market realigned the trade routes. On the other hand, there is the view stemming from Fletcher and earlier presumed by Chinese border administrators, that an increase in trade injured nomad societies by encouraging consumerism, sedentarization and class division, which destroyed the solidarity of the nomads, a major source of their strength. Fletcher, like the Chinese experts before him, saw a mutual exclusiveness of *imperium* and *emporium*. These two views appear mutually exclusive both as to facts and interpretation. However, they could be reconciled by arguing that there were two fundamentally different kinds of trade in Central Asia: one, which supported empires, which was in decline; another which disrupted nomadism, which was on the increase. Furthermore, there may have been a relationship between the decline of the first and the rise of the second. If this relationship in turn was rooted in the rise of the world market, it may not necessarily have worked out to Central Asia's disadvantage. For the world market conveyed benefits as well as imposed costs.

It will be argued below that such was the case. There was a fundamental difference between the east–west trade, long distance, concerning luxuries, irregular and largely irrelevant to nomadism, though taxable by its empires, and the north–south trade, concerning necessities, regular, having a real impact on nomadic society, though less useful to empires. The first affected the state, the second affected society. The rise of the world market from the beginning of the sixteenth century shaped these two trading networks in four distinct ways. First, in the sixteenth century, it gave the east–west trade, the central land route in particular, a final period of relative prosperity. Second, its first major contraction, the world wide depression of the seventeenth century, struck the central land route a blow from which it never fully recovered. The decline of east–west trade, however, stimulated the north–south trade which eventually, because it was trade in necessities, came to outdistance the east–west trade in volume and value. Third, the recovery of the world market in the eighteenth century, surcharged this local revival of realignment, so that, on balance, trade increased in Central Asia between 1300 and 1800, though it was a different sort of trade. Finally, by the early nineteenth century, world economic recovery and expansion had produced a revival even in the east–west routes, and it was along these that after 1850, a new phenomenon, the industrial revolution, or higher poly-technic, was to be conveyed to Central Asia. Though Central Asia may have been relatively passive with regard to the world market, it is not clear that its participation did any lasting economic injury. There are passivities of growth as well as diminution.

THE WORLD MARKET: CONNOTATION AND DENOTATION

The concept of a world market was first adumbrated by Pierre Chaunu in 1959.[3] Since 1959, the concept has been extended, delimited in relation to other world institutions, and refined, both in theory and application, not least by the work of Chaunu himself.[4] Yet despite criticism, constructive and destructive, it remains the best hypothesis in the field which it itself created.

Connotation

A world market involves goods or services traded world wide, but they are not sufficient to constitute it. Before the sixth century AD, China was the only source of silk. Before the eighteenth century, it, or rather its Central Asian province of

Chinghai, was the only source of medicinal rhubarb, in pre-modern conditions the only effective drug against infantile dysentery, the number one killer. These commodities were widely traded, through Central Asia, but they did not constitute a world market. A market is more than frequent commercial connections. It is essentially a phenomenon of information, 'the first computer available to man' as has been said. It implies a regular interplay of signals between producers, distributors and consumers. It is a semiotic device which, like language itself, is established less by design, *taxis*, than by the involuntary interaction of many designs, *intertaxis*. A market is a system of what von Mises and Hayek called indeterminate teleology. This is the ground of its ability to generate and process more information about a given subject than a more determinate system of, say military intelligence, industrial espionage or consumer research.

A world market is an institution with a recognized location for the intertaxic generation and processing of information about resources traded worldwide. Resources covers both goods and services. For, to take traditional London examples, in addition to fish, fruit and meat markets at Billingsgate, Covent Garden and Smithfield, there were shipping markets at the Baltic Exchange and insurance markets at Lloyd's, as well as different money markets throughout the City. Goods may further be subdivided into raw materials for intermediate demand, as for example on the London Metal Exchange, and commodities for final demand: the direct satisfaction of human material needs in food, clothing and shelter. Thus rhubarb, silk and porcelain, the three staples of the central land route, were commodities: a foodstuff, a textile and a furnishing. Strictly, a market may not require a market place, though even data banks, telephone and computer screens still require some physical embodiment. Yet in practice, even though its participants are restricted, a market must be public. Part of the information it processes must be information about itself. A secret market is an impossibility. Even a black market must be known to the *cognoscenti* and thieves need to have a kitchen. It is to this public character of a market that the postulate of a recognized location points.

For a world market in this sense to exist, a number of conditions must be met. First, there must be world resources, i.e.

commodities, raw materials and services, either from a single source, as was once the case with silk, porcelain and rhubarb, or from a variety of sources. For eventually, information, the ultimate resource, allows anything to be produced anywhere. This condition is necessary but not sufficient. The resource may be of too little significance economically, or its distribution routes too long, expensive or too frequently interrupted to generate sufficient information to constitute a market. Second, therefore, there must be relatively cheap, quick and uninterrupted means of communication between producers, distributors and consumers. In pre-modern circumstances these could only be maritime communications. Before the railways, sea transport was between twenty and forty times cheaper than land transport. It was quicker over long distances and, although it had its own hazard of piracy, it was less vulnerable to political interruption. When Anthony Jenkinson visited Bokhara in 1558, no caravan had come through from China for three years because of 'incessant and continual warres'. It would be an unlucky port which was blockaded for so long. Third, to constitute a world market, resources must possess a critical mass or value. They must not be, as in Gibbon's characterization of ancient trade, splendid and trifling, but equally not too down to earth. Neither diamonds nor potatoes would do.[5] It was because of this condition that precious metals played such a crucial role in the genesis of the world market. Precious metals were not only in demand everywhere, but in their monetary function as liquidity, medium, measure and store, they resonated beyond themselves to other resources. Combing both mass and value, precious metals, and perhaps precious metals alone, were in a unique position to ground a world market.

Finally, a world market required appropriate enterprise, to process the information, to act on it, and to take the risks that would generate further information. A market is not a machine even though, once in motion, it will produce, as its sub-systems, mechanisms of the market. It is not deterministic. On no set of assumptions can its functioning be predicted. It is Gödelian or chaological, an open universe not a closed one. What keeps it open is risk. Without risk taking, markets grind to a halt, and risk taking is creative not mechanical. The capacity for risk, its assessment, acceptability and accountability, is a variable between societies and between groups and individuals within societies. Into such capacity enter both institutional and ideological factors: liquidity preference, legal predictability, temporal orientation, and the mentality expressed by the Hanseatic motto *navigare necesse est, vivere non necesse*. Traditional Chinese business sought to minimize risk by short turnover cycles, subdivision of functions, guild guarantees and personalized arrangements.[6] Traditional European business, on the other hand, while no stranger to these practices, was more willing to manage risk. It was no accident that the insurance industry was better developed in traditional Europe than in traditional China. A higher tolerance of risk was a major reason why it was European rather than Chinese business which created a world market. With its long maritime routes and lengthy turnover cycles of several years, a world market demanded an increase in risk capacity, based on an extension of institutions of risk management. Without these, the Great Discoveries would have been of no more commercial significance than were the voyages of Cheng Ho. World resources, oceanic routes, critical mass and value, sufficiency of risk capacity were interlocking preconditions for the semiotic system which was the world market. Risk and knowledge are correlative. A commercial venture, like a scientific hypothesis, puts itself willingly in danger of being refuted by events. In this way it generates further information for the system on which it is based.

A world market is not the same as capitalism. One should distinguish here between capitalists, capital and capitalism. Capitalists are the entrepreneurs, the risk takers. But, they do not necessarily operate with capital. In China, with a view to the minimization of risk, much business operated on the basis, not of capital, but of brokerage, commissions and bridging loans, such as are familiar in the property, stock and insurance markets in the West. Second, if by capitalism is meant a system of free entry to a market, then it is not necessarily an arrangement desired or produced by capitalists. What capitalists most frequently want is monopoly. Historically, most markets, whether local, regional, interregional or world, have not had unrestricted entry. Capitalism is an arrangement to limit the monopolistic proclivities of capitalists in the public interest. It was the invention, not of businessmen, but of moral theologians, university professors, civil servants and statesmen, though businessmen were not slow to see its long term advantages. Third, capital may be used in business without capitalists or capitalism. In Roman antiquity and early Islam, capital was employed by household freedmen or privileged slaves within the framework which has been called euergetism, while in China it was employed, for example in the salt monopoly, by state servants, responsible to neither master nor market but to the throne. A world market may involve capitalism, capitalists or capital, but it may not. Of these capitalists are the most likely to occur in its context, because household freedmen, privileged slaves and state servants are unlikely to generate sufficient risk capacity.

Finally it should be re-emphasized that a world market, like other world institutions, need not be evenly spread or everywhere dominant. Chaunu's second hypothesis, that all economic rhythms followed that of the world market centred on Seville, has not stood the test of time. The conjuncture of Seville was a very powerful one, but there were other conjunctures which were not dependent on it as was first shown by Richard Gascon in his study of Lyon.[7] As Braudel put it, America did not command everything. Particularly one might expect this to be so outside Europe, and especially in areas, like Central Asia, remote from oceanic routes. Even where the presence of the world market may be detected, as on the China coast and in the Levant, the degree of its dominance remains an open question. The notion of a world market does not imply even ubiquity or equal pressure.

Denotation

From its beginnings in the Great Discoveries, the world market, though not without setbacks and periods of contraction, expanded to include more resources. Five overlapping phases in its development may be distinguished, superimposed upon each other to make an even more complex reality.

First, there was a phase of precious metals, when the epicentre was Seville and relayed by those more capitalistic centres, Antwerp and Genoa.[8] Here the essential was American silver and in particular the silver of Potosi. From the 1560s American silver was produced by the new *patio* of amalgamation of ore with mercury and salt, which transformed these commodities into industrial catalysts.[9] Between 1500 and 1600, the quantity of silver available to Europeans roughly doubled, from 20,000 tons to 40,000 tons, doubling again between 1600 and 1800. Inside Europe, the main effect was not the once vaunted prices rise, which in the light of later inflations looks more like price stability, but avoidance of the two diseases of the monetary system, internal thesaurization and external flight.[10] Chaunu reckons that of the increase, roughly one third found its way to China.[11] Probably another third was absorbed by the Ottoman empire and India. Two kinds of evidence confirm this wide diffusion of Peruvian and Mexican silver. First, there was the increasing homogeneity of the gold to silver ratio, formerly 1:10 in Europe, 1:5 in China, at around 1:15 or 1:20[12] Second, in its infancy but giving promising results, there is nuclear analysis of coins and ingots to uncover the associated trace elements which fingerprint silver from different sources. Thus Potosí silver is associated with traces of *indium* and contains a lower percentage of gold than silver from Mexico or Europe.[13]

Second, there was a phase of commodities, whose epicentre was successively Lisbon, Amsterdam and London. Commodities, goods destined for final demand in food, clothing and shelter, figured in many markets. Building materials, water and fish were local. Cereals and meat were regional. Salt, emergency grain, naval stores and high grade wool were interregional. Sugar, coffee, tea, cocoa, silk, porcelain and fur, many medicines and some dyestuffs were international. The new emphasis on world commodities reflected an increase in consumptivity, propensity to consume, which was generated by renaissances and reformations and sustained by the influx of liquidity. A band of sumptuousness was spread across Eurasia in the days of Philip II, Elizabeth I, Rudolf II, Selim II, Shah Abbas, Akbar and Wan-li which was not coincidence but conjuncture. Of these world commodities, the most significant was sugar.[14] Sugar had long been an object of interregional commerce: in the Levant, in India and in Southeast Asia. It was a modest luxury, an indication of a threshhold of affluence. However, its progress was frequently accompanied by an increase in dental caries, so medical archaeology has an important rule to play in chronicling its diffusion.[15] Lisbon brought its cultivation to Brazil, whence it spread to the West Indies, the classic sugar islands. Amsterdam, however, gave sugar a world market where changes in price could affect events at the other end of the world. Thus in 1637, a rise in the price of Brazilian sugar on the Amsterdam market led Captain Weddell, the commander of the first English voyage to China, to make sugar his principal return cargo from Canton.[16]

Third, there was a phase of services, especially financial services, whose epicentre was first Amsterdam and then London. The financial services provided by London in the eighteenth century included letters of exchange, discounting of 60-day bills, long term state bonds, stock market transactions, equity flotation, freight charter and marine, fire and life insurance. Not all these activities functioned world wide, but City facilities enabled English nabobs to repatriate their profit from the government of India, itself generated by English government loans, by selling cotton or opium at Canton, transferring the proceeds to the supercargoes, who used it to buy tea for the London market, in return for a draft on the City paid out of the returns when the teas was sold there: all without physical movement of bullion. Financial services, however, did not merely supplement and extend liquidity in a first step towards the demonetarization of precious metals. They also represented a major extension in the management of risk. Particularly was this the function of marine insurance.[17] Though it had its precursor in the bottomry loans of antiquity, marine insurance in its modern form of underwriting dated from thirteenth century Genoa, from where it passed to Ragusa, Venice and other maritime centres. It was not only maritime centres, however, which were involved in underwriting. In the sixteenth century, Burgos underwrote policies for Castilian wool going from Bilbao to the Low Countries, for Portuguese ships going to Brazil, and for Spaniards involved in the *Carrera.* By the middle of the seventeenth century, Paris had become a major centre of marine insurance and aristocrats contributed to it via the insider dealing of *finance.*[18] The foundation of Lloyd's around 1686, the development of the London insurance market, and its reform by Sir John Angerstein from 1756, were, nevertheless, landmarks in the rise of a world wide insurance industry. Insurance was the risk business par excellence. It was risk on risk, indeed, in reinsurance, which goes back to before the sixteenth century, triple risk. By accepting risk and spreading it, insurance made risk more manageable for everyone else.

Fourth, after 1800, and especially from the mid century,

there was a phase of raw materials and energy sources. Its epicentre was London where it was symbolized by the Coal Exchange in Lower Thames Street, one of the earliest cast iron buildings in the City, erected in 1847–49 and demolished in the 1960s. This phase of the world market was associated with the distinct but allied phenomenon of the industrial revolution. The industrial revolution was not simply a mechanization of techniques and a multiplication of energy sources. It also involved a new attitude to raw materials: a world wide mobilization of resources, stockpiling of reserves, pinpointing of sources for subsequent development, the search for substitutes, the establishment of future markets. The most conspicuous of the modern industrial markets for raw materials is that for oil, but the London Metal Exchange, established in 1877 handles aluminium, copper, lead, nickel, zinc and tin. In the nineteenth century nitrates were another international raw material.

Finally, as the twentieth century ends, the world market is increasingly concerned with marketing its own infrastructure: information, software, hardware and the personnel who handle them. New York or Tokyo might seem the epicentre, but one of the properties of the latest phase of the world market may be that it has no centre, but only a diffused field of force. Industry is no longer dependent on natural resources. Given appropriate information, anything can be manufactured anywhere. Industry too is relativized by services in health, education and leisure. Saint Simon's forecast that the government of men would be replaced by the administration of things looks increasingly unlikely. On the contrary, international headhunting has become a service in its own right. The development of computers has only highlighted the distinction between persons and machines.[19] The world market involutes upon itself from information to information.

THE WORLD MARKET IN THE HOMELANDS

If the above account of the world market is accepted, its operations in the homelands can now be considered. As already emphasized, these operations were neither even nor always dominant. They coexisted with other conjunctures of equal or greater significance.

The Ottoman Empire

The economic history of the Ottoman empire in the early modern period has been presented as a classic case of peripheralization, incorporation into a world economic system in a dependent position with resulting impoverishment.[20] It will be argued here that this is at best a half truth. In the light of the concept of the world market, an alternative pattern may be suggested with parallels both in the other homelands and in Central Asia.

First, while it may be accepted that the Ottoman empire did join the world market, its participation was limited and had positive as well as negative effects. The Ottoman empire lay athwart the three major transverse routes which, prior to the Great Discoveries, linked Europe and China: the northern land route, the central land route, the southern sea route. It was, therefore, already involved in long-distance international trade. In particular, the pepper trade from Indonesia found its western outlets in Aleppo and Alexandria, which by 1520 were Ottoman cities. It was one of Braudel's achievements to show that this route was not destroyed by the Portuguese opening of the Cape route to the east. It maintained its vitality until at least the end of the sixteenth century. It was not until the middle of the seventeenth century, when the Dutch secured possession of the sources of pepper and fine spices and imposed a monopoly for the Cape route, that the old links were broken. The Ottoman empire, therefore, participated in the bullion phase of the world market through its entrepot trade in pepper. It drew considerable imports of silver from the West. These will have benefited its economy as well as allowing it to buy more cottons from India and raw materials from the Black Sea. The decline of the pepper trade, as a result of the configuration the world market took under Dutch leadership, no doubt injured the empire. It was, however, compensated in the commodity phase of the world market by the development of an export to the west first of raw cotton and then of tobacco. These exports gave rise to the essentially new towns of Smyrna, 'the New Orleans of the eighteenth century' and Salonika. In the service phase of the world economy the Ottoman empire made use of European, especially French, shipping in its coastal traffic. It is not clear that this use was at the expense of local craft. On the contrary, Greek shipping ports like Hydra remained prosperous in this period. The use reflected an increase in demand for shipping which the world market could supply most cheaply and effectively. Ottoman participation in the world market, therefore, was real, but, except episodically in raw cotton, was not central to it.

Second, there is reason to think this participation was not the dominant element in the Ottoman economy. Indeed, because of the decline of the pepper route, international trade may have been relatively less important in 1800 than in 1600. As in all traditional societies, statistics are hard to come by for the Ottoman empire. There is, however, one source of evidence which suggests that local and regional trade, mainly north–south, was more important than international trade, mainly east–west. This source is Daniel Panzac's investigation of plague and cholera in the Ottoman empire.[21] Plague was diffused from its reservoirs by couriers, commercial travellers, caravans, nomads and soldiers. Plague routes were trade routes and the plague map is therefore also a map of commercial circulation. Cholera too needs human agents for its diffusion. The two major plague reservoirs were Kurdistan on the east–west corridor and Constantinople itself on the north–south line. Most outbreaks of plague in the Ottoman empire between 1700 and 1850 were the result of diffusion from Constantinople. This suggests that intra-imperial trade was more important than extra-imperial trade, even in ports like Smyrna and Salonika which were export centres and liaison areas for the world economy. The picture which emerges of the Ottoman economy is therefore, one, not of dependence, but of limited participation, counterbalanced by the articulation of new vertical north–south links between the capital and its provinces. These probably more than compensated for the decline of the horizontal east–west routes from which the empire had formerly benefited.

Third, while these changes produced both loss and gain, they are better characterized as portfolio rearrangement than as impoverishment. From the late seventeenth century, the Ottoman empire became a Balkan or Levantine rather than a world power. It had lost Hungary. It had given up its ambitions in the Western Mediterranean and no longer received large numbers of renegades. No more did it seek to reactivate the central land route, overcome the Shah and unite with the Sunni Turks of Central Asia. It abandoned hegemony in the Ukraine. The empire turned in upon itself and became implosive rather than explosive. The era of Selim III was less splendid than the era of Selim II, but that does not mean that it was less prosperous. The growth of Smyrna and Salonika, the continued prosperity of Alexandria and Cairo, while it may have stored up trouble politically, is not evidence of impoverishment. The Ottoman empire was more injured by the ongoing ravages of the microbian common market in the form of plague than by the onset of the world market. The injury was compounded by the reluctance of Muslim authorities, now reinforced by the religious international of the Naqshbandiyya, to take action against plague by quarantine. It was only when the plague was surcharged by cholera, coming by the north–south route from the Holy Places, that the Ottoman authorities, already half convinced by the European consuls, were forced to move.

China

In its relation to the world market, China shows a pattern of greater participation, less dependency, and a different sort of portfolio rearrangement.

First, greater participation.[22] In the bullion phase of the world market, China not only received one third of the production of the American mines, but also kept it. Though the import of opium, by both the central land and southern sea routes, was eventually to lead to an outflow of silver, this was more than compensated for by the invisible inflow of remittances from overseas Chinese, which equilibrated China's balance of payments down to the Communist period. The Ottoman empire may have received as much, but it did not keep it. Much silver went to India to pay for muslins via rather than from Mosul or to the Black Sea to pay for 'Baltic goods' and naval stores.[23] In the commodities phase of the world market, the raw cotton and tobacco supplied by Smyrna and Salonika was of only secondary importance. China's contribution of silk in the sixteenth century, especially via the new Amoy–Manila–Acupulco–Mexico route, was of more global significance. In the eighteenth century, China provided, in tea, one of the central items of world trade, rivalling sugar. In the services phase of the world economy, Western shipping not only entered China's north–south coastal traffic after the first treaty settlement in 1842, but went on to play a role in China's inland navigation after the second treaty settlement in 1860. Western insurance business, conducted by the agency houses at Canton, penetrated China earlier than the Ottoman empire and underwrote more vessels. In money matters, the Hong Kong and Shanghai Bank cut more ice than the Ottoman Bank, its western equivalent.[24] In the raw materials phase of the world market, while the Ottoman empire supplied little, China supplied useful if not crucial soya beans, wood oil and scarce minerals such as antimony. In the world market generally Canton and Shanghai outweighed Smyrna and Salonika.

Second, less dependency. Although China participated in the world market to a greater extent than did the Ottoman empire, its impact on the Chinese economy was less. The basic reason for this was scale. In 1800, the Ottoman empire had a population of 20 million, the Ch'ing empire a population of 300 million. The Ottoman empire, if Arabia and part of North Africa are included, covered two million square miles, the Ch'ing empire four million. For the world market to have had the same impact on China as it did on the Ottoman empire, its pressure would have had to have been many times greater. The Western presence on the China coast, through diplomats, merchants, professional people, synarchs and missionaries, was fundamentally undynamic. It was unsustained from home, muffled by Ch'ing diplomacy and circumvented by Chinese social inertia. Western firms adopted Chinese ways of doing business and were infiltrated by Chinese capital. Consequently, Chinese economic history, like its history generally, continued to be made in China. It was made either down on the farm in the innumerable villages of the agricultural frontier, or up in the massive new cities which, while they might be served by steamships and railways of foreign origin, had been inflated as much by Chinese as world factors. The treaty ports were not really like Salonika and Smyrna. Canton would have been a great port without the East India companies because of its trade with Vietnam and Siam. Shanghai grew as much by native banks, salt smuggling, prostitution, gambling and racketeering as by foreign trade.[25] Tientsin was already the port for Peking, the terminus of the Grand Canal, and the headquarters of a salt division. Hankow was the product, not of foreign, but of interregional trade. Treaty ports were selected because they were dynamic: they did not become dynamic because they were selected. Where growth points were misidentified, as in the case of Ningpo, world trade alone could not make them grow.

Third, different portfolio rearrangement. Unlike the Ottoman empire which underwent a process of verticalization, reorienting its trade routes from east–west to north–south, the Chinese empire retained the articulation it had assumed in the Sung period: a major east–west axis along the Yangtze and a minor north–south axis along the Grand Canal and the waterways which effectively extended it to Canton. Two major changes took place within this framework: an extension of the Yangtze route to include the newly opened agricultural frontier of Szechwan; an extension of the Grand Canal and its prolongation by the Liao river to include the colonial frontier of Manchuria. The first was an addition to the already widely radiating trade of Hankow; the second to the already considerable redistribution function of Tientsin.[26] Both routes involved an exchange of primary products for manufactured goods and business services: a pattern of urban domination and rural compensation familiar in China. A third change lay outside this framework and involved the world commodity of tea. Where the Ottoman empire contracted its horizons in the early modern period, China expanded its horizons with the Ch'ing conquest of Inner Asia. This conquest gave rise on the east–west line to a revival of the central land route for part of its run, and, on the north–south line to a new route across Mongolia. Both routes carried tea, though most tea, of course, exited via Canton and Shanghai. The extension of the tea trade to include customers in Western Europe, Russia and Central Asia, however, changed nothing in principle. It simply added European East India companies, Tibetan lamas, Uzbek *aksakals* and Tsarist officials to the usual long line of compartmentalized intermediaries, between producers and consumers. China in the eighteenth century therefore did not alter radically its portfolio. It took up options in stock it already held, and for the rest was content with its blue chips. After all they had allowed her to triple her population between 1700 and 1850 at probably gently rising standards of living.

India

The participation of the Indian subcontinent in the world market is difficult to assess. More than in China, there is the problem of regional economies: the basic division of north and south, the secondary division within each of east and west. India was a collection of continental islands only federated by whoever ruled in Delhi. Often when India is spoken of, Bengal is meant.

In the bullion phase of the world market, India drew a stream of silver through its exports of cotton textiles to the Ottoman empire and the West. The diminution of this stream in the seventeenth century did not have the consequences sometimes ascribed to it in China. India was one of the few major countries (Japan was another) not to experience a seventeenth century general crisis. This suggests that the Indian economy, however deeply involved, was not strongly dependent on the world market. In the commodities phase, India, like the Ottoman empire, was not an important supplier. What started as East India companies became China companies or, in the case of the Dutch, a Southeast Asia company. In the services phase, Anglo-Indian business, especially Parsee, collaborated to develop the country trade in raw cotton and opium to Canton. The *raj* itself may be regarded as a gigantic provision of services, especially as its real costs were largely met by the English rather than the Indian taxpayer. In the raw material phase, India's major contribution was jute, which in the nineteenth century substituted itself for Baltic hemp. Jute was paid for by imports of salt, first from Cheshire and then from the Red Sea. These had the effect of ruining the Bengal artificial boiling salt industry. This pattern of disindustrialization, frequently noted for the Indian textile industry, may however, have been confined to Bengal, the precarious core of the Indian *économie-monde*. Maharashtra and the Tamil Nadu with its own colony in Ceylon indicate a happier pattern. Yet even Bengal was not a complete loser. Calcutta, no less than Bombay and Madras, were creations of the foreigner, ultimately of the world market. They were more like Smyrna and Salonika than Canton, Shanghai and Tientsin. Like China, India, through the *raj*, had a greater participation in the world market than the Ottoman empire, but unlike China, that participation produced more than portfolio additions.

Russia

In contradistinction to India and China, and more like the Ottoman empire, Russia's participation in the world market was limited. Moreover, its degree of dependence was not large. It was an *économie-monde* in Braudel's sense, a world apart or island economy. Nevertheless, participation was of significance not so much to the *esse* of the Russian economy as to its *bene esse*. It provided export surplus and consequent ability to import.

Russia began as Muscovy. With the Ukraine, White Russia and Lithuania, it formed part of the Baltic macroregion. From the middle ages, the Baltic supplied Western Europe with timber and potash, tar and pitch, amber, hemp, honey and wax, and above all, fur, in return for salt, wine and manufactured goods.[27] In addition to this east–west route, fur also went north–south to Constantinople, Tabriz and Khiva.[28] In the macroregion, Muscovy's role was that of guardian of the deep forest, the *taiga*, the home of bees, martens, northern lynx and mink. Its acquisition of Novgorod in the fifteenth century and of Lithuania in the eighteenth put it in control of the *tundra* with its sables and the middle forest with its squirrel and ermine. It became an effective fur monopolitan for Europe, and, by its acquisition of Siberia in the seventeenth century, for Asia too. This monopoly lasted effectively till the development of Canada successively by the St. Lawrence, Hudson's Bay and the Pacific coast. Fur was Russia's major export commodity. Unlike Ottoman spices, Indian cotton and Chinese tea, fur did not draw in much silver, except from the Ottoman empire, because the proceeds were needed for other imports. In the commodity phase, Russian fur traded at Kiakhta drew in Chinese brick tea from Hankow to make Russia one of the great tea-drinking nations.[29] Exports of fur to Constantinople paid for incense from Arabia for the Orthodox church. In the field of services, Russia paid its subscription to the ecumenical patriarchy in fur. This connection drew in the stream of Greek ecclesiastics, so important to Muscovy in the age of the religious assault, of the West, the Nikonite reform, and the Raskol.[30] Long before Peter the Great founded St. Petersburg, fur was Russia's window not only to the west and east, but also to the south, the lands of Central Asia.

THE WORLD MARKET IN CENTRAL ASIA

The impact of the world market in Central Asia was mediated through the Ottoman empire, the Ch'ing empire, India and Russia. It was therefore indirect and oblique. Moreover, it was further deflected by the conjuncture of Central Asia, in particular by its political conjuncture. Assessment of participation, degree of dependency and consequences must begin with political developments.

Since the ending of Timurid dominion, Central Asia had been divided between steppe and oasis and within steppe and oasis. Such unity as it possessed was due to society and culture: especially to the Naqshbandiyya on the one hand, and the Gelugspa on the other. In the period 1750 to 1850, these divisions were compounded by a further tripartition between east, west and south.

In the east, Zungharia, part of Semirechie, and Eastern Turkestan were reunited under Ch'ing control as Sinkiang, the new dominion. The headquarters of the *chiang-chün*, or military governor, was at Ili or Kuldja, the former Zunghar capital, with deputies at Urumchi and Kashgar. Until 1884, and a second conquest following a rebellion, Sinkiang was not a Chinese province, but a Manchu military region. Although *lebensraum* for China's bounding population which worried Ch'ien-lung, was one of his objects in conquest, immigration was not encouraged, except for a few military units at Ili and some Chinese Muslim or Tungan merchants and clerks who, it was hoped, would act as a buffer between the authorities and the natives.

As in their other dominions, the Ch'ing in Sinkiang operated a sophisticated colonial system. They kept their military profile low and their fiscal presence light. They tried always to mobilize a maximum of friends against a minimum of enemies. After the dissolution of the Zunghar confederacy and the physical extermination of many Zunghars through the deliberate introduc-

tion of smallpox, the Ch'ing identified their number one enemy as the Afaqi Makhdumzadas. These they could not win
over, like the Gelugspa, or root out. When the Ch'ing moved
in, the Khojas fled west. They were arrested by the sultan of
Badakhshan, who, to ingratiate himself with the Ch'ing, executed them, but, not wishing to inflame Muslim opinion, allowed their sons to escape to Kokand, where they established a
government in exile. From Kokand, their descendants launched
a series of incursions into eastern Turkestan where they retained support and organization. Yet down to 1864 all these
incursions ultimately failed. Against a single enemy, the Ch'ing
found many friends, especially when against that enemy, the
Ch'ing looked like winning. Not everyone was Muslim. The
Torghud Mongols of Karashahr were Gelugspa lamaists who
could provide useful light cavalry. Not all Muslims favoured the
dervishes. There were the secular Chaghatai princes of Hami in
a key communications area and the conservative *ulema* in many
of the oases of the Tarim basin. Not all dervishes were
Naqshbandi. There were also branches of the Khiva based
Kubrawiyya and the Baghdad based Qadiriyya and independent
or Uwaysiyya Shaikhs. Not all Naqshbandis were Makhdumzadas:
there was an earlier line at Kucha. Not all Makhdumzadas were
Afaqi: the Ishaqiyya continued to exist at Yarkand. Moreover,
the Ch'ing learnt to neutralize external support for the Afaqi
jihad by giving trade privileges to the khan of Kokand, on the
implicit condition that he keep the exiled Khojas on a leash.
More generally, the encouragement of trade was a Ch'ing technique for keeping the region quiet. Tungan merchants, based
on Ninghsia, Lanchow and Sining, acted as intermediaries in a
revival of the central land route for interregional traffic between Sian and Kashgar. Yarkand was allowed to develop a
substantial north–south trade with India. In 1851, by the treaty
of Kuldja, Chuguchak (Tarbagatai) and Ili were opened to
direct Russian trade. During its first century in the Ch'ing free
trade area, Eastern Turkestan enjoyed one of its most prosperous periods economically. It was criss-crossed by routes both
east–west and north–south along which were transmitted the
pulsations of the distant world market.

In the west, steppe and oasis had different histories. On the
steppe, the three Kazakh hordes came under increasing Russian control. In the first half of the eighteenth century, the

Kazakhs, threatened by the Zunghars, accepted a largely formal Russian protectorate. When the Zunghars were overthrown and Ch'ing forces appeared, the khans hastened to pay tribute to them too. As enemies of the Zunghars and relatively non-dervish Muslims, the Kazakhs were acceptable to the Ch'ing. In the period after the Napoleonic wars, the Russians began to turn their formal protectorate into a real one. The khans were forced to live in Russian border fortresses and Cossack garrisons were established out in the steppe. This increased presence provoked a series of strongly Islamic revolts led by lesser nobles and diehard nomads, of which the most famous was that of Kenesari Khan of the Middle Horde between 1837 and 1847. These revolts were supported from the south by the oasis states. Russia, preoccupied elsewhere, could only respond by building fortresses south of the steppe as well as north of it.

In the oases, the Uzbek polity became divided in the second half of the eighteenth century into the three city states of Khiva, Bokhara and Kokand. In appearance a further fragmentation of power, in reality it was a new concentration. The last Shibanids had lacked either revenue or an army. Such power as there was fell to local *obogh* chiefs and dervish leaders in the various oases. The new city states, with a single *obogh* chief as ruler – Qunggirat in Khiva, Manghit in Bokhara, Ming in Kokand – provided regional centralization. They were effective, even reforming, and fell into the pattern of successful medium sized states which Bayly has found in other parts of the Muslim world.

The three city states were different. Khiva was a military state which defeated Russian expeditions in 1717 and 1839, and extended control over the Turkmen to the south. It also maintained a high level of Islamic culture. Bokhara was a clerical state. The founder of the Manghit dynasty was educated as a canonist, continued as ruler to wear dervish dress, and strictly enforced the *sharia*. It also had a commercial dimension. It sent a tribute mission to China in 1764 and imported tea via Yarkand and Badakhshan. In 1830, Alexander Burnes reported, the 'country is flourishing, trade prospers and property is protected.'[31] Kokand was a mercantile state. Established in the 1740s to protect Ferghana from the Zunghars, Kokand entered into tributary relations with the Ch'ing in 1759. Between 1762 and 1821, it sent a total of 48 missions, sometimes to Peking, sometimes to Kashgar. On one occasion the ambassadors returning from Peking were accompanied by eighty-eight wagons carrying tea, pepper, silks and ceramics. These imports were paid for with horses, cattle, skins, indigo, opium from both Persia and India, and above all fur, imported from Russia. This return trade was so brisk that there was a net outflow of silver from China. The Kokand khans secured the allegiance of the mountain Kirghiz and added a military dimension to their state. They used the diplomatic leverage of the presence of the Afaqi Makhdumzadas to force the Ch'ing authorities in 1835 to sign what Joseph Fletcher called China's first unequal treaty. This gave them privileged access to Sinkiang and extraterritoriality for their merchants. Under Omar Khan (1798–1822) and Muhammed Ali Khan (1822–1842), Kokand built itself unto a major entrepot linking Persia, India, China and Russia.[32]

In the south, Herat and most of Afghan Turkestan found itself from 1750 in the hands of the new Afghan state constructed by Ahmad Shah Durrani (1747–1773). Its construction offers parallels to the story of the Zunghars. Like the Zunghar empire, the Afghan kingdom was new. It had never existed before and the people it embraced were not united by either language or religion. Modern Afghanistan contains both Turkish and Persian speakers: three kinds of Persian, indeed, Parsa, Pashtun and Tajik. It contains both Sunnites and Shiites, among whom are the descendants of the Mongol armies, the Hazaras. Like the Zunghar empire, the Afghan monarchy was originally based on pastoralists: not so much nomads, as these are rare in the hills of Afghanistan, as transhumants and fixed ranchers. Like the Zunghars, the early Afghan state, which started round Kandahar, was associated with a religious organization, the Rawshaniyya. Like the Zunghar empire, the Afghan monarchy was military and expansionary. In 1760, its threat of an international *jihad* intimidated Ch'ien-lung into halting Manchu advance on the Tien-shan instead of going on to the Caspian as he had planned. Yet here the likeness with the Zunghars ceased. The Afghan rulers turned cautious. After early campaigns in India, they contented themselves with their transmontane state and avoided military disaster and internal dissensions. Unlike the Zunghars, the Afghans moved in the direction of sedentarization, shifting their capital from pastoral Kandahar to mercantile Kabul. Unlike the Zunghars, the Afghan rulers

inclined to secularism to escape clerical domination. This was a
further reason for the move from Kandahar to Kabul. The
Naqshbandiyya existed in Afghanistan, but it did not have the
power it had in Transoxania. Finally, unlike the Zunghars, the
Afghans had to face the British for whom Central Asia was
marginal, while for the Manchus it was essential. For all these
reasons, Afghanistan survived while Zungharia did not. Yet there
was also an element of luck. In 1800 the Afghan monarchy was
tearing itself apart in succession disputes which lasted twenty-
five years. The likelihood of eventual British annexation was
high. However, good foundations had been laid. In particular,
Kabul was well placed to exploit a north–south route between
India and Russia with links to the world market at both ends.
We can now approach the impact of the world market in Central Asia directly.

First, the participation of Central Asia in the world market.
From antiquity Central Asia had participated in world trade
through the northern and central land routes. This participation reached a high point in the Timurid period. Clavijo noted
that: 'Every year to the city of Samarqand much merchandise of
all kinds from Cathay, India, Tartary, and from many other
quarters besides, for in the countries round the Samarqand
territory commerce is very flourishing.'[33] Tamerlane promoted
trade actively and invested in it through the construction of
central markets for which traders paid rent. This policy was
continued by Shah Rukh and Husayn Bayqara at Herat, notably
in the building of the *chahar su*, later echoed in the spice
market of Constantinople. Although the Timurid courts were
places of conspicuous consumption, the greater part of this
trade was transit rather than terminal. Of the three commodities characteristic of the central land route, silk, porcelain and
rhubarb, only rhubarb originated in Central Asia and that marginally. Central Asia also produced exportable textiles, notably
the *saqalet* of Samarkand and Herat, 'scarlet', a fabric before
being a colour, but it was not these which sustained the route.
Samarkand was essentially an entrepot, as was Herat.
    This pattern was not initially disturbed by the emergence of
the world market. The best evidence for the central land route
in the sixteenth and seventeenth centuries is provided by the
Chinese tribute lists.[34] Trade and tribute were correlative and

often were identical. The Chinese tribute lists show a high level of connection with Hami, Turfan, Samarkand, Arabia and Rum (the Ottoman empire) throughout the sixteenth century, though no expansion. The period 1600 to 1643 shows a falling off in relations, followed by an almost complete collapse in the early years of the Ch'ing until the revival of tribute from Hami in the eighteenth century. It was not the emergence of the world market which injured the Central Asian routes, but rather its contraction in the seventeenth century depression. Moreover, when expansion resumed in the eighteenth century, it did so in different channels. Those who operated the central land route – the Armenians, the Jews, the Bokharans, the Tungans, the Shansi Chinese – switched their capital to the new north–south routes which were developing: across the Caucasus, over the Caspian, through the Hindu Kush, via the T'ien-shan, across the Gobi, over the Tibetan plateau, along the Manchurian rivers. Because this trade was in humbler, less luxurious commodities such as salt, flour, grain, wadded cloth and ironmongery, it had greater growth potential than the more glamorous east–west traffic.

As the world market turned from bullion to commodities, a further significant change occurred. Central Asian trade shifted from transit to terminal. Kokand might constitute itself a mini Samarkand, but the growth area of Central Asian trade in the early modern period was the import of tea for local consumption: brick tea from Szechwan and Hunan for Tibet and Mongolia, green tea from Fukien for Transoxania. Alexander Burnes noted that the 'love of the Bokharans for tea is, I believe, without parallel', and Mongolian scholars have traced the growth in tea consumption in their country from twelve bricks a year per family in 1778 to thirty-six in 1910.[35] At the same time, Central Asians developed a taste for other new international commodities such as sugar, tobacco and opium. Alexander Burnes has a nice conceit of American and Chinese sugar meeting in the markets of Khiva.[36] Behind this new consumerism lay the victory of society over the state and the rise of the religious internationals. In Europe, tea, coffee and cocoa were associated with a feminization of consumption. In Asia, the new beverages were associated with clericalization: coffee and tea with the *tariqats*, tea with lamaism. Turkish dervishes and Tibetan lamas, travelling widely, were the representative of the service aspect of the world economy, but they also carried its commodity phase. Of course, because of its low population, Central Asia's share of the global tea market was not large. It may, however, have equalled Russia's share of 10 per cent. Mongolia's per capita consumption at one time equalled Britain's.

Second, the degree of dependency of the Central Asian economy on the world market. Mongolian scholars of the communist era portrayed Sino-Mongolian relations in the early modern period in terms of the Leninist theory of Imperialism. In particular, the so-called *tunsh* or *t'ung-shih* agreements relating to Mongol debt were seen as exploitive. Similar theories could have been advanced about Russian relations with Western Turkestan, though in fact Soviet scholars were reluctant to admit that their country had ever been imperialistic even under the tsars. Moreover, both views could easily be transposed into world-systems dependency theory. In fact, such interpretations are misplaced. Sino-Mongolian trade was initiated as much by the Mongols as by the Chinese. Indeed, the Ch'ing authorities started by opposing it. The *tunsh* agreements now look more like Third World credit recyclement to avoid bank default than debt peonage. The rise of consumerism on the steppe via the monasteries may have been socially divisive and politically weakening, but it was probably advantageous economically to increasing numbers of nomads. Nomad diet, clothing and shelter all became diversified. Yet this did not imply dependence in the Wallerstein sense. Mongolia exported more to pay for its imports, but it did so by raising existing production rather than by a switch in capital investment. It would not have been difficult to go back to the old autarky. As with Russia, it was the *bene esse* of Mongol life which was at stake, not the *esse*. That sedentary Central Asia was not dependent was shown by the favourable balance of trade it ran with China. It was Kokand which was the colonialist in Sinkiang not the Chinese.

Finally, the consequences in Central Asia. The short answer to the view that Central Asia declined because of the impact of the world market is that Central Asia did not decline. Muslim scholars in the Soviet Union have long rejected the view that their countries were sunk in some specially non-progressive form of feudalism from which only Tsarist and Soviet assistance freed them for advance towards capitalism and socialism. In the period 1800 to 1850 Central Asia was experiencing a modest renaissance. The world portrayed by Alexander Burnes and Arminius Vambéry was not sunk in economic torpor. As with the Ottoman empire, the economic changes in Central Asia in the early modern period are best described in terms of port-folio rearrangement. Latitudinal east–west transit trade in luxu-ries declined. Longitudinal north–south terminal trade in necessities increased. Some of the decline was due to the world market, e.g. the decline of the silk route, but so too was some of the advance, e.g. the advance of the tea routes. As with China, Central Asia would probably have benefited from greater par-ticipation in the world market, though, as always with economic growth, there would have been social costs and political prob-lems, as well as need for cultural readjustment. More economic growth and wider contacts might have alleviated what was prob-ably Central Asia's greatest problem in the early modern pe-riod: its low demography. Mongol demography was restricted by syphilis, the latest ramification of the micobian common market, and possibly by excessive clericalism, though it is not certain that celibacy was fully practised by all who claimed lama status. Muslim demography was restricted by the canonists' doctrine that birth control was justified, indeed made manda-tory, by 'bad times.'[37] More economic growth would have helped here, just as wider contacts had already brought the modern form of vaccination to Central Asia, as the Russian traveller and Kazakh prince Chokan Valikhanov reported. Today Muslim natality in the Soviet Union is higher than that of the Christian population. Before 1850 it was lower, because Orthodox doc-trine favoured early marriage and high natality. The great Rus-sian advance, which was to bring Central Asia into yet another world institution, was powered in part by this demographic differential.

9 The Higher Polytechnic and Modern Central Asia

In the second half of the nineteenth century, Central Asia began to receive the effects of the industrial revolution. This has continued to the present in descending degree in Western, Eastern and Afghan Turkestan and their associated steppe. The industrial revolution created an assemblage of tools, techniques, energy sources, processes, programmes and allied institutions which may be termed the higher polytechnic and, in its widest dimensions, be regarded as a further world institution. This terminology allows one to distinguish between the industrial revolution as a process, whether local, regional, interregional or international in production, distribution or consumption, and the higher polytechnic as the result of that process. In his systematic processual archaeology, Colin Renfrew distinguishes between the subsistence subsystem (artefact–nature) and the technological subsystem (man–artefact).[1] In the modern world, where information has become the primary resource, the higher polytechnic represents a combination of these two subsystems, now only notionally distinct, into a technosphere. To a future archaeologist, the higher polytechnic will be part of both the material and cognitive archaeology of our culture. It was the end-product of the more familiar concept of the industrial revolution. Jonathan Clarke has criticized this concept, particularly with regard to the micro and medio levels of English political and social history in the eighteenth century.[2] Here industrial evolution, transformation or undercurrent might be more adequate to the realities. Nevertheless, at the macro level of world history, the term industrial revolution, suitably delimited, has a proper application as shorthand for the transition between Renfrew's lower, subsystemic, polytechnics and the higher, overarching, polytechnic, operative universally today, though, like other world institutions, unevenly and not necessarily dominant.

THE HIGHER POLYTECHNIC: CONNOTATION AND DENOTATION

The scope of the term may best be indicated, on the one hand, in relation to concepts, and on the other hand, in relation to facts, in particular the facts of the industrial revolutions which established it.

Connotation

The concept of the higher polytechnic as a world institution may be signified both by what it was and by what it was not. First it was something which affected not only production and distribution but also consumption. Certainly production was central. A massive increase in both gross and per capita production is intuitively part of the notion of an industrial revolution. Four criteria have been proposed to determine whether a process is industrial or preindustrial: powered machinery; new sources of power beyond the traditional wood, wind, water, sun and muscle; assemblage in factories; and application of science. An example would be the Leblanc process for the manufacture of soda which was adopted in factories in Paris, Widnes, St. Helens and Glasgow in the late eighteenth and early nineteenth centuries to become the foundation of the modern chemical industry.[3] Soda, an alkali, was a raw material used in the textile, paper, glass and soap industries. Previous to the Leblanc process, alkali had virtually been a natural substance, being derived from kelp or potash. Now it became a manufactured product. The manufacture was effected by the application of sulphuric acid, a non-traditional agent, to salt. To avoid the transportation of this dangerous substance and to acquire the space for dealing with the noxious waste products, production had to be in factories. The process itself, invented by Nicholas Leblanc in 1789, was the application of earlier advances in pure chemistry, notably by Lavoisier. The Leblanc process, however, did not involve the mechanization and re-powering of transportation, which intuitively is another part of the notion of an industrial revolution. Leblanc factories were located near the coalfields which supplied the large quantities of fuel required. The other raw material, salt, was less costly to transport and generally travelled on its traditional water routes. At Widnes, for example, salt was brought from the salines of Nantwich and Northwich by a pre-industrial transportation route, the partially canalized River Weaver. Most soda left Widnes via the Mersey and Liverpool.

It was different with the Solvay process which from 1861 increasingly replaced the Leblanc process in the manufacture of soda. The Solvay process, invented in Belgium, substituted ammonia for sulphuric acid and brine for salt and reduced the requirements for fuel. As brine was then difficult to move, it located its plant near saline sources. As its fuel requirements were less than those of the Leblanc process, it could afford to bring in coal, in continental circumstances chiefly by rail. Rail was also used to distribute the soda produced. Solvay had started at Couillot east of Charleroi because of its coal and limestone for which he imported rock salt, but he soon moved to Dombasle south of Nancy on the Lorraine saltfield for which he imported coal from the Saar. In England, Brunner and Mond obtained the patent from Solvay and placed their works at Winnington near Northwich, to which they imported by rail Staffordshire and North Wales coal and Derbyshire limestone. Similarly, their soda was diffused by rail. Where Leblanc had been industrial only in production, Solvay was industrial in distribution as well. It belonged to the era of the steamship, the railway and the automobile.

While production and distribution have generally been recognized as part of industrialization, consumption has been much less studied by economic historians. Yet consumption – antecedent, concomitant and subsequent – can never be divorced from production and distribution. Again, the alkali industry is a good illustration. Its customers were the textile, paper, glass and soap industries, but they in turn served the public. Behind the pre-industrial and fully industrial development of textiles in northwest Europe, lay two important social changes. First, there was a shift in consumer preference from heavier to lighter fabrics: furs and woollens to silks and cottons; which was accompanied by a greater distinction between indoor and outdoor clothes. This shift may be associated with improvements in housing, especially in the adoption from the Renaissance of the ideal of the warm and heat conserving 'heavy' house built of stone.[4] Second, again from the Renaissance, but more particularly in the eighteenth century, there was a rise in expenditure on female clothes, whether as a result of increased male willingness to spend on their womenfolk (this looks like the factor in the Lyon black velvet market in the sixteenth century) or the command of greater resources by women themselves (this may be the explanation in eighteenth century Bath and the world of Jane Austen). Paper consumption rose through the expansion of literacy, especially to women, in Chaunu's cerebral revolution. The glass industry too was affected by the changes in housing, just as its elimination of window draughts furthered the change in clothing and its improvement of lighting encouraged habits of reading. The increased use of soap may be related, on the one hand, to the refinement of manners, and, on the other, to the reduction of child mortality effected through putting cleanliness next to godliness. Smoking factory, puffing train, earnest school room, animated salon and quiet night nursery were all interrelated in the industrial revolution. It involved high-energy consumption as much as powered production and mechanized distribution.

If these be the positive attributes of the higher polytechnic it may also be characterized negatively.

First, the higher polytechnic should not be identified with the world market. Unlike the world market, the higher polytechnic did not presuppose global action. Moreover, it spread toward it, not as a continuous field, but as discontinuous points of production, distribution and consumption. Indeed, by providing import substitutes, industrialization might work against the world market. Thus the development of the European potteries by Wedgwood and others reduced the international trade in Chinese porcelains from Ching-te-chen.[5] Similarly, in the middle ages and the early modern period, salt both in Europe and China, had been traded interregionally in *ordines salis* and *yin-ti*. In the nineteenth century, it became briefly a world commodity when Cheshire, able to exploit favourable conditions of fuel and ballast, exported to every continent. Then, as salt changed from alimentary commodity to chemical raw material and as deep drilling made it possible to develop brine sources almost anywhere, international trade in salt contracted sharply. True, industrialization created new world commodities in automobiles and high fashion articles, as well as new world raw materials such as rubber or petroleum, but such creations were not of its essence. In itself the higher polytechnic tended as much to autarky as to world market.

Second, the higher polytechnic should not be identified with capital, capitalists or capitalism. True, the industrial revolution frequently involved a substitution of fixed capital for floating funds, machinery for labour, but the finance might come from loans or taxation rather than from genuine risk capital. As Saint-Simon saw, for the early stages of industrialization, particularly in continental countries without a tradition of large scale private business, public enterprise might be a more appropriate framework than private enterprise. In Central Asia, for example, industry was the product of socialism, not its precursor. Elsewhere social overheads had to be provided by public authority. In few countries were railways built without a considerable degree of state participation. Many individual enterprises sought and obtained virtual monopolies or at least protection from competitors. Industrialization is as favourable to command economy as to market economy. Except in Britain and the United States, capitalist industry was at first something of a rarity. What Saint-Simon, Marx and their Soviet disciples did not appreciate was that the command economy would cease to be an appropriate framework for industry as its complexity increased, the information content rose and consumer preference became more decisive. Socialism could initiate industrialization, it could not sustain it. Insufficiently interested in the forces of consumption and distribution as compared to the forces of production, they mistook the birth pangs of capitalism for its death throes. It was only in its developed forms that the higher polytechnic came to require capitalism and the world market.

Third, the higher polytechnic should not be identified with economic development, modernization, or Europe's precocious dominance within the modern world order. First, already in 1800, perhaps 1750, even 1700, Europe was, both absolutely and per capita, very much richer, consumed more energy, had higher rates of literacy than Islam, India or China. The gap between Europe and the rest of the world was striking before even a breath of the industrial revolution. Industrialization was a result of European supremacy before being a cause of it. Second, the industrial revolution was a much slower and above all later phenomenon than has generally been allowed. In England, steam did not replace water as the principal prime mover until the 1820s and in the United States coal did not overtake wood until 1887. If this was what things were like there, what must they have been like in Austria, Poland or Russia? The Victorians lived and worked their amazing achievements in education, social organization and politics, in a largely preindustrial world. The horse, for example, maintained its role in transport. In 1914, there were more horses in the world being used by more people than ever before or since. The multiplication of horses outside the steppe, indeed, was one reason for the relative decline of Central Asia in world energy, and specifically military potential. Third, one must not confuse the industrial revolution with the medical revolution which, through the dramatic fall in death rates it effected, did almost as much to create the modern world as the technological changes. Today, of course, industry and medicine are inseparable: X-rays, cobalt treatment, chemotherapy, artificial organs, laser beams, etc; but it was not so at the beginning. The basic medical breakthroughs: the conquest of plague by quarantine, of smallpox by vaccination, of cholera by sanitation, of infantile dysentery by cleanliness; the microbian theory of disease, the identification of pathogenic agents, the development of specific antibodies; had little to do with industrialization, much with the republic of letters. Their hero, Louis Pasteur, came from one of the countries least receptive to the industrial revolution. Similarly, the rapid world wide diffusion of vaccination, the discovery of a country doctor from Gloucestershire, is to be attributed to neither industrialization, nor world market, nor capitalism, but to the basic information circuit as extended by the Enlightenment.[6] The emergency of the higher polytechnics was important and beneficial, but it was not *the* great discontinuity in world history, nor the unique source of Europe's pre-eminence within it.

Denotation

Conceptual definition leads on to ostensive definition: where is a technosphere concretely located? The higher polytechnic points both to present facts and to past events. Among present facts, it points to tools, equipment, machines and plant; to trade secrets, apprenticeships, training on the job or formally, schools of engineering, colleges of technology and professional associations; to users' manuals, patents, brand specification, blueprints and scientific abstracts. The higher polytechnic is composed of lower polytechnics. It is a mixture of hardware and software: World I objects and World III objects to use Karl Popper's terminology. Among past events, the higher polytechnic may be identified with the five stages of the industrial revolution in time and space.[7]

First, it began in the late eighteenth century in northwest England with the application of coal and steam to the salt and cotton industries. From Cheshire and Lancashire this application was extended to the woollen industry of Yorkshire and the metallurgy of Birmingham. Second, during the Napoleonic Wars, the English industrial complex was copied in Belgium: at Ghent by Bauwens and Bossaert in cottons, at Verviers by William Cockerill in woollens, at Seraing by John Cockerill in machine making and metallurgy; all making use of the ancient coal mines of Liège now expanded. Third, industrialization spread up the Rhineland to the Ruhr conurbation, Ludwigshafen and Basel and over the Alps to Piedmont and Lombardy. Hither it came in two waves: an initial wave of coal and steel, the empires of Krupp and Thyssen; a subsequent wave of chemicals – Unilever in Rotterdam, Bayer in Cologne, Hoechst in Frankfurt, BASF in Ludwigshafen. Fourth, in the second half of the nineteenth century, industry spread from the backbone of old Europe to the new Europes of the inland United States, coastal Brazil and Australia, and continental Russia. These were the years when Chicago became hogbutcher to the world, when Sao Paulo began its astonishing one-hundred-year rise from 50,000 to 10 million, when Sydney became wool broker to the world. It was in this phase of overseas agricultural processing and steamer transportation that the higher polytechnic and the world market joined forces. Finally, only a little later than in America and Russia, industry implanted itself in the non-European world: in Japan preeminently; in China, India, and the Ottoman empire more hesitantly; and eventually, via external vectors in Central Asia. Concurrently, chemicals gave way to consumer durables as the cutting edge: automobiles, airplanes, refrigerators, washing machines, T.V., word processors, microwaves, personal computers and all the denizens of Silicon Valley. From being a means, information became an end. The technosphere rejoined the noosphere.

This record prompts four further delimitations of the process of industrialization and the higher polytechnic as its outcome. First, despite the importance of the factory, its presence was neither sufficient nor necessary to make a process industrial. Large assemblages of workers existed before the industrial revolution: in shipyards, building sites, mining camps, or in industries based on traditional sources of fuel such as breweries or solar salt works. Equally, if the solitary typist or manual operator of a Singer sewing machine is non-industrial, it is less easy to deny the title to her more modern sister with a word processor or an electrically operated model. Coal gathered into factories but electricity created the possibility at least of industrial diffusion, as a number of Italian and Soviet theoreticians saw. Second, as a consequence, industrialization should not be identified with urbanization. Industry did not always concentrate, concentrations were not always due to industry. On the one hand, megalopolitan growth in London, Paris, Constantinople, New York and St. Petersburg, was due as much to politics, administration, finance or commerce as to industry. Indeed, characteristically supercities today are not industrial. On the other hand, as Franklin Mendels and Alain Dewerpe have shown in their theory of rural proto-industrialization, much industry started as rural and in some cases has remained so. Paper mills, aluminium smelters and nuclear reactors are characteristically non-urban.

Third, despite the importance of coal for early industry, their histories are independent. As John U. Nef was the first to document, English production and consumption of coal increased dramatically in the sixteenth century. This, however, did not constitute an industrial revolution because, although some of it was used in the Tyneside salt and glass industries, most of it went south for the domestic fires of London. Equally, early industry did not always use coal as its source of non-traditional energy. We have already noted the use of sulphuric acid in the Leblanc soda process. One might also cite the use of mercury in Potosi and the other *patio* process silver towns of

Spanish America. If these be questioned as energy sources in a strict sense, the same cannot be done with the use of natural gas at the salt works of Tzu-liu-ching in Szechwan. Tzu-liu-ching was the first urban industrial centre, just as the small producers in northern Szechwan which used coal in brine boiling might be regarded as the first industrial villages. Petroleum makes an earlier appearance than one might expect. A Celtic salt works at Gaulter Gap near Kimmeridge in Dorset used oil shale as fuel in evaporation. Baku oil was in use from an early date and Greek fire apparatus is a kind of primitive blow lamp. The Tibetan sufflator, or steam-jet fire-blower, forms part of the prehistory of the steam engine. The industrial use of gunpower too should not be overlooked. It was used in the papal alum mines at Tolfa in 1588 and even earlier in road building in the Tyrol. In the seventeenth and eighteenth centuries, there were several attempts to design gunpowder machines and it was even considered in 1807 by Sir George Cayley, the father of aerodynamics, as the power source for an airplane. Coal was vital in the early industrial revolution, but it never stood alone. What was essential was the search for new energy sources.

Finally, in the diffusion of industrialization and in the establishment of the higher polytechnic as a world institution, stress should be placed on mechanized distribution: the steamship, the railway, the automobile and the airplane. These were crucial not only for their backward and forward linkages economically, especially to coal and steel, but also in their demonstration and educational effects. The new means of communication were the most visible aspects of the higher polytechnic. They were seen by a wide range of consumers. Their basic technology was not too difficult to understand. Especially in the station and the garage, they provided hands-on education at a basic level. They broke the speed barrier of old humanity where nothing went faster than a horse. They revolutionized perspectives of space and time. They reduced the gap between town and country, coast and inland. They brought new cultural phenomena: the day trip, the shipboard romance, the backseat driver, train spotters, Bradshaw addicts, the jet set. The decline of church going in the West owes more to Daimler than to Darwin. The bicycle and the car combined to kill rural endogamy. In Central Asia, far from the sea, the railway in particular was the purveyor of the higher polytechnic. The development of modern communications, and especially the railway, will serve as a thread for following the expansion of the higher polytechnic into the homelands which surrounded Central Asia. Production was private, consumption was domestic, but distribution was public. It acted as a multiplier.

THE HIGHER POLYTECHNIC IN THE HOMELANDS

The development of modern communications in the home-lands, as it related to Central Asia, was uneven. First, there was a contrast, on the one hand, between Russia and China which developed intercontinental railways, and, on the other, the Ottoman empire and India which did not. Second, there was a contrast between the strong development of Russia and the weak development of China and between the distance of the Ottoman empire and the proximity of India. The order of impact was therefore Russia, China, India and the Ottoman empire.

The Ottoman Empire

In the nineteenth and early twentieth centuries, the Ottoman empire was the homeland most in contact with Central Asia. To and through its territories came thousands of Central Asians each year on the *haj*. The authority of the sultan as caliph was widely accepted, though frequently criticized for its spineless-ness in the face of the *giours*. The empire was linked to Central Asia by politics as well as religion. Panturkism was one of the options for its reconstruction along with Panislamism, Ottomanism and Anatolianism. The Sublime Porte was in dip-lomatic contact with Khiva, Bokhara and Kokand. When the Kokandian adventurer Yaqub beg dislodged the Manchus and established the Kashgar emirate in Sinkiang between 1864 and 1877, he received a measure of Ottoman recognition and was sent Turkish military instructors and rifles.[8] Under the Commit-tee of Union and Progess, the minister of the interior, Talaat Bey, took a particular interest in Central Asians who came to Constantinople and arranged for a Turkish teacher to go to Kashgar to found a modern school.[9] During World War I, Ottoman aims included the annexation of Azerbaijan, possibly

Turkmenistan (also Anatolian Turkish speaking), and the turn-
ing of Khiva and Bokhara into clients. Ottoman agents were
present in Sinkiang and on several occasions alarmed 'Chinese'
Morrison by their anti-Allied propaganda.[10] After the war, Enver
Pasha, the wartime Ottoman chief minister and a leading
Panturkist, died fighting the Bolsheviks in Western Turkestan.
In the 1930s the radical Muslim warlord Ma Chung-ying who
invaded Sinkiang from Kansu, was advised by a Turkish officer,
an exiled anti-Kemalist, Kamal Kaya Efendi.[11] Between the wars,
defeated Turkish nationalists, such as Muhammad Amin Bughra
from Khotan, often found refuge in Constantinople or Ankara.
After World War II, the Kazakh opponent of Chinese rule in
Sinkiang, Ali Beg Rahim, was resettled in Anatolia. Subsequently
Turkey gave asylum to the Pamir Kirghiz fleeing from the Soviet
invasion of Afghanistan.[12] Even the republic – Kemalist,
Anatolian, secular and increasingly European – did not turn its
back on Central Asia.

Despite these ongoing political and cultural ties, the economic
impact of the Ottoman empire on Central Asia was least of all
upon the homelands. The reason was distance and the fact that
railway construction in the empire followed the north-south
routes of imperial articulation and internal trade rather than
the east-west routes of religion and external trade.

Serious construction began after Sultan Abdulaziz's return
from his European tour in 1867. Between 1867 and 1876, 1200
km of track were laid down, of which the principal were the
Constantinople–Edirne, Salonika–Skopje, and the beginnings
of the Haidar Pasha–Ankara lines, though this last was only
finished in 1888. Between 1876 and 1906, 4000 km were added
under the auspices of the Ottoman Public Debt Administration
set up in 1881 following the empire's near bankruptcy. The
OPDA provided kilometric subsidies to the railway companies.
The revenues it controlled were mainly internal; the tobacco
and salt monopolies and agricultural tithes in certain areas. It
was chiefly concerned with internal trade, with communications which would promote the sale of its tobacco, salt and
agricultural produce within the empire. Its 1907–8 report declared: 'Railway development creates prosperity, brings security
and better government, has great strategical and commercial
advantages, and in the long run increases the revenue of the

state.'[13] Most of the lines it assisted with fell into this pattern: Haidar Pasha to Ankara 1888, Salonika to Monastir 1890, Constantinople to Salonika 1892, Eskisehir to Konia 1893, Rayah to Hama 1900. The Administration took pride in its achievements: 'where railways have been built they have brought with them increased civilisation, tranquility, better administration, followed at once by increased production and prosperity.'[14] In addition to these local developments, there were the two transimperial lines, the Berlin to Baghdad (to which the OPDA contributed) and the Hejaz railway to the Holy Places. Both ran from north to south. Neither brought the industrial revolution any closer to Central Asia. In 1914 there were no railways in eastern Anatolia and no plans to create a railway equivalent to the central land route. The Ottoman empire remained a Balkan and Levantine state, its two circles of Rumelia and Anatolia intersecting at Constantinople. Had the Central Powers won the first World War and the Ottomans achieved their Panturkist ambitions, it would have been different with the empire reoriented along an east–west axis Constantinople–Baku–Bokhara.

India

The economic impact of India on Central Asia was greater than that of the Ottoman empire because of proximity and the continued use of traditional north-south routes. By 1980 these had been supplemented by the modern Karakoram highway from Gilgit to Kashgar over the Khunjerab pass. Moreover railway building was more seriously considered.

In 1873 Ferdinand de Lesseps suggested to General Ignatiev, then Russian ambassador in Constantinople, the construction of one of the great nineteenth century Utopian railways: the Calais to Calcutta. In Central Asia, Orenburg to Samarkand was to be built by Russia, Samarkand to Peshawar by Britain. Nothing came of the suggestion, but it put Central Asian railways on the agenda. During the Anglo-Russian crisis leading to the Congress of Berlin in 1878, Britain considered a Central Asian railway as a means of countering Russian pressure on India. Salisbury in particular took the idea of a line from Quetta via Girishk to Herat seriously.[15] Beaconsfield made his last speech in the House of Lords in 1881 to advocate the retention of

Kandahar with this end in view. Thus was born the notion of the
Seistan railway: Quetta–Helmand delta–Bandar Abbas, with
possible branches to Herat, Kerman, Yazd, Isfahan, Shiraz and
Bushire; a dogleg across southern Persia with access to Central
Asia. Curzon was its strongest advocate. He added economic to
military arguments:

> such a railway would be essentially a commercial and not a
> strategic undertaking, inasmuch as it would not merely open
> up Seistan, but would provide a southern way of entry into
> Khorasan itself, which would be brought into nearer commu-
> nication with the Indian Ocean. At the same time its execu-
> tion might act as a deterrent to any Russian operations against
> Herat . . . Of all the possible suggestions for counteracting
> Russian menace to India by pacific and honourable means,
> the construction of such a railway is at once the least aggres-
> sive, the cheapest and the most profitable.[16]

In the event the Seistan railway was never built. Even advocates
of a forward policy like Curzon, came to feel that bad communications were a better protection from the Russians than
good communications, a conclusion already come to by the
Ottomans in eastern Anatolia. No Trans-Afghanistan line was
ever constructed. Its parallel cousin, the Trans-Iranian, was
only completed by Reza Shah Pahlavi I just before World War
II. The proposal by Reza Shah Pahlavi II in 1977 for a line from
Meshed via Herat and Kandahar to Kabul found no support in
Afghanistan. India's own considerable railways development
was turned inward rather than outward and when outward
towards the sea. India participated in the world market less
through commodities and raw materials than through services,
the *raj* itself. Economically the *raj* was undynamic. It sought
neither to exploit India nor to develop it. Thanks to the *raj*,
industrialization could take root in India, but it was not
exported by land routes.

China

The role of China in the introduction of industrialization to
Central Asia was greater than that of India or the Ottoman
empire. Given that China had been in political control of
Sinkiang since 1759, one might think that this was only to be

expected. In fact, China's political structures delayed the introduction of railways in particular, not only in Sinkiang but also in China itself.

Modern transportation in the form of steamships was initially well received in China. Merchants and travellers were quick to take advantage of the greater speed and lower insurance afforded by the foreign shipping which developed after 1860 on the Yangtze and on the Shanghai to Tientsin run.[17] In 1872, to link the two halves of his regional empire in Anhwei and Chihli, Li Hung-chang founded the China Merchants Steam Navigation Company, which was soon offering tough competition to the foreigners. Railways, however, took longer to acclimatize. They were opposed by officials on strategic grounds, by traditional transport interests, and by the public on grounds of *fengshui*. In 1877, an admittedly unauthorized line from Shanghai to Woosung, opened the year before by Jardine Matheson and others, was purchased by the Nanking governor-general Shen Pao-chen and destroyed. The first two ongoing railways, the Taipei to Kelung line in Taiwan and the Kaiping mines line in Chihli, were purely local and coastal. It was not until 1889 when railway building received the support of Hukuang governor-general Chang Chih-tung that interior and interregional lines were attempted. Thereafter, allowing for the interruptions of the Sino-Japanese war and the Boxer rebellion, construction was rapid. Between 1900 and the revolution of 1912, 18 new railway trunk lines were opened, with a mileage of over 5000. These included the Manchurian T (Chinese eastern railway, South Manchuria railway), the north China A (Peking–Hankow, Tientsin–Pukow, Kaifeng to Loyang) and the Peking to Mukden reversed L which linked them north–south. Indeed most of the development was on China's north–south axis. In addition to the lines built, many others were projected. For a decade, a fever of railway building as profitable and prestigious gripped all levels of Chinese society.[18] Financial mismanagement, revolution and the first world war cut short this boom, and except for the Wuhan–Canton line, few major projects were completed in the interwar period. Under the Kuomintang, interest shifted to road building and air transport. The drive for the permanent way was not resumed until the first Five-Year Plan of the Communists, in this, as in much else, the heirs of the late empire rather than the early republic.[19]

Modern communications took a long time to reach Sinkiang. Between 1862 and 1877 China lost control of the territory to the local Muslim rebellion which was taken over by Yaqub beg and the Kokand immigration. Sinkiang was reconquered in 1878 and became a full Chinese province in 1884, but the early governors did little to improve communications with China. In 1898, Belgian entrepreneurs began to show an interest in Kansu, 'the Katanga of China.'[20] In June 1907, a leading political figure, Ts'en Ch'un-hsuan, who had recently been president of the ministry of posts and communications, suggested the construction of a railway trunk line from Shansi to Ili.[21] This presumably would have run via Sian, Lanchow and Urumchi. Earlier, in 1903, an agreement had been made with a Belgian company, which was looking towards Kansu, to build an east–west line from Kaifeng to Loyang. In 1912, after the establishment of the republic, a further agreement provided for the extension of the line at each end, to Haichow on the coast and Lanchow in Kansu. This Lunghai line, as it was called, was obviously aimed at Chinese Central Asia. It had the explicit support of Sun Yat-sen, then in a phase of grandiose railway plans.

The quasi-independent governors of Sinkiang between the wars, however, had no wish to bring the central government closer, nor had the Muslim warlords of Kansu. By 1937 the Lunghai line had only got a little beyond Sian. The first form of modern transport to operate in Sinkiang was the airplane. In 1932, a German company, Eurasia Aviation, planned a route between Berlin and Shanghai via Urumchi and in September 1933 Nanking's foreign minister Lo Wen-kan touched down there. In January 1934, Soviet air strikes, called in by the governor, played a major part in the defeat of Ma Chung-ying. From July 1937, Soviet military aid began to be sent to the Nanking government. The central land route was improved so as to carry the trucks which served the Russian airbase at Lanchow. It gradually became a road rather than a route. Railway development, however, had to await the Communists and the First Five-Year Plan. The Plan gave a high priority to the Lanchow–Sinkiang railway: 'Linking up with the Lunghai Railway, this will become the main east–west artery of our country. It will also be an important international line linking the Soviet Union and China. It is also essential to exploitation of the resources of Sinkiang.'[22] The line was begun in 1955 and reached Urumchi in 1962 but the link-up with the Soviet branch line of the Turksib from Aktogai to Druzhba was long delayed by the Sino-Soviet dispute and was not re-pursued till the détente following the summit in Peking in May 1989. By the 1990s Sinkiang was linked by air, road, rail and, on the Irtysh, steamship, to both China and the Soviet Union.

Russia

Because of its further degree of railway development, the economic impact of Russia in providing a liaison between Central Asia and the higher polytechnic was greatest of all. Railway development was a major factor in the consolidation of Russian power in Central Asia. It intensified it from a political and military presence to a demographic and economic presence. Between 1822 and 1848 Russia had turned a nominal suzerainty over the Kazakh hordes into a real one. Between 1865 and 1884, Russia advanced from the steppe into the oases to conquer Transoxania, the core of sedentary Central Asia. In 1865, Tashkent, the link between the steppe and the sedentary world, was occupied and annexed from Kokand. In 1868, Kokand and Bokhara were forced to accept protectorate status and Samarkand was detached from Bokhara and annexed to Russian Turkestan. In 1873, Khiva too was compelled to become a protectorate. In 1876, Kokand, which had become destabilized, was dissolved and placed under direct rule as the province of Ferghana. In 1881, the Turcomans were defeated by a Russian army brought across the Caspian and reinforced by a railway. In 1884, Merv, under Turcoman rule the last independent oasis, was occupied. Among defenders of British India, this gave rise to the bouts of 'Mervousness' which prompted the plans for the Seistan railway.

In this advance, local initiative by military men played an important part. Here the leading figure was Konstantin Petrovich von Kaufman, governor-general of Turkestan (1867–82), and the real architect of Russian Central Asia. St. Petersburg was often not keen. It worried about diplomatic complications and financial costs. Compensation for Russia's setbacks in the Balkans, however, attracted, as it had the possibility of threatening the British in India to obtain concessions elsewhere. Among army officers, too, there was a strong sense of civilizing mission,

of bringing Christianity and/or enlightenment to dispel
dervishism and slavery. Unlike the British, the Russians were
seldom pro-Islamic or romantic about tribespeople. From the
start, the Russians aimed at assimilation, i.e. Russification, even
though von Kaufman insisted it must be gradual. He ruled
indirectly through native intermediaries and worried about a
jihad if Russian migration came too fast. Till the last quarter of
the nineteenth century, the Tsar's government too was hesitant
about encouraging Russian emigration, despite bounding demography produced by vaccination acting on the traditional
high Slavic birth rate. In European Russia, landlords were reluctant to lose tenants and serfs, while in Central Asia officials
feared to stir up Pan-Islamic revolt. The abolition of serfdom in
1861 and the conquest of Transoxania from 1865, reduced
these fears, while Tso Tsung-t'ang's reconquest of Sinkiang,
plus a confrontation in 1881 with Russian forces at Ili, convinced many Russians that if they did not fill up their empty
spaces, the Chinese would do it for them. Kaufman's gradualism
was therefore replaced by the policy of the other great colonial
administrator, Alexei Nicolaievich Kuropatkin, of actively encouraging Russian immigration and modern economic development.

The instrument was the railway, specifically the four major
lines which cross-hatched Central Asia. First, in the south, there
was the Trans-Caspian, predominantly a military line: begun at
Krasnovodsk in 1881, reaching Samarkand in 1888, Tashkent in
1889, Ferghana in 1899. Second, in the north, there was the
Trans-Siberian from Moscow to Vladivostok, but skirting Central Asia. It was the brainchild of Utopian technocrats, notably
Count Witte: planned in 1886, begun in 1891, finished in 1903.
Third, from northwest to southeast, there was the Orenburg to
Tashkent, or Trans-Aral, line. It was built between 1900 and
1906, a business route for cotton and textiles. Fourth, from
northeast to southwest, there was the Turksib, the Turkestan-
Siberia line: started 1912, resumed 1927, completed 1930. It
was the work of commissars and the Soviet First Five-Year Plan.
These four lines put Russia in a position to dominate the
economy of its share of Central Asia and, for a time, its demography too. A considerable inflow of Russians and Russian industry followed, particularly to Kazakhstan and to Tashkent. Farmers
went to Kazakhstan, businessmen and administrators went to
Tashkent. Yet by the time the railway network was completed in

1930, Russia's demography had been undermined by the 'bad times' of the Bolshevik revolution and by the policy once described as taking women out of reproduction to put them into production. Central Asia's demography, on the other hand, was surcharged by modern medicine and the reduction of infant mortality. Only the economic domination remained in the form of Soviet command economy.

THE HIGHER POLYTECHNIC IN CENTRAL ASIA

We may now assess the degree and character of the participation in the higher polytechnic of the three areas into which the events of the nineteenth century had split Central Asia. The degree was greatest in Soviet Central Asia, less in Sinkiang, and least in Afghanistan. In character, while participation in Afghanistan and Sinkiang remained segmental and unabsorbed, in Soviet Central Asia, Uzbekistan in particular, it was general and internalized.

Afghanistan

Here the story is quickly told. Although Afghanistan participated least in the higher polytechnic, by the 1990s it had a genuine if subordinate participation, not unlike its neighbour, Tadjikistan.

The Afghan kings sought survival through isolation. Exports, mainly *karakul* lamb skins, were necessary to pay for imports of tea and sugar, but autarky rather than development was their ideal. It was not until after World War II, as the costs of minimal medicine and education modernization rose, that a modest degree of industrialization was encouraged for import substitution. An example here would be the Spinzar cotton company and associated businesses founded by the Nashir family of Kunduz around 1945.[23] Such people formed the basis of King Zahir's attempt to introduce a measure of constitutionalism to Afghanistan in the period 1964 to 1973. The King's failure indicates that the basis remained narrow, but the narrowness was not the only reason for the failure. In particular, his last prime minister, Muhammed Moussa Shafia, who had founded an industrial bank, made himself unpopular by the Helmand waters treaty with Iran and the measures necessary to secure its ratification by parliament. Under the Daud republic, 1973 to 1978, in effect a return of the old royal bureaucracy against the king, a more active policy of industrialization was pursued.[24] A petroleum industry in the northwest, begun around 1965, was further developed with more emphasis on heavy industry. Among the projects envisaged were a petroleum refinery, chemical fertilizer plants, oil seed presses, a dye factory and copper smelter: all to be achieved with Soviet aid. Yet the aim continued to be autarkic, a source of Soviet disenchantment with Daud, and the achievements were modest. In 1975–6, industrial activity was only 6.7 per cent of GNP and even as planned by 1983 it would only have amounted to 8.7 per cent.

With the Communist republic from 1978, similar policies continued minus the autarky. All policies, however, were distorted by the needs of revolution, civil war and foreign military assistance. Under the Khalq, economic development was subordinated to cultural revolution. Under the Parcham regimes of Babrak Kamal and Najibullah, some economic development was resumed if only to pay for imports of military hardware. In particular, the Shibargan natural gas field west of Mazar-i-Sharif was developed, but with the Soviet rather than the Afghan consumer in view. The protection of Shibargan played a part in the strategy of the Kabul government in the Civil War.[25] Together with the capital, it formed one of the centres of the hour-glass shaped perimeter linked by the Salang tunnel, which the central authorities sought to defend against the *mujahidin* outside. By 1990 Afghan industry was comparable to that of Tadjikstan whose hydro-electricity was allocated not to local industry but to aluminium smelting for the Union economy. Both were increasingly dependent members of the Soviet economic community. Whether autarky, or community membership, or some mixture of the town, optimizes Central Asian economic circumstance is a matter of dispute and ultimately politics. Many Afghans would have agreed with the remark attributed to Ahmed Shah Masud that 'Afghans need only two things: the Koran and Stingers.'

Sinkiang

In Afghanistan, with no railway communication with the outside world, industrialization remained marginal. In 1990, there was no true industrial city there, only the industrial centre of Shibargan. In Sinkiang, on the other hand, linked to China by the line from Lanchow to Urumchi completed in 1962, industrialization went much further. In 1990, Urumchi was an industrial city with a population of over a million and there were secondary industrial centres at Lop, Karamai and Shih-ho-tzu. Moreover, agriculture as well as manufacturing had been affected by industrialization. Yet industrialization remained within a parallel economy created from without rather than from within. It was implanted in Zungharia rather than Eastern Turkestan, in the Han rather than the Uighur sector of the economy, and it was the work of the state rather than society. In Sinkiang, communism behaved as a mixture of command economy and colonialism. For, unlike Afghanistan where the only migration was a massive emigration of five million because of the Civil War, in Sinkiang industrialization was accompanied and effected by an immigration of over three million Chinese, forced, organized and spontaneous.[26]

Industrialization began before the People's Republic.[27] It began with Soviet penetration during the warlord regime of Sheng Shih-ts'ai between 1933 and 1944. Under Sheng's predecessors Yang Tseng-hsin and Chin Shu-jen, the Soviet Union had become predominant in Sinkiang's foreign trade. In the absence of improved communications with China or across the Himalayas, this was unsurprising and only continued Tsarist trends. Foreign trade did not affect a large percentage of the province's economy. Under Sheng, Soviet penetration took an industrial and not merely commercial turn. Sheng was a Manchurian, part of the military empire of Young Marshal Chang Hsüeh-liang, which since its expulsion from Manchuria in 1931 had become increasingly pro-Soviet. He had also acquired leftist ideas as a student in Peking in the May 4 era. Moreover, he was more beholden than his predecessors to the Soviet Union which had intervened militarily on his behalf more than once against the forces of the radical leftist Muslim warlord from Kansu, Ma Chung-ying. In return for this support, Sheng allowed Soviet geologists to make a survey in 1934. In 1935 oil drilling was commenced at Tu-shan-tzu, near Manas, in Zungharia. In 1938, as part of Soviet assistance to Chiang Kai-shek, an airplane assembly plant was erected in Urumchi, the capital's first industrial plant except for the coal mines which already existed for domestic consumption. In November 1940, Sheng signed the so called tin mines agreement, really about petroleum, tungsten and uranium, which gave a fifty year concession to a privileged Soviet company Sin-tin. By that time the Tu-shan-tzu field was producing 50,000 tons of crude oil a year. When Sheng Hsuan-huai changed sides in 1942 and a degree of Kuomintang rule in Sinkiang was established, the Soviets continued their control through their protégé, the East Turkestan Republic, set up in Ili late in 1944.

The coming of Communism to China brought changes. The Soviets accepted Chinese sovereignty. They liquidated their satellite, much of whose leadership was conveniently killed in an air crash in August 1944, though they insisted Peking keep the remaining leader Saifudin as part of the new local regime. Sovereignty, however, was attenuated by the Sino-Soviet treaty of 1950. This provided for the continued existence of joint companies in petroleum and non-ferrous metals.[28] It was not until 1954 that these companies passed completely to China. Chinese control did not change the formula of Soviet technology and Han labour they implied. Under the First Five-Year Plan, which stressed heavy industry, Sinkiang figured for its non-ferrous metals (probably tungsten for the steel industry), for two hydroelectric power stations, for oilfields, especially the development of a new field at Karamai in northwest Zungharia, and for the railway from Lanchow to Urumchi, which was placed first in the list of new railway projects for the whole country. The programme of the plan continued Soviet perspectives, except for the change to Chinese management and an extension of Han immigration organized through a state production and construction corps founded in 1954. Not all the immigration, however, was forced or organized. Because Sinkiang never abandoned the Soviet Model and avoided the worst disruptions of both the Great Leap Forward and the Cultural Revolution, it continued to attract independent immigration, permanent or migrant, by its available land and employment opportunities.

The programme gave results. The population of Sinkiang rose from 5 million in 1954 to 13 million in 1984. In 1954 10 per cent of the population was Chinese, in 1984 nearly 40 per cent. By 1984, Urumchi, with a population of 132,000 in 1949, had

become a city of over a million. It now contained plant for non-
ferrous metals, petroleum, iron and steel, machinery, motor
repair, cement, textiles and flour. Its government department
stores were full of modern consumer durables. It was the headquarters of a thriving construction industry. It was the management centre in charge of petroleum extraction to the north,
nuclear testing to the south, and a local government made
more centralized by the railway and the adherence to the Soviet
Model. Yet only 15 per cent of its population was non-Chinese
and the Muslim population referred to it as Kafir city.[29] Sino-
industrialization was largely confined to a sourthern strip of
Zungharia and did not involve the bulk of the Uighur population. It was an excrescence. Not a malignant excrescence, it is
true, for under the Communist peace, as under the Ch'ing
peace, Kashgar and its trade prospered, and would prosper
further if China's great leap outward was maintained. It was
simply that the two economies, traditional and modern, ran in
parallel but uncommunicating channels. In Sinkiang, Communism was colonialism carried on by other means, not necessarily
to the natives' disadvantage, but also without their active participation. As Chinese population growth slackened under the
constraints of the birth control campaign, while that of the
natives did not, this imbalance was of growing significance.

Soviet Central Asia

Cross-hatched by four railway systems, Soviet Central Asia sur-
passed Sinkiang in the degree of its participation in the higher
polytechnic. The character of industrialization too was much
more profound, especially in the case of Uzbekistan, where
even agriculture was deeply affected by industry. Its capital
Tashkent, the Soviet equivalent of Urumchi, had a population
in 1979 of 1,700,000 which made it the fourth largest city in the
USSR, roughly half and half natives and Russians. Since industrialization had only limited impact on Turkmenistan and
Kirghizia, the focus will be on Kazakhstan and Tadjikstan where
it was significant, and on Uzbekistan where it was crucial.

Kazakhstan followed a pattern not unlike Zungharia.[30] Similarities included massive immigration (in 1979 40 per cent of
the population were Russians), industrialization from without,
presence of oil and non-ferrous metals, and the close proximity

of nuclear testing facilities. Karaganda, in north-central Kazakhstan and connected to the Trans-Siberian by a branch line, was the leading centre. Its coal and copper resources were first developed in the 1850s by a British firm using imported Russian and Ukrainian labour. By 1914 it was already a considerable industrial site. In the period of the first two five year plans, it was a centre for KGB industry using convict labour. By 1950, its coal production reached 10 million tons. Most of this was exported to the Ural iron and steel complex. With its immigrant population and external outlet, Karaganda was eccentric to the life of the region. It was in Kazakhstan rather than of it. Kazakhstan, however, was also affected by the industrial water policies of its neighbour Uzbekistan. These contributed to the increasing dessication of the Aral sea which threatened the agricultural and pastoral economy of central Kazakhstan. Kazakh nationalists therefore came to feel that not only did their republic draw little direct benefit from Karaganda, but that it was being forced to meet part of the cost of Uzbek cotton monoculture. Added to these discontents were worries about the management competence and ecological effects of the Semipalatinsk nuclear testing site. Although the Kazakhs were the least separatist of the peoples of Soviet Central Asia, they were not content with the industrialization process to date.

Tadjikstan was late in industry. It only became linked to the Trans-Caspian line in 1929. Dushanbe, the capital, with a population in 1979 of nearly half a million, was an administrative rather than industrial centre. In 1984, however, there finally opened, after twenty years planning and construction subject to innumerable postponements and delays, the Tadjik aluminium smelter at Tursun-zade on the railway west of Dushanbe. It was a typical think-big project of the kind beloved by Soviet planners both in Moscow and in the republics. Its rationale was the abundant hydroelectricity resources of Tadjikstan: 50 per cent of those in Central Asia, 8 per cent of those in the Soviet Union. Bauxite would be brought in by rail, processed by cheap electricity, and shipped out as aluminium ingots for final processing in European Russia or the Urals. Since 1984, the plant has experienced numerous teething troubles due to faulty engineering, but even assuming these can be overcome, it is viewed ambivalently by many Tadjiks. Massive quantities of water have to be appropriated, pollutant side effects appear to have been insufficiently considered, and the end product is essentially a raw material for Russian rather than local industry. The multiplication effect of Tursun-zade in Tadjikstan was small. It was comparable to Shibargan in Afghanistan.

Uzbekistan

Of all areas of Soviet Central Asia, Uzbekistan has been most radically affected by industrialization or, in another sense, by non-industrialization.[31] Both under the Tsars and the Soviets, Uzbekistan has been developed in industrial agriculture as a massive cotton plantation which exported raw cotton to textile mills elsewhere. In 1983, Uzbekistan produced two-thirds of all cotton grown in the Soviet Union. The cultivation and processing of cotton accounted for 65 per cent of the republic's GNP and employed 40 per cent of the labour force. Cotton monoculture was not a Bolshevik invention. It went back to the 1860s when Russian and world markets experienced an acute shortage of raw cotton on account of the American Civil War. Systematic promotion of cotton cultivation in Central Asia thus became fixed Russian policy. In Ferghana, the best irrigated part of Uzbekistan, the area sown to cotton rose between 1885 and 1915 from 14 to 44 per cent. Socialism, however, surcharged the system. In 1985, 60 per cent of all resources in Uzbekistan – water, energy, fertilizer, etc. – went into the cotton economy. Cotton was not only king but leviathan. In Uzbekistan, Communism was colonialism aggravated by command economy, which not only assigned physical quotas, but also fixed prices and decided terms of trade. Cotton monoculture was the condition of entry into the higher polytechnic.

It is not easy to draw a balance sheet for cotton monoculture. Five separate issues are involved. First, there is the issue of regional specialization versus autarky. Sympathizers with nationalism often take it for granted that autarky is best, that trade inevitably involves winners and losers, and that it should be avoided. Despite the attraction of local self-sufficiency to some minds, the economic arguments against it are powerful. Regional specialization is simply the application of the principle of the division of labour to larger units. Cotton specialization in Uzbekistan is not more misguided *a priori* than wine specialization in Burgundy. Second, there is the issue of command economy versus market economy. Economists from Adam Smith have generally preferred market economy and the arguments in its favour have been strengthened by epistemological and information considerations. Nevertheless, Adam Smith was willing to make strategic exceptions to market economy. Keynes advocated intervention in interest rates and capital investment, and even Hayek would allow that *intertaxis* presumes *taxis*, spontaneous order presumes purposeful activity. Soviet command economy may be misguided generally, but cotton may be a legitimate field for intervention. If the former Soviet Union moves toward a market economy, Uzbekistan may still find it in its interest to operate cotton specialization. Third, there is the issue of the specific *Soviet* economic community and command economy. It is possible to prefer command economy to market economy, but still consider Soviet cotton planning mistaken in view, say, of the water resources. Fourth, in all these issues, there is the further issue, difficult to resolve in economic terms, of short run and long run benefits. It cannot be settled by Keynes' dictum, that in the long run we are all dead, because people have children and risktakers in particular are addicted to the Hanseatic principle of *navigare necesse est, vivere non necese.* Uzbekistan may gain tomorrow from its losses of today. Its future might be considered better than that of Afghanistan or Sinkiang.

Finally, there is the issue of balancing economic considerations against sociological, political and cultural considerations. Questions such as, how much increased GNP balances, how much increased unemployment or is a bigger cake worth more unequal shares, constantly occur in economic debate. The case against capitalism, for example, has shifted from economic efficiency to human cost. As Keynes pointed out, it is not sufficient for capitalism to be demonstrably more efficient than socialism, if it continues to be perceived as immoral or unaesthetic. Similarly, all the economic arguments might point in favour of Uzbek cotton monoculture, but a nationalist might reject them on non-economic grounds. In the last resort, an economy exists for non-economic reasons and is judged by non-economic criteria. If the facts of Central Asia's participation in the higher polytechnic are reasonably clear, its evaluation will rest on social, political, and cultural factors. In particular it will rest on the shaping of those factors by Central Asia's involvement in yet another world institution: the common consensus.

10 The Common Consensus and Contemporary Central Asia

In the previous chapter, the impact of modern technology on Central Asia, as mediated through the higher polytechnic, was considered. It was concerned with the material end of the world order, the infra-red so to speak. In the present chapter, the impact of modern thought-patterns on Central Asia, as mediated through what will be called the common consensus, will be considered. It will be concerned with the intellectual end of the world order, the ultra-violet so to speak. The common consensus is the keystone of the current world order. The set of world institutions considered in earlier chapters obviously did not amount to a world empire, a universal state, and perhaps never will. For, as Wallerstein had argued, the evidence of the past suggests that the world order, with all the advantages it brings, is weakened by any attempt to turn it into a world empire.[1] Indeed, the world order does not yet amount to a world system. Its various institutions have grown up too haphazardly, are not sufficiently interrelated, and do not follow an architectonic plan, whether taxic or intertaxic. Yet the world order is already more than global factors, such as figure in geology and meteorology. Its institutions form a set and not simply a collection. The common consensus has a particular, unifying function here. Although an independent institution with its own origins and activities, it also functions as the co-consciousness of all the institutions. It is a recognition of the world order and its overarching role in the contemporary world. For this reason, it is basically a political consensus, a consensus about institutions and the proper sphere of politics. It is a common consensus because, although beginning in the West and still centered there, it is increasingly accepted throughout the world and not only by an educated elite. Even the continued opposition to it in some quarters is really a witness to its widening strength. The present chapter, therefore, is about modern politics in Central

Asia, but politics conceived as a wider consensus of thought-patterns which formed a world institution in its own right.

THE COMMON CONSENSUS: CONNOTATION AND DENOTATION

Since this chapter, like the two previous ones proceeds from outside to inside, it will be helpful to locate the common consensus conceptually and factually, in connotation and denotation, before considering its relay through the homelands to the three constituents of contemporary Central Asia.

Connotation

During the May 4 movement in China, one of the most radical efforts to bring a traditional mind-set into the common consensus, the slogan was 'Down with Confucius and sons, up with Mr Science and Mr Democracy'.[2] The slogan was crude, its terms undefined and probably misunderstood, but it was effective shorthand for the intellectual revolution it proposed. For although modern politics was the most visible part of the common consensus, that consensus was basically intellectual. It was a consensus of methods before being a consensus of conclusions. For this intellectual consensus, science was too narrow a definition, just as democracy was too narrow a definition for the political consensus. Science had metaphysical presuppositions. It presupposed, for example, that the universe was both rational and contingent, so that scientific theories about it (including theories that it was neither rational nor contingent) could be both mathematical and empirical.

The consensus of methods was primarily critical, in Kant's sense of *Kritik*: reflective, second order, transcendental. As a method, criticism began in cognitional analysis, advanced to epistemology and concluded in metaphysics. Though philosophy has always been thinking about thinking as well as thinking about the world, and logic may be regarded as a particular form of methodology, the immediate origins of critical philosophy of method are to be found in scholasticism's reflection upon itself in the later middle ages.[3] From there, after the anti-intellectual-ism of the Renaissance, in particular Erasmus who rejected later scholasticism too easily on account of its barbarity of language and apparent irrelevance to living, it passed to Descartes in the *Discourse on Method* of 1637 and then to Kant in the *Critique of Pure Reason* of 1781.

Critical enquiry, however, has never been confined to philosophy in a technical sense. St Augustine looked inward to his own intellectual processes as well as outward to God. Many Reformation debates about authority were implicitly arguments about method. *The Grammar of Assent* was an essentially critical work, Newman on one occasion declaring that he had been a Kantian before reading Kant.[4] Since Pythagoras, mathematicians have been divided as philosophers over the ontological status of their discipline.[5] The self-reflection natural to physicists such as Ernst Mach and Ludwig Boltzmann, was only reinforced by the relativity, quantum and time theory revolutions. Few historians deny themselves comment on methodology, as in Ranke's ambiguous and misleading 'as it actually was' aphorism or Acton's more helpful 'think in terms of problems not periods'. Critical thinking is one of the foundations of the modern world. It avoids the extremes of scepticism and credulity, it unifies different branches of knowledge, it demarcates the different moments in the learning process, and it ensures an appropriately full range of intellectual operations. Critical theories may differ: as in philosophy of science between Popper and Kuhn, or in religion, in different philosophies of theology; but they concur in favour of criticism itself, not as a criterion of truth (that is the province of particular branches of knowledge), but as its further appropriation of 'the dynamic structure immanent and recurrently operative in human cognitional activity.'[6]

The content of the Western tradition of politics was more Latin than Greek and more medieval than either. The Greeks, one is tempted to say, contributed nothing to politics except the concept of politics itself. From this foundation, schematized by Roman concepts of law and consent, the Western political tradition made three distinctions more sharply than in the worlds of Islam, India or China. First, it distinguished between church and state. By church here is meant not just religious corporations, but also institutions of the intellect generally: the religious internationals, yes, but also the components of the republic of letters – universities, professional schools, corresponding societies, publishing houses, newspapers, learned journals, theatres, academic and aesthetic groups of every kind. Western states were non-ideological, secular in the sense that they did not ask for their subjects' ultimate allegiance, but only for their conditional, intermediate and instrumental loyalties. Beyond the state lay Christendom, the community of science, the world of the arts, the vanity fair of pleasure and leisure. Kings did not need to be philosophers, nor philosophers kings. Second, the Western political tradition distinguished between state and society. True, the frontier between them was not fixed and was susceptible of fresh demarcation. But beyond the state was property in a wide sense: the farm, the firm, the trade union, the club, the salon and the drawing room. Not all questions were political. Beyond politics lay other worlds with their own rules. Politics was therefore limited, externally by international communities, internally by the co-presence of social institutions. Since politics did not touch either the church in a wide sense, or society broadly conceived, it was free to develop expertise in its own sphere. It could make itself the art of the possible, escape absolutes which must lead to violence, and emphasize relatives which might lead to compromise. Third, within society, the Western political tradition distinguished between sociology and economy. It separated institutions which were ends, such as the family, from institutions which were means, such as the factory. Keynes' dictum that economists are the guardians not of civilization but of the possibility of civilization expressed this distinction.[7] It opened the way to mixed economy as a compromise between command economy committed to non-economic values and market economy committed only to economic values.

These three distinctions were the basic methodology for the conduct of politics. They were projected by the Greeks and Romans, given institutional content by the middle ages, and formulated by the moderns from Hobbes and Locke via Adam Smith to Keynes, Popper and Hayek. From them may be derived the four chief ingredients of the current political consensus: the non-ideological limited state, constitutional government, autonomous civil society, and mixed economy.

Denotation

If it is relatively easy to demarcate the conceptual reference of the common consensus, it is much harder to indicate its factual reference. The common consensus, as methodology and content, has become the precondition of all modern institutions. Since water, it has been said, is the last thing a fish will discover, the common consensus is the most elusive of the world institutions because the most pervasive. Thus, within the microbian common market and antidotes, institutions, such as WHO, national health services, the International Psychoanalytic Association or *Médécins Sans Frontières* could hardly exist without distinctions between ideology and state, government and society, sociology and economy. Effective quarantine, for example, postulated action according to its own criteria, for preference transnationally, if necessary contrary to both governmental and commercial interests. For this reason, Western governments and merchants were not always wholehearted in support of the introduction of quarantine elsewhere, for example in the Ottoman empire and on the China coast. Pervasive factors are often most clearly perceived by the resistance to them. Similarly, the action of the common consensus is best indicated by hostile or ambiguous reaction to it.

Hostile reaction is most fully exemplified by the phenomenon of totalitarianism. The sudden emergence of totalitarian regimes, in contradiction to the political tendencies of the nineteenth century, remains one of the most puzzling phenomena of the twentieth century. Most of the analyses, whether political, social or economic, either do not apply to all cases, or they explain features rather than the phenomenon itself. All the totalitarianisms, however, were hostile to the world order in general, the common consensus as its keystone in particular. All persecuted the religious internationals, disrupted the republic of letters, rejected the world market and impeded the basic information circuit. If they accepted world health institutions, the global arsenal and the higher polytechnic it was only with qualification and within their own priorities. Against the common consensus, in methodology the totalitarians were *terribles simplificateurs,* as Burckhardt had foretold they would be. In content, they affirmed the ideological state, denied the autonomy of civil society, and confounded the social and economic in a variety of socialisms. Whatever its other dynamisms and necessary circumstances, totalitarianism was a revolt against the nineteenth century emergence of a world order. Though it might make professions of universalism, it was really hostile to any world order, not just the Victorian one. This was evident in its pseudo-polarities, both between totalitarianisms (fascists versus communists) and within a single totalitarianism (party line versus deviation, Khrushchev versus Mao). Pseudo-polarity obscured similarity and created division, because schism was the essence of totalitarianism. It was Rauschning's revolution of destruction or Orwell's boot forever on the face. In the violence of its revolt, however, totalitarianism was solid witness to the reality of the world order in general, the common consensus in particular.

Ambiguous reaction is best exemplified by nationalism. Here nationalism should be distinguished from national sentiment or patriotism. National sentiment is the perceived existence of a community called a nation. This may be defined in terms of territory, history, language or culture. Nations in this sense go back to the barbarian armies of the later Roman empire, which claimed, or were given, an ethnic unity whether real or fictitious. National sentiment can exist for long periods without any political repercussions, as in the case of the German nation under the Holy Roman Empire. Nationalism, on the other hand, is the proposal that states be founded on national sentiment. In the West, it was mainly a nineteenth and twentieth century phenomenon, directed against the dynastic states of the Habsburgs, Romanovs or Ottomans, or in the case of Irish nationalism against the less obviously dynastic state of the Hanoverians. Irish nationalism was unusual, too, in that, unlike German, Italian, Magyar, Polish, Czech, Rumanian, Finnish and Greek nationalisms, it was non-linguistic, Modern Irish being a consequence rather than a cause. It was not unique in being cultural rather than linguistic as may be seen from the cases of Switzerland, Belgium, Norway and Iceland.

In the nineteenth century, nationalism was generally associated with liberalism, that is the liberal state and its coexistence with civil society and some degree of market economy. It might therefore be regarded as part of the Western political tradition. Yet from the beginning it contained elements inconsistent with the common consensus. First, being a proposal about the foundations of the state, it had little to say about the style of state to be built. It demanded home rule, but did not specify what kind of rule. If most nineteenth century leaders constructed liberal states, that was not because they were nationalists, but because they were Victorians. Second, nationalism was implicitly conservative since, in addition to language, an ambiguous criterion since a person might speak different languages at home, at work and at worship, most definitions of nationhood made reference to indefeasible traditions. Nationalism, pace Mazzini, could easily turn into xenophobia. Third, nationalism contained no principle of conflict resolution between nations. This was noted as early as the Frankfurt parliament of 1848 when justice to Germans seemed to involve injustice to Danes, Poles and Czechs. The Wilsonian principle of self determination was no remedy, since what was often at issue was precisely the unit which was to exercise the right. Nationalism bred absolutes. Fourth, nationalism at home emphasized sovereignty, a difficult notion hardly compatible with the limited state, autonomous civil society and market economy.

The illiberal aspects of nationalism were magnified when the idea was used outside Europe. There it was territorial rather than linguistic and it was aimed not so much against dynasticism as against colonialism, that is, a manifestation of the world order. Nationalism outside Europe, it should be remembered, was not simply a European transplant. National sentiment already existed in the Islamic, especially Persian, notion of *shuubiyya*, in the Chinese sense of cultural, even racial, superiority over surrounding barbarians, and in the Japanese conviction of their own uniqueness. As C. A. Bayly has shown, prototypical nation states existed in Asia before the Europeans, as prosperous peripheries seceded from decaying imperial cores. Nationalism too could appeal to the strain of isolationism and xenophobia in Asia shown by the hermit kingdoms of Yi Korea and Tokugawa Japan. In favourable circumstances, anticolonialist nationalism could spell continued Westernization by other means, as in India and Egypt. But just as frequently, it reacted against the world order and fell into nativism (Bokassa's Central African empire), isolationism (Burma), anti-Americanism (Libya) or absorption into totalitarianism (Vietnam). Moreover, it was conservative. It did not change the frontiers imposed by imperialism or the bureaucratic character of the colonial regimes. It simply turned them to other ends. Nationalism became a means of de-Westernization without modernization.[8]

A second ambiguous reaction to the common consensus was the Green movement. This deserves attention, less for its immediate significance in parliamentary systems where single issue movements seldom retain continued electoral support, than for its potential importance in Central Asia. Here, in Kazakhstan and Uzbekistan in particular, in conjunction with Muslim resurgence, it could become what might be called a double green movement of resentment against the Soviet Union. Such a movement would be diverse. It would contain elements of nationalism, religion and protest of sociology against economy, in addition to pure environmentalism. Even in England, Greens show considerable variety, so that they have been characterized as urban, county, primitivist, quality of life, etc. Broadly, however, two main tendencies may be detected in the movement. On the one hand, there is a tendency which is part of the Western political tradition, which can accommodate plural life styles, careful management of resources, avoidance of injurious technological side effects, and the assertion of meta-economic values. On the other hand, there is a tendency which is hostile to the Western political tradition in that it rejects the higher polytechnic and the world market, repudiates the global arsenal, is indifferent to the republic of letters, denigrates the achievement of scientific medicine, and asserts itself as a new religious international. In this Utopian form, the Green movement, like totalitarianism, of which it is a potential successor, bears reactive witness to the common consensus.

Finally, more direct witness is borne to the common consensus by what might be called the Anglophone overlay: the increasing universality of the English language. In 1500, with a world population of 500 million, less than 1 per cent spoke English. In 1990, with a world population of 5000 million, some 10 per cent spoke English to some extent: 350 million native English speakers in England, the United States and the Old Dominions, 150 million elsewhere, making use of English to greater or less degree. No other major language can show a comparable rate of growth. If it continues, by 2500 no other language but English will be spoken! What is most striking is the growth of English as a second language. Already during World War I, some units of the Habsburg army used English as the language of command.[9] During the Sino-Soviet dispute in the 1960s negotiations between the two Communist powers were conducted in English. Few international conferences meet in which English is not one of the official languages. Japanese mathematicians are advised to write their papers in English, not merely with a view to publication, but to achieve maximum intelligibility. Increasingly the world cannot think but in English, just as in former times it could not think except in Greek, Latin, Sanskrit or Chinese. Unlike these predecessors, however, English, as the language of the media and of pop art, has spread far beyond the literocratic elite. The Anglophone overlay, becoming thicker daily, is the most conspicuous testimony to the common consensus as a contemporary fact.

THE COMMON CONSENSUS IN THE HOMELANDS

In the case of the higher polytechnic, the order of importance of the homelands as liaison areas with Central Asia was, from the least: the Ottoman empire, India, China and Russia. In the case of the common consensus, the order was different: India, China, the Ottoman empire and Russia. The difference highlighted that the two were separate world institutions. Modern technology and modern politics did not necessarily coincide.

India

More than any other of the homelands, India absorbed the common consensus, yet it influenced Central Asia least, except in the diffusion of the English language. The *raj* was favourable terrain for the inculturation of the Western political tradition. It provided for India, at largely English cost, what China possessed, but India, absorbed in its social institutions, had never developed: political unity and an a-political civil service. Within this framework, an English version of bureaucratic absolutism, English forms of opposition, and the English language easily took root. Indian nationalism was territorial not linguistic. It did not seek to change the foundations of the state, but simply to take over its management. Its greatest quarrel with the *raj* was not whether the British should leave, but whether Pakistan should leave as well. Towards this goal of constitutional instead of absolutist bureaucracy, Congress moved along English lines. In *satyagraha*, it mobilized the out of doors opinion which had been a recognized element of the unreformed constitution. It followed in the footsteps of the Catholic association, the Anti-Corn Law League, the Education League and the Irish Home Rule movement. Like them, and unlike Chartism, it was successful because its goals were limited and attainable without social revolution. Force only entered the Indian revolution with the non-political communal violence attending partition in 1947. Nehru was a more successful Parnell: an English educated member of an ascendancy, who knew how to keep lieutenants, henchman and clerics in order. Continental nationalists overthrew dynasties. Nehru, a nationalist in an English mode, founded one, though as a Whig he might not have approved of it.

Because of its Anglicized framework, the Indian version of the common consensus found little resonance in Central Asia. Neither the *raj* nor Congress were interested in events beyond India. Their politics were not for export. Britain renounced interest in Afghanistan after a single bomb had ended the Third Afghan War in 1919. In 1934, she lent no support to the Turkish-Islamic nationalists in Sinkiang against the pro Soviet warlord Sheng Shih-ts'ai. In 1959, Nehru offered no opposition to the Chinese reoccupation of Tibet and allowed his frontiers to be eroded in the Aksai Chin and the northeast frontier. In 1979, the Indian government saw in the Soviet invasion of Afghanistan only an opportunity to reseal its alliance with Moscow and to embarrass Pakistan. Rajiv Gandhi's subsequent attempt to impose a settlement in Ceylon was unhappy. Pakistan, for its part, was more generous in its treatment of the Afghan *mujahidin*, despite the disruption they caused, but its generosity arose more from Islamic solidarity than from commitment to the common consensus. Pakistan had some English roots, especially in the army, but its basis in religious communalism rather than language or territory was not characteristic of Europe. Jinnah's approach to politics was legalistic. He wanted to do the best he could for his client, the Muslim community, in the face of both secular and Hindu pressure from Congress. He was to that extent Westernized. If Nehru was Parnell, Jinnah was Carson.

Neither spoke to Central Asia's condition, but both at least spoke in English. Peshawar became a liaison area for bringing the Afghan *mujahidin* into the Anglophone overlay.

China

If India adopted nationalism in its more pro-Western form, China succumbed to totalitarianism in its Communist and specifically Maoist form. Neither Communism nor Maoism were predetermined for China. Late imperial China with its limited state, autonomous civil society, and a wide sector of market economy monitored by guilds, looked like a good candidate for transition to the common consensus. That China rejected both tradition and modernity in favour of totalitarianism was a matter of conjuncture rather than structure.

In the nineteenth century, Chinese diplomacy had been all too successful in muffling the impact of the world order. In contrast to Japan, modernization therefore remained limited, promoted by the regional viceroys rather than by the central government. At the intellectual level, the formula 'Chinese learning for the substance, Western learning for practical use' or Chinese values, Western technology, appeared adequate to the situation. It was not until China's defeat in the Sino-Japanese war of 1894–5 that the need for more radical modernization, not least in education, was perceived. In 1898 a university at Peking was sketched out. A Shanghai missionary college and a Tientsin private high school were encouraged to turn themselves into tertiary institutions. From 1901 a modern state school system was initiated. State and provincial scholarships were awarded to study overseas, notably Japan. In 1908, Tsing Hua college was founded out of the American share of the Boxer indemnity to prepare students to go to the United States.

The revolution of 1911 only accelerated the process. In 1915, the Rockefeller Foundation took over Peking Union Medical College and turned it into an approximation to Johns Hopkins.[10] From 1917, under a new chancellor Ts'ai Yüan-p'ei, the Peking proto university was turned into a real one with a proper faculty. Three of that faculty: Hu Shih a philosopher, Ch'en Tu-hsiu a literature man, and Li Ta-chao a historian were the leaders of the intellectual awakening known as the May 4 movement. They were not nationalists, though many of their students were. They sought a new universalism to replace Confucianism. Hu Shih found it in pragmatism, Ch'en Tu-hsiu and Li Ta-chao found it in Marxism, Ch'en in a hard headed rationalistic form, Li in a soft hearted, though strong willed, romantic form. Mao Tse-tung was one of Li's students. Without his leadership and the intellectual nucleus provided by May Fourth, China would never have gone Communist, whatever the circumstances of warlordism, Japanese invasion and rampant inflation. China went Communist via a massive flight from society on the part of the middle class in the period 1945 to 1949, but there had to be something for it to fly to. That something was an intellectual Communist party entrenched in the North China countryside and newly implanted in the North Manchurian cities.[11]

The Communists first came into contact with Central Asia when their forces entered Kansu in 1935, at the end of the Long March. The Chinese Muslim community enjoyed a golden age under the republic in terms of autonomy and contact with the rest of Islam.[12] Kansu, Ninghsia and Chinghai were ruled by four Muslim warlords, the *Ssu-Ma*, descendants and affiliates of a military clique which had established itself under the late empire. A fifth, Ma Chung-ying, was endeavouring to take control of Sinkiang. The Tungans were provincial but not isolated. Between fifty and a hundred went annually on the *haj*, the warlords supported students at the al-Azhar university in Cairo, and the Naqshbandiyya still formed an international brotherhood. The community therefore reflected currents of thought in Islam generally. In particular it reflected the critical current, which had been flowing strongly in Muslim theology since the seventeenth century. As in parallel Christian currents, Muslim criticism discriminated between the respective roles in theological method of scripture, tradition, reason and authority. In the 1930s Chinese Muslims were divided between three schools. First, there was the *lao-chiao* or old teaching. Its core was the original *khafiyya* Naqshbandiyya brought to China by the sons and grandsons of the Makhdum-i Azam. With it were associated conservative *ulema* and the *jahriyya* Qadiriyya. The *lao-chiao* was traditionalist. Second, there was the *hsin-chiao* or new teaching. Its core was the revivalist *jahriyya* Naqshbandiyya introduced by Ma Ming-hsin in the late eighteenth century from the pilgrimage places of Arabia. With it were associated some Wahhabite and Shiite elements. The *hsin-chiao* was fundamentalist and in one particular line, authoritarian, i.e. Mahdist. Third, there was the *hsin-hsin chiao*, the newest teaching. Its core were those who had been in contact with Constantinople or Cairo. With it were associated those mullahs who wanted to take advantage of the new educational opportunities in China to open more Muslim schools with a broader curriculum. Promoted by the warlords, the *hsin-hsin chiao* was modernist-secularist. These were not identical terms, but represented an alliance against traditionalism, fundamentalism and authoritarianism. Thus, among the warlords, Ma Pu-fang tended to modernism and ended his days in Mecca, while Ma Chung-ying tended to secularism and ended his days in Moscow.

In this trichotomy the role of the communists was unexpected but logical. The *Ssu-Ma* had no wish to share the northwest with the party. They opposed it militarily and inflicted on the Red army some of the most serious setbacks it ever experienced. The party therefore could not look to modernist Muslims who wished to adapt to the world order. Since traditionalist Muslims were also unlikely to be attracted to the party, Communist propaganda was forced to appeal to the fundamentalists, who at least had a background of miltancy. The propaganda was not conspicuously successful, though it did make some recruits among the mullahs. However, as the party found new openings in China after 1937, it could turn its back once more on Muslim Central Asia, where for a moment it had seemed that its future lay. Nevertheless, the episode was indicative of the curvature of political space. Muslim fundamentalism and Chinese communism shared an enemy in the emerging world order and the common consensus. Both were negative reactions to it.

Ottoman Empire and Turkish Republic

Until the abolition of the Caliphate in 1924, Turkey was the centre of the Sunni world of which Central Asia (except for its Buddhist fringes in Zungharia) was a part. Like Rome, it was a centre which both attracted and repelled, but was never a matter of indifference. The Ottoman empire had been in contact with the European-centred world order since the sixteenth century. Its first response, expressed particularly in its attempt to reopen the central land route by military and naval action, had been to construct a world order of its own in the form of a tricontinental empire from Poland to the Yemen and from Algiers to Bokhara. The impossibility of the design in terms of costs and manpower led the empire in the late seventeenth century to contract its horizons and become a Balkan and Levantine dynastic state. In the eighteenth century, the empire, through foreign advisers, renegades and minimum changes, adapted to the world order with what amounted to a formula on Chinese lines of 'Islamic learning for the substance, Western learning for practical use', Muslim values, European technology. As the nineteenth century developed, however, this solution became inadequate as the need for Western institutions and ideas as well as technology became apparent. Moreover, like the dynastic states of the Habsburgs and Romanovs, the Ottoman empire was challenged by the nationalism of its component *millets*, or national-religious communities: Greeks, Armenians, Jews, and of those beyond the *millet* system – Slavs, Albanians, Kurds, Arabs.

In the face of nationalist pressure, the empire had four options. First there was Ottomanism: a reassertion of the dynastic character and historical unity of the state, but with greater concessions to the *millets*, especially since the Greek and Armenian communities had been antagonized, to the Jewish *millet*. This was the policy of Djavid bey, minister of finance in the government of the Committee of Union and Progress. Today, with economic communities and functional alternatives to the state, it might seem an attractive solution, but it was open to the objection that it pleased nobody but the Galata bankers. Second, there was Pan-Islamism: a reassertion of the sultan's role as caliph to revive Islamdom to counter the European world order. This was the policy of several sultans, notably Abdulaziz, some Albanians and the Naqshbandiyya. It was open to the objection that it offered nothing to the non-Muslim *millets*, weakened the empire in the Balkans, and jeopardized modernization. Third, there was Pan-Turkism: the reconstruction of the empire as a *Gros-Türkei*. This was the policy of some sultans, notably Abdulhamit II, of the Committee of Union and Progress, and in particular of Enver and Talaat. It was open to the objection that it wrote off the Albanians, the Kurds and the Arabs and required military expansion for its realization. Finally, there was Anatolianism: the reconstruction of the empire as a *Klein-Türkei* confined to Asia Minor. Until 1918, this was no one's policy of first preference. It was open to the objection that it required major surgery, the abandonment of Constantinople as capital, and the loss of great power status. This was the option which eventuated, but it was only post-World War I circumstances and the determination of Mustafa Kemal which brought it about.

Consideration of the political options was intertwined for Muslims at least, with concurrent critical debate. Ottoman Islam had originally been modernistic in the liberal dervish orders, the Mevleviyya and the Bektashiyya. The rise of the Naqshbandiyya, however, shifted it in a traditionalist direction. This move was consolidated by the dissolution of the Bektashi order in 1826, concurrent with that of the Janissaries. The dropping of the Bektashiyya was serious. Former Bektashis found their way into Albanian nationalism (Tirana had been a Bektashi capital) or into secular republicanism, especially in Central Anatolia, where the Alevi community was a Bektashi front. The Janissaries had become an incubus, but Bektashi liberalism might have been a better support for modernization under the Tanzimat and Abdulhamit II than Naqshbandi conservatism. Ottoman Islam, traditionalist in theory but increasingly secularist in practice, left itself vulnerable both to real secularism and to the various fundamentalisms – Wahhabite, Senussi, reformed Naqshbandi – coming out of Arabia. Mustafa Kemal, with his usual decisiveness, resolved this duality by plumping for radical secularity. His decision, however, left the Turkish republic with another duality, still unresolved, of a secular state seeking membership of the basically Christian European community, and a religious society whose Islam was increasingly infiltrated by fundamentalism. Yet religious fundamentalism did not necessarily imply hostility to modernity. Indeed, its hostility to traditionalism might make it sympathetic. The Nurist movement, the strongest fundamentalist force in Turkey today, a kind of Muslim *Opus Dei*, was in origin a reformed Naqshbandi offshoot with a *jahriyya dikr*. Yet, it was enthusiastic about science, repudiated theocracy as a Christian aberration, accepted secular democracy, favoured mixed economy, admitted women among its activists and supported President Turgut Ozal.[13] The spectra of methodologies and politics did not coincide in Islam anymore than in Christianity. *Aggiornamento* could have more than one intellectual basis.

Russia

It was not so much Russian thought and institutions which brought modern politics to Central Asia, but those of Muslims in Russia, notably those of the Volga Tatar community of Kazan.[14] This in turn was influenced by the intellectual *problematik* of the Ottoman empire. Kazan, however, was more than a provincial outpost. It stood at the head of the Jadist or modernist movement (*usul-i-jadid* 'new method') which did most to shape Central Asian ideas in the contemporary period.

Kazan became Muscovite in 1552. Initially, its Muslim Tatar community was persecuted by its new Christian masters and sank to a low ebb. Subsequently, however, with the more tolerant and secularist policy of Catherine the Great, the Tatar community revived as the intermediary for Russian trade with Central Asia, one of the north-south routes developing in this period. It became a natural bridge between the European centred world order and the isolationist Muslim east. The founder of the Jadist school was Abunnasir Kursavi (1776–1812), a Muslim law doctor: born in Kazan, studied in Bokhara and reacted against it, and died of cholera, half in exile, in Constantinople. Kursavi was a modernist in that, in Koranic hermeneutics, he championed *ijtihad*, judgement, against *taqlid*, obedience. Revelation was open, not closed. New judgements could be derived from it, old judgements could be revised. Kursavi laid the critical foundations for innovation. His views did not command much acceptance in his lifetime, whether in Kazan, Bokhara or Constantinople, but he left disciples and sub-disciples who built on his foundations in the next generation.[15]

The next important Kazan Tatar thinker was Shihabeddin Mardjani (1818–1889). He wanted the repristinization of Islam by a return to the sources critically examined. He thus combined fundamentalism and modernism and became one of the first higher critics in the Muslim world. In the secular field, he was most significant as a historian whose work created what is still the self identify of the Volga Tatars as the successors of the Volga Bulgars. He thus founded the first historicist nationalism among the Muslim peoples of Russia. His presentation, however, did not exclude the Volga Tatars from a wider community of Turkish speaking peoples or from the universal *umma* of Islam. These more inclusive memberships were emphasized by the Crimean Tatar publicist Ismail Bey Gasprinski (1851–1914), who had spent some time in his youth in Constantinople where both Pan-Islamism and Pan-Turkism were under discussion. Gasprinski was primarily an educator. He founded a chain of Muslim schools where modern as well as traditional subjects were taught and insisted on education for girls as well as boys. Gasprinski was an irrepressible optimist who always thought he had won over the people he talked to and that reason must prevail. He saw the future of the Muslims in Russia in terms of a single Turkist state, in partnership with a Russian state, inside a Tsarist confederation, which should be simultaneously the greatest Christian and the greatest Islamic power. A third significant thinker of this period was another Volga Tatar, Rizaeddin Fahreddin (1858–1936); Jadist, Pan-Turk, Pan-Islamist. Like the Persian publicist Jamal ad-Din al-Afghani, he stressed the social dimension of Islam as an *umma* or community. He admired the Hanbalite fundamentalist Ibn Taimiya, who defined the true Muslim by his political and social attitudes, and his work looked towards Islamic socialism.

When the Russian revolution came, the Jadists appeared to have four choices: a single large Turkestan, either autonomous within a Russian state or independent outside it; a number of small Turkestans similarly either autonomous or independent. In fact, there were only two choices: with the Whites or with the Reds. As the Whites, proto fascists rather than defenders of the 'old order, made no concessions to national sentiment and remained resolutely Great Russian chauvinists, most Muslims preferred the Reds, who at least had a nationalities policy. Muslim units organized by the Volga Tatar Bolshevik Mir Said Sultangaliev (1892–1940) played a significant role in the defeat of Kolchak. Yet in the end, Sultangaliev found he had no choice. He wanted a single large Turkestan inside the Soviet Union, with a Muslim Communist party parallel to the European, and recognition of the Muslims' inherent proletarian status as victims of imperialism, an anticipation of Mao's claim that the Chinese were inherently proletarian. All Stalin would grant, however, was a number of small Turkestans with limited autonomy. Sultangaliev himself, the first major Asian communist theoretician, was condemned in 1923 and shot in 1940. Though a Marxist and not a liberal, his Islamic socialism allowed for some limitations on the state and was closer to the common consensus than what Stalin had to offer.

THE COMMON CONSENSUS IN CENTRAL ASIA

It is possible now to examine the extent to which political forces active in Central Asia participated in the critical awareness and political discrimination of the common consensus. Since all three areas of Central Asia were subject to Communist rule, it might be expected that the extent would not be great. Opposition to communism, however, continued to exist, and Marxism too, no more than Christianity or Islam, has been able to escape the critical urge. Scripture, tradition, reason and authority all have analogues in Marxism. Critical awareness may one day bring Marxism back to the Western political tradition with which it started. The mere fact of Communist rule does not exclude from the common consensus. The totalitarian revolt is parasitic and draws its life blood from its host. The same could be said of anti-Western forms of nationalism and of the Green movement. All are excrescences on a body which will isolate, contain and eventually reabsorb them.

Afghanistan

In 1990, following the Soviet withdrawal – in fact more of a transference of responsibilities from the Red Army to the KGB – Afghan politics was doubly divided between four main groups. First, there was the division between the government and the opposition, i.e. the Kabul authorities and the *mujahidin*. Second, within each of these entities, there was an ideological division, which divided the government into Parcham and Khalq, the opposition into Jamiat-i Islami (Islamic association) and Hezb-i Islami (Islamic party). The first division related to a difference of political register. The Kabul government was a modern state, though an imperfect and embryonic one, whose writ did not run much beyond the double circles centred on Shibargan and the capital and joined by the Salang highway. The *mujahidin* were part of a premodern society, the fish in the sea of classical Maoist guerrilla theory. The Afghan sea was a collection of suboptimizing *qawms*: local communities, lineage solidarities, religious affiliations and personal retinues. These basically opposed not Communist government but government. It was a struggle, not between similarly equipped opponents, but between *gladiator* and *retiarius*. The second division, however, that within each camp, was related to differences in the philosophy of politics, that is, to critical awareness.

The Afghan Communist party originated from within the royal bureaucracy. It developed under Daud, the King's cousin, who was prime minister (1953–63) and president (1973–78). In politics, Daud was a Pashtun nationalist (Pashtun is the majority language in Afghanistan and it is also spoken in the Northwest Frontier province of Pakistan and parts of Baluchistan), in religion a secularist, and in diplomacy an ally of the Soviet Union. As part of that alliance, he accepted an Afghan Communist party as a reversionary interest. In time, divisions developed in the party which crystallized round two newspapers, *Parcham* (The Banner) and *Khalq* (The Masses). The division was both social and intellectual. Parcham was composed of young bureaucrats who had actually been to the Soviet Union or could hope to do so. It was a ginger group which stuck closely to the seats of power and under Daud was known derisively by its opponents as the royal Communist party. Khalq, on the other hand, was composed of young school teachers, whose adherence to Marxism was based on experience at home. It was a mission team, which in Narodnik fashion, went to the people both to teach and to learn. In intellectual method, Parcham was fundamentalist and traditionalist: the basic Western texts of Marxism as interpreted by Soviet practice. Khalq, on the other hand, was modernist and authoritarian: the Afghan situation today as interpreted by local charismatic leaders. Parcham wanted an instituional revolution. Khalq wanted a cultural revolution. Parcham was rationalistic, Khalq was romantic. The division transcended Afghan circumstances. It was rooted in older and wide polarities: the old Marx against the young Marx, Plekhanov against Lenin, Stalin against Trotsky, Ch'en Tu-hsiu against Li Ta-chao, Brezhnev against Mao. These polarities in turn rested upon divergent critical evaluations of the cognitive process in politics. Of the two, Parcham was closer to the common consensus, because the Soviet practice, which it followed, could include *glasnost* and *perestroika*. Its traditionalism could be *traditio juvenescens*, a return to a wider world.

The two chief *mujahidin* groups – for there were others associated with *ulema* traditionalism and Shiite authoritarianism – originated in the king's initiatives outside the royal bureaucracy. In particular, they originated in his phases of liberalism which allowed theological students to go to study at al-Azhar in Cairo.[16] The Islamist movement, as Olivier Roy calls it, i.e. the application of Islam to politics, began among returned students in the religious science faculty in Kabul university. It spread to their students in the university, the state *madrasa* and teachers' training colleges. While Marxism appealed to young bureaucrats and secular school teachers, Islamism appealed to young military and civilian professionals and to religious school teachers. The predominant influence at al-Azhar was modernist, the same kind of Islamic emphasis as in Kursavi, Mardjani and Gasprinski. But there was also a fundamentalist current associated with the Muslim Brotherhood and the Ibn Taimiya revival. It emphasised the Koran alone and political and social criteria for true Islamic membership. The wings of the *mujahidin* divided along these lines. Jamiat was modernist. It left the future open. It wanted a loose coalition. It sought the maximum of friends against the minimum of enemies. The defeat of the enemy was the top priority. Internal divisions could be ignored. The immediate aim was collaboration between groups. Hezb was fundamentalist. It knew what the future must be. It wanted a tight party. It sought committed members and regarded all who were not for it as against it. The victory of its own organization was the top priority. Internal divisions could not be ignored. The immediate aim was centralized leadership over groups. In practice, Jamiat and Hezb often collaborated, but sometimes they fought, and Hezb was prepared to make a truce with the enemy, while Jamiat was not. Jamiat was stronger on the ground and in Afghanistan. Hezb was stronger in organization and in Peshawar. Jamiat was more sympathetic to the common consensus. While Hezb admired Ayatollah Khomeini and Saddam Hussein, Jamiat welcomed Western journalists and sent a token force to the Gulf coalition. Its intellectual leader,

Burhanuddin Rabbani, an admirer of Jami as well as an ex-student leader in Ankara and Cairo, appealed to the Persian elements in Afghan culture, while his opposite number in Hezb, Gulbuddin Hekmatyar, was more provincial and Pashtun. An open Islam was ranged against a closed. In 1992 Kabul became the prize.

Sinkiang

Ruled by a conservative party machine with only token Uighur participation, Sinkiang in 1990 was not good terrain for dissidence. Nevertheless, dissidence existed below the suface, and in suitable circumstances could build on an earlier political movement which was not without contact with the common consensus. This was the movement associated in 1933 with the brief Turkish-Islamic Republic of Eastern Turkestan (TIRET), with the governorships of Masud Sabri (1947–48) and Burhan Shahidi (1948–55), and with a group of exiles in Turkey.

The revolt of Yaqub beg eliminated the Makhdumzada khojas from religious politics in Sinkiang. It also reduced the power of the dervish orders in general, the Naqshbandiyya in particular, except among the Tungans. Ma Shao-wu, a son or nephew of a noted Kansu *hsin-chiao* leader Ma Yuan-chang, who, so it is said, was swallowed up in an earthquake in 1920 with 150,000 of his supporters on the eve of an eschatological rebellion, served as taotai or subgovernor of Kashgaria in the 1920s and 1930s. The place of the orders was taken by the traditionalist *ulema* in Altishahr and by the lay nobility of the khanate of Hami in Uighuristan. But modernist influences from Constantinople and Kazan were beginning to make themselves felt.[17] In 1914, as a result of Talaat's support, a Turkish educationalist from Rhodes, Ahmed Kemal, founded a modern school in Kashgar. Relocated in Urumchi, it functioned till 1920 and had a number of distinguished pupils. Among its supporters in Urumchi were the Tatar merchant Burhan Shahidi who had received a Jadist education in Kazan and Masud Sabri, member of a rich Uighur merchant family, who had studied in Constantinople.

TIRET was proclaimed in Khotan in 1933, a chaotic year in Sinkiang between the governorships of Chin Shu-jen and Sheng Shih-ts'ai. It briefly dominated most of Kashgaria. It was interpreted at the time by Western observers such as Peter Fleming as purely traditionalist. Andrew Forbes has shown that this was not so.[18] Though its constitutions laid stress on the *sharia* as the basis of the state, the fact of a constitution was untraditional, as was the provision for a legislature and membership of the League of Nations. Muhammed Amin Bughra, its principal architect though he remained in the background, had been associated with the circle of the Jadist school, and after Communist victory, chose Turkey as his place of exile. The prime minister, Sabit Damullah is 'reported to have travelled extensively in the Soviet Union, Turkey, Egypt and India' and two of his ministers were among those who had worked with Ahmed Kemal.[19]

TIRET did not last long. It was overthrown by the secularist Tungan warlord Ma Chung-ying who in turn was eliminated by the leftist Sheng Shih-ts'ai. As TIRET was strongly anti-Soviet, there was no place for it in Sheng's Sinkiang. Its leadership therefore went to Nationalist China, where it was joined by another exile, Isa Yusuf Alptekin, from the same Kashgar merchant Jadist background as Masud Sabri. From thence, they emerged in 1944, on the removal of Sheng Shih-ts'ai by Chiang Kai-shek, to join the relatively liberal regimes of Masud Sabri and Burhan Shahidi. These tried to mediate between the Uighur population and first the Kuomintang and then the Chinese Communists. Masud Sabri died in an Urumchi prison, Burhan Shahidi was kicked upstairs by his Communist patrons, but Alptekin, like Bughra, went into exile in Turkey. Bughra founded a *waqf*, a charitable trust for his countrymen, which still operates in Ankara. In February 1991, an Erkin Alptekin, probably a son or grandson of Isa Yusuf, was reported as a vice-chairman of the alternative United Nations at the Hague, a body purporting to represent peoples without states, such as the Kurds and Uighurs.[20] The movement behind TIRET, therefore, was a mixture of traditionalism and modernism, just as the Nurist movement in Turkey today is a mixture of fundamentalism and modernism. If political initiative is ever again possible in Sinkiang, and the balance of demographic advantage is beginning, as in the Soviet Union, to swing to the Muslim population, then there are leadership and precedents to follow which could provide links to a wider world and the common consensus.

Soviet Central Asia

Here, to evaluate links with the common consensus, one needs to consider first the general context and then the particular situations in Kazakhstan and Uzbekistan.

The general context in 1990 was still that laid down by Stalin. The most he was prepared to offer the nationalities was plural republics with limited autonomy. In practice, this amounted to the policy known as *korenizatsia* or indigenization.[21] Policies decided in Moscow, in the economic sphere by Gosplan, were to be implemented by elites recruited locally, though often Russian led. In return, the elites were given a share of the spoils of office, the preservation of their languages, and membership of the wider if still claustrophobic world of the Soviet Union. To prevent the elites becoming too powerful or indispensable, national units were kept small and in some cases artificial, and periodic purges were conducted against nationalist deviations or the slightest sign of Pan-Turkism or Pan-Islamism. Any Islam was forced to keep low key. Till the 1980s the system worked well and the Soviet empire looked solid and immovable.

Nevertheless, it had its disadvantages even from Moscow's point of view. These became clear as Soviet power, after the abortive reformation of Khrushchev, sank into the inertia of Brezhnev, Andropov and Chernenko. First, the local elites were corrupt and inefficient. These characteristics they shared with the whole Soviet *nomenklatura*. But whereas in European Russia, corruption and inefficiency were unpopular, so that they could be attacked by reformers from above in the name of *perestroika*, in Central Asia they were popular as surrogates for autonomy. Given the degree of central planning, *korenizatsia* left the republic governments little function except to be corrupt, indeed forced them to be so to fulfil their obligations under the plan. When in December 1986, Gorbachev dismissed the notoriously corrupt and inefficient, but deeply entrenched, Kazakh leader Dinmukhamed Kunaev, who had been in charge of the republic since 1959, the result was riots in Alma Ata. Moreover, Moscow was unable to sustain its own candidate for the succession. Second, the local elites secreted national sentiment. Through the vested interests of their republic's apparatus, the spurious nationalities created by Stalin gradually turned into real nationalities. Thus while Uzbeks and Kirghiz spoke the same language, lived in the same areas, followed the same religion and had common histories, by 1989 they were rioting against each other in Ferghana. The Kremlin was the victim of its own success. There were too many units in the Soviet Union with endless possibilities for friction. The obvious remedy was the KGB, but resort to it would only inaugurate a fresh cycle of centralization, *korenizatsia*, and inertia. The other alternative, to turn the Soviet Union into a common market with a confederated core and a periphery of independent states, was unacceptable to the army, which had too many interests on the frontiers.

Despite the Alma Ata riots, the situation was least serious in Kazkhstan.[22] According to the 1979 census, Kazakhs comprised only 36 per cent of the population of their republic, and the addition of Tatars, Uzbeks and Uighurs only pushed the Muslim population up to 41 per cent.[23] Secession on a Muslim basis therefore was impossible without partition. This would be difficult since division would be between Muslim country and non-Muslim town. Moreover, the secularist Kazakh elite did not want to secede. What it wanted was a more equal partnership with the Soviet elite: recognition of the Turkish contribution to the common pre Soviet past, long term commitment to the language, action on the ecological problems of the Aral Sea and the Semipalatinsk nuclear testing sites, reconsideration of the Sibaral water scheme, genuine toleration for Islam. If only some of these demands were met, the current Kazakh party leader Nursultan Nazarbayev indicated his willingness to enter a confederation along with Russia, White Russia and the Ukraine under Yeltsin, or to operate the kind of uncorrupt, efficient *korenizatsia* favoured by Gorbachev. Some Kazakh intellectuals, such as the controversial poet Okhas Suleymenov, insisted that all must be met and implicitly demanded that the state be non-ideological, limited and concerned for sociology as well as economy.[24] In Suleymenov, who believed the Turks were descended from the Sumerians and had saved Russia from both Islam and the Tatar yoke, Kazakh modernism and secularism reached an extreme which challenged Soviet fundamentalism and traditionalism, yet could still accommodate to them. On such a basis Kazkhs and Russians might enter the common consensus together.

In Uzbekistan the situation was more intractable. According to
the 1979 census, Uzbeks comprised 69 per cent of the population of their republic, while the addition of Volga Tatars,
Karakalpaks, Kazakhs, Tadjiks and Kirghiz raised the Muslim
population to 85 per cent.[25] Secession therefore on a Muslim
basis was possible. Both official and unofficial Islam were strongly
organized. The Naqshbandiyya, the Yasawiyya, the Kubrawiyya
and the Qadiriyya were all active. Since Uzbek Islam was traditionalist or fundamentalist, however, there were points of contact with Soviet attitudes. Sharaf Rashidov, who was Uzbek party
chief from 1959 to 1983, was an almost perfect *korenizatsia*
leader.[26] He supported cotton monoculture, insisted on bilin-
gualism, praised Russian as world language, repudiated Islam
as a superstition to be overcome by Marxist-Leninist science,
but still kept local backing. Yet serious difficulties were only just
below the surface. After the death of 'Grand Vizier' Rashidov,
Moscow insisted on the removal of many of his cadres. Cotton
monoculture only operated through the activities of so-called
cotton barons who manipulated state investment funds in conjunction with organized crime.[27] Its ecological and health costs
were increasingly criticized, while the decline of Soviet cotton
exports in the fact of Chinese competition on the world market
made it harder to justify economically. Unemployment, real
and concealed, was at a high level, thanks to under-education
and Union investment policy. Uzbeks, on the other hand, were
unwilling to export their population to other parts of the Union as the central authorities wished. Politically, Uzbekistan was
further from the common consensus than Kazakhstan. Both
Moscow and the Uzbek leadership in 1990 really wanted the
status quo, but that is an option which is seldom on offer.
Uzbeks outside the leadership felt that time was on their side.
Whatever the griefs of the past and the problems of the present,
they were confident that the future would restore them to their
place of leadership in Central Asia and Central Asia to its
position as a crossroads in world history. Whether Central Asia
would continue to be passive in that history, or once again, as in
the days of the Timurids, become active, only that future would
decide. Central Asia was still very much a factor in world history.

Notes

1 World History and Central Asia – Time, Place and People

1. Joseph Fletcher, 'A Bibliography of the Publications of Joseph Fletcher', *Harvard Journal of Asiatic Studies*, Vol. 46, no. 2, June 1986, pp. 7–10.
2. Robert Delort, *Le Commerce des Fourrures en Occident à la fin du Moyen Age*, 2 Vols., École Française de Rome, Rome, 1978.
3. Sylvain Bensidoun, *Samarcande et la vallée du Zerafshan*, Anthropos, Paris, 1979.
4. Arminius Vambéry, *Sketches of Central Asia*, Allen, London, 1868.
5. Eden Naby, 'The Uzbeks in Afghanistan', *Central Asian Survey*, Vol. 3, no. 1, 1984, pp. 1–21.
6. Martha Brill Olcott, *The Kazakhs*, Hoover, Stanford, California, 1987.
7. Joseph Fletcher, 'Ch'ing Inner Asia c.1800', in John K. Fairbank (ed.), *The Cambridge History of China*, Vol. 10, Cambridge University Press, Cambridge, 1978, pp. 33–106, especially pp. 62–9.
8. L. N. Gumilev, *Searches for an Imaginary Kingdom: The Legend of the Kingdom of Prester John*, Cambridge University Press, Cambridge, 1987.
9. Sechin Jagchid, Paul Hyer, *Mongolia's Culture and Society*, Westview, Boulder, Colorado, 1979; Elizabeth E. Bacon, *Central Asians under Russian Rule*, Cornell, Ithaca, New York, 1966.
10. John Masson Smith, 'Mongol and Nomadic Taxation', *Harvard Journal of Asiatic Studies*, Vol. 30, 1970, pp. 46–85.
11. Joseph Fletcher, 'Blood Tanistry: Authority and Succession in the Ottoman, Indian Muslim and later Chinese Empires', The Conference for the Theory of Democracy and Popular Participation, Bellagio, 1978.
12. Ludwig W. Adamec (ed.), *Historical and Political Gazetteer of Afghanistan*, Vol. 3, *Herat and Northwestern Afghanistan*, Akademische Druck-u Verlagsanstalt, Graz, 1975.
13. Firdausi, *The Epic of the Kings, Shah-Nama*, Reuben Levy (trns.), Routledge and Kegan Paul, London, 1965.
14. Richard W. Bulliet, *The Camel and the Wheel*, Harvard, Cambridge, Mass., 1975.

2 Central Asia and Temporary World Institutions

1. Colin Renfrew, *Archaeology and Language. The Puzzle of Indo-European Origins*, Cape, London, 1987; Marija Gimburtas, 'Accounting for a great change', *Times Literary Supplement*, June 24–30, 1988, pp. 71–4.
2. Owen Lattimore, 'La Civilisation, mère de Barberie', *Annales, Économies, Sociétés, Civilisations*, 17:1, Jan–Feb. 1962, pp. 95–106.
3. Philip L. Kohl, *Central Asia: Palaeolithic Beginnings to the Iron Age*, Éditions Recherche sur les Civilisations, Paris, 1984, p. 241.

4. Renfrew, *Archaeology and Language*, p. 12; A. L. Basham, *The Wonder that was India*, Grove, New York, 1954, p. 233.
5. Jack Goody, *The Interface between the Written and the Oral*, Cambridge University Press, Cambridge, 1987.
6. David N. Keightley (ed.), *The Origins of the Chinese Civilisation*, University of California Press, Berkeley, 1983.
7. Henri Goblot, 'Dans L'Ancien Iran, Les Techniques de L'Eau et La Grande Historie', *Annales, Économies, Sociétés, Civilisations*, 18:3, May–June 1963, pp. 499–520.
8. Bulliet, *The Camel and the Wheel*, Harvard, Cambridge, Mass., 1975, pp. 141–75.
9. Kohl, *Central Asia*, pp. 241–2.
10. Mary Boyce, *A History of Zoroastrianism*, Vol. I, *The Early Period*, Brill, Leiden, 1975, p. 190; Vol. II, *Under the Achaemenians*, Brill, Leiden, 1982, pp. 1–3.
11. Boyce, Vol. I, p. 22.
12. L. N. Gumilev, *Searches for an Imaginary Kingdom*, Cambridge University Press, Cambridge, 1987. pp. 260–82.
13. Jean Doresse, *The Secret Books of the Egyptian Gnostics*, Hollis & Carter, London, 1960; R. L. Gordon, 'Mithraism and Roman Society: Social factors in the explanation of religious changes in the Roman Empire', *Religion*, Vol. 2, 1972, pp. 92–119; R. Beck, 'Mithraism since Franz Cumont', *Aufstieg und Niedergang der Romischen Welt*, II, 16, 4, Berlin, 1984, pp. 2002–115.
14. Samuel N. C. Lieu, *Manichaeism in the Later Roman Empire and Medieval China, A Historical Survey*, Manchester University Press, Manchester, 1985.
15. R. C. Zaehner, *Zurvan, A Zoroastrian Dilemma*, Clarendon Press, Oxford, 1955; Joseph Needham, *Science and Civilisation in China*, Vol. V, *Chemistry and Chemical Technology*, Part 4, *Spagyrical Discovery and Invention: Apparatus, Theories and Gifts*, Cambridge University Press, Cambridge, 1980, pp. 210–79.
16. Samuel N. C. Lieu, 'Captives, Refugees and Exiles. A Study of Cross-Frontier Civilian Movements and Contacts between Rome and Persia from Valerian to Jovian', Philip Freeman, David Kennedy (eds.), *The Defence of the Roman and Byzantine East*, B. A. R., Oxford, 1986, pp. 475–505.
17. Pierre Briant, *L'Asie Centrale et Les Royaumes Proche-Orientaux du Première Millenaire (c. VIIIᵉ—IVᵉ siècles avant notre ère)*, Editions Recherche sur les Civilisations, Paris, 1984, p. 7.
18. N. G. Gorbunova, *The Culture of Ancient Ferghana*, B. A. R., Oxford, 1986, pp. 22–3.
19. F. L. Holt, *Alexander the Great and Bactria*, Brill, Leiden, 1988; Firdausi, *The Epic of the Kings, Shah Nama*, Reuben Levy (trns.), Routledge and Kegan Paul, London, 1965, pp. 229–50.
20. Amélie Kuhrt, Susan Sherwin-White (eds), *Hellenism in the East*, University of California Press, Berkeley, 1987, pp. 6–7.
21. Donald W. Engels, *Alexander the Great and the Macedonian Army*, University of California Press, Berkely, 1978.

22. Claude Lévi-Strauss, *Tristes Tropiques*, Penguin, Harmondsworth, 1970, pp. 516–19.

23. E. Zurcher, *The Buddhist Conquest of China*, 2 Vols., Brill, Leiden, 1989; Zenryu Tsukamoto, *A History of Early Chinese Buddhism from its introduction to the death of Hui-yuan*. Kodansha, Toyko, 1985.

24. Liu Ming-wood, 'The *P'an-chiao* system of the Hua-yen school in Chinese Buddhism', *T'oung-pao*, Vol. LXVII, 1–2, 1981, pp. 10–47.

25. J. Needham, Lu Guei-djen, *Trans-Pacific Echoes and Resonances, Listening Once Again*, World Scientific, Singapore and Philadelphia, 1985.

26. Edward H. Schafer, *The Golden Peaches of Samarkand*, University of California Press, Berkeley, 1963; Christopher J. Beckwith, *The Tibetan Empire in Central Asia*, Princeton University Press, Princeton, 1987.

27. R. de Rotours, Lin Lu-tche, *Le Règne de L'Empereus Hiuan-Tsong (713–756)*, Institut des Hautes Études Chinoises, Paris, 1981, pp. 331–2, 415–16.

28. Patricia Crone, Martin Hinds, *God's Caliph, Religious Authority in the First Centuries of Islam*, Cambridge University Press, Cambridge, 1986.

29. Beckwith, *The Tibetan Empire in Central Asia*, p. 39.

30. Patricia Crone, *Slaves on Horses. the Evolution of the Islamic Polity*, Cambridge University Press, Cambridge, 1980; Daniel Pipes, *Slave Soldiers in Islam. The Genesis of a Military System*, Yale University Press, New Haven, 1981. Denis Sinor (ed.), *The Cambridge History of Early Inner Asia*, Cambridge University Press, Cambridge, 1990.

31. Omeljan Pritsak, 'The Khazar Kingdom's Conversion to Judaism', *Studies in Medieval Eurasian History*, Variorum, London, 1981, pp. 271–8.

32. Aziz S. Atiya, *A History of Eastern Christianity*, Methuen, London, 1981, pp. 260–2.

33. Jacques Bureau, 'L'Espace Politique Ethiopien', *Annales, Économies, Sociétés, Civilisations*, 40:6, Nov.–Dec. 1985, pp. 1379–93, p. 1393.

34. Marco Polo, *The Travels of Marco Polo*, R. E. Latham (trns.), Penguin, Harmondsworth, 1958, pp. 271–2.

35. Atiya, *A History of Eastern Christianity* pp. 265–6; P. Y. Sacki, *The Nestorian Documents and Relics in China*, Toyko, 1951.

36. Charles Hartman, *Han Yü and the T'ang Search for Unity*, Princeton University Press, Princeton, 1986.

3 The Mongolian Explosion and the Basic Information Circuit, 1200–1300

1. Ruth Wilton Dunnell, *Tanguts and the Tangut State of Ta Hsia*, Princeton, New Jersey, 1985; Herbert Franke, 'The Forest Peoples of Manchuria: Kitans and Jurchen', 1991, Sinor, *The Cambridge History of Early Inner Asia*, pp. 400–23; Tao Jing-shen, *The Jurchen in Twelfth-Century China, A Study in Sinicization*, University of Washington, Seattle, 1976.

2. Paul Kahn, *The Secret History of the Mongols*, North Point, San Francisco, 1984.

3. L. N. Gumilev, *Searches for an Imaginary Kingdom*, Cambridge University Press, Cambridge, 1987, pp. 221–43.

4. Karl A. Wittfogel, Feng Chia-sheng, *History of Chinese Society: Liao*

(907–1125), American Philosophical Society, Philadelphia, 1949, pp. 650–5.

5. Ata-malik Juvaini, *The History of the World Conqueror*, John Andrew Boyle (tr.), 2 Vols., Harvard University Press, Cambridge, Mass., 1958, I, pp. 77–128.
6. Juvaini, Vol. I., pp. 130–78, Vol. II, pp. 896–911.
7. Juvaini, vol. I., p. 131.
8. Viscount Montgomery of Alamein, *A Concise History of Warfare*, Collins, London, 1972, pp. 13, 117–22.
9. Ellsworth Huntington, *Pulse of Asia*, Houghton Mifflin, Boston, 1917; *Mainsprings of Civilisation*, Wiley, New York, 1945.
10. Wittfogel and Feng, General Introduction; Karl A. Wittfogel, *China und die Osteuraisische Kavallerie Revolution*, Harrasowitz, Wiesbaden, 1978; *Oriental Despotism: A Comparative Study of Total Power*, Yale University Press, New Haven, 1957.
11. Wittfogel and Feng, p. 533.
12. Wittfogel and Feng, p. 507.
13. John Masson Smith, 'Ayn Jalut: Mamluk Success or Mongol Failure', *Harvard Journal of Asiatic Studies*, Vol. 44, 1984, pp. 307–45.
14. Juvaini, *The History of the World Conqueror*, Vol. I., p. 162.
15. V. V. Barthold, *Turkestan down to the Mongol Invasion*, Probsthaine, London, 1928.
16. Thomas J. Allson, *Mongolian Imperialism, The Policies of the Grand Qan Mongke in China, Russia and the Islamic Lands, 1251–1259*, University of California Press, Berkeley, 1987.
17. John D. Langlois (ed.), *China under Mongol Rule*, Princeton University Press, Princeton, New Jersey, 1981; Morris Rossabi, *Khubilai Khan. His Life and Times*, University of California, Berkeley, 1988.
18. Marc Gaborieau, 'Les Oulémas/Sufis dans L'Inde Moghol: Anthropologie Historique de Religieux Mussulmans', *Annales, Économies, Sociétés, Civilisations*, 44:5, Sept.–Oct. 1989, pp. 1185–204; Olivier Roy, *Islam and Resistance in Afghanistan*, Cambridge University Press, Cambridge, 1986.
19. John Fennel, *The Crisis of Medieval Russia 1200–1304*, Longman, London, 1983; Charles J. Halpern, *Russia and the Golden Horde. The Mongol Impact on Medieval Russian History*, Indiana University Press, Bloomington, 1985.
20. Uli Schamioglu, *Tribal Politics and Social Organization in the Golden Horde*, Columbia University, Ph.D. thesis, 1986.
21. John D. Barrow, Frank J. Tipler, *The Anthropic Cosmological Principle*, Oxford University Press, Oxford, 1988; J. L. Simon, *The Ultimate Resource*, Princeton University Press, Princeton, 1981; Rupert Sheldrake, *A New Science of Life*, Paladin, London, 1983.
22. L. Olschki, *Marco Polo's Asia*, University of California Press, Berkeley, 1962.
23. Sir Henry Yule, *Cathay and the Way Thither*, 4 Vols., Hakluyt Society, second series, n. XXXVIII, London, 1915, Vol. II; I. de Rachelwiltz, *Papal Envoys to the Great Khans*, Faber and Faber, London, 1971; Jean Richard, *La Papauté et les Missons d'Orient au Moyen Age (XIIIe-XVe siècles)*, École Française de Rome, Rome, 1977.

24. Allan Evans (ed.), *Francesco Balducci Pegolotti, La Practica della Mercatura*, Medieval Academy of America, Cambridge, Mass., 1936.
25. F. Hirth, W. W. Rockhill (tr.), *Chao Ju-kua. His Work on the Chinese and Arab Trade in the twelfth and thirteenth centuries entitled 'Chu-Fan Chih'*, Imperial Academy of Sciences, St. Petersburg, 1911.
26. J. V. G. Mills (tr. & ed.), *Ma Huan, Ying-yai sheng-lan. The Overall Survey of the Ocean's Shores*, Hakluyt Society, Cambridge, 1970.
27. Morris Rossabi, 'A Translation of Ch'en Ch'engs *Hsi-yü fan-kuo chih*' *Ming Studies*, Fall 1983, pp. 49–59.
28. John Andrew Boyle (tr.), *The Sucessors of Genghis Khan, Rashid al-Din Tabib*, Columbia University Press, New York, 1971.

4 The Chaghatai Khanate and the Microbian Common Market, 1300–1370

1. Andrew D. W. Forbes, *Warlords and Muslims in Chinese Central Asia*, Cambridge University Press, Cambridge, 1986.
2. Emmanuel Le Roy Ladurie, 'L'historie immobile', *Annales, Économies, Sociétés, Civilisations*, 29:3, May–June 1974, pp. 673–92, p. 681.
3. Pierre Darmon, *La Longue Traque de la Variole*, Perrin, Paris, 1986.
4. Juvaini, *The History of the World Conqueror*, John Andrew Boyle (tr.), 2 Vols., Harvard University Press, Cambridge, Mass., 1958, I., p. 271.
5. Herbert Franz Schurmann, *Economic Structure of the Yüan Dynasty*, Harvard University Press, Cambridge, Mass., 1956, p. 63; Ch'i-ch'ing Hsiao, *The Military Establishment of the Yüan Dynasty*, Harvard University Press, Cambridge, Mass., 1978.
6. Juvaini, I., p. 114.
7. Juvaini, I., p. 272.
8. Juvaini, I., p. 273.
9. Morris Rossabi (ed.), *China Among Equals, The Middle Kingdom and its Neighbours, 10th–14th Centuries*, University of California Press, Berkeley, 1983.
10. Hsiao, *The Military Establishment of the Yüan Dynasty*, pp. 45–50, 224–7.
11. Marco Polo, *The Travels of Marco Polo*, R. E. Latham (tr.), Penguin, Harmondsworth, 1958, pp. 3, 50.
12. Ibid., p. 50.
13. J. A. Boyle (ed.), *The Cambridge History of Iran*, Vol. 5, *The Saljuq and Mongol Periods*, Cambridge University Press, Cambridge, 1968, pp. 374–6.
14. John W. Dardess, *Conquerors and Confucians. Aspects of Political Change in Late Yüan China*, Columbia University Press, New York, 1973.
15. Joseph Needham, *Science and Civilisation in China*, Vol. 4, Part III, Cambridge University Press, Cambridge, 1971, Plate CDXII and text, following p. 656.
16. Michel Balard, *La Romanie Génoise (XIIᵉ– Debut du XVᵉ siècles)*, 2 Vols., École Française de Rome, Rome, 1978.
17. G. A. Fyodorov-Davydov, *The Culture of the Golden Horde Cities*, B. A. R. International Series 198, Oxford, 1984.
18. Mirko D. Grmek, *Les Maladies de l'Aube de la Civilisation Occidentale*, Payot, Paris, 1983; J. Ruffié, J. C. Sournia, *Les Epidemics dans L'Histoire de*

L'Homme, Flammarion, Paris, 1984.

19.   Asa C. Chandler, Clark P. Read, *Introduction to Parasitology*, Waley, New York, 1961.

20.   Darmon, *La Longue Traque de la Variole*, p. 12.

21.   C. Carrière, M. Courdurié, F. Rebuffat, *Marseille Ville Mort, La Peste de 1720*, Garcon, Marseille, 1968; Wu Lien-teh, *Plague Fighter. The Autobiography of a Modern Chinese Physician*, Heffers, Cambridge, 1959.

22.   Jean-Noël Biraben, *Les Hommes et La Peste en France et dans les pays européens et méditerranéens*, 2 Vols., Mouton, Paris, 1975–6; Michael W. Dols, *The Black Death in the Middle East*, Princeton University Press, Princeton, New Jersey, 1977; Daniel Panzac, *La Peste dans L'Empire Ottoman 1700–1850*, Peeters, Louvain, 1985.

23.   Graham Twigg, *The Black Death, A Biological Reappraisal*, Batsford, London, 1984; Mary Kilbourne Matossian, *Poisons of the Past. Moulds, Epidemics and History*, Yale University Press, New Haven, 1989.

24.   A. Colborne Baber, *Travels and Researches in Western China*, Murray, London, 1882, pp. 178–9.

25.   Helen Dunstan, 'The Late Ming Epidemics, A Preliminary Survey', *Ch'ing-shih wen-t'i*, Vol. 3, no. 3, November 1975, pp. 1–59.

26.   Ann Bowman Janetta, *Epidemics and Mortality in Early Modern Japan*, Princeton University Press, Princeton, New Jersey, 1987.

27.   Samuel Pepys, *The Diary of Samuel Pepys*, Henry P. Wheatley (ed.), Bell, London, 1920, Vol. VII, p. 124.

28.   B. F. Musallam, *Sex and Society in Islam*, Cambridge University Press, Cambridge, 1983.

29.   Jean Delumeau, *Le Péché et La Peur. La Culpabilization en Occident XIIIe – XVIIIe siècles*, Fayard, Paris, 1983.

30.   M. L. Aimé Martin (ed.), *Lettres Edifiantes et Curieuses*, Paris, 1853, Vol. III, pp. 535–7.

5   Tamerlane and the Global Arsenal, 1370–1405

1.   Walter J. Fischel, *Ibn Khaldun and Tamerlane*, University of California Press, Berkeley, 1952, p. 47.

2.   Uli Schamioglu, *Tribal Politics and Social Organization in the Golden Horde*, Columbia University, Ph.D thesis, 1986, pp. 41–5, 91.

3.   Beatrice Forbes Manz, *The Rise and Rule of Tamerlane*, Cambridge University Press, Cambridge, 1989.

4.   Ernst J. Grube, Eleanor Sims (eds), *Between China and Iran, Colloquies on Art and Archaeology in Asia No. 10*, University of London, London 1980, pp. 51–3.

5.   Francois-Bernard Chamoy, *Expedition de Timour-i-lenk (Tamerlane) contre Toqtamiche en 1391 de J. C.*, St. Petersburg 1834–5, Philo Press Reprint, Amsterdam, 1975.

6.   M. M. Alexandrescu-Dersca, *La Campagne de Timur en Anatolie (1402)*, Bucharest 1942, Variorum Reprints, London, 1977; J. Buchan Telfer (ed.), *The Bondage and Travels of Johann Schiltberger*, Hakluyt Society, First Series 58, Burt Franklin, New York, 1970.

7. Guy Le Strange, *Clavijo, Embassy to Tamerlane 1403–1406*, Routledge, London, 1928, p. 287.

8. Richard William Jelf (ed.), *The Works of John Jewel, D. D., Bishop of Salisbury*, Vol. VIII, Oxford University Press, Oxford, 1848, pp. 288–321.

9. Giovanni Botero, *The Reason of State* and *The Greatness of Cities*, Routledge and Kegan Paul, London, 1956, pp. 210, 263.

10. Radek Sikorski, *Dust of the Saints*, Chatto and Windus, London, 1989, p. 167.

11. Le Strange, op. cit. pp. 269, 360.

12. John Ure, *The Trail of Tamerlane*, Constable, London, 1980.

13. Le Strange, op. cit. pp. 7, 43, 362.

14. Peter Jackson and Laurence Lockhart, *The Cambridge History of Iran*, Vol. 6, *The Timurid and Safarid Periods*, Cambridge University Press, Cambridge, 1986, pp. 72–80.

15. Atiya, *A History of Eastern Christianity*, Methuen, London, 1981, pp. 210, 276.

16. Le Strange, op. cit. p. 130.

17. Daniel Pipes, *Slave Soldiers and Islam, The Genesis of a Military System*, Yale University Press, New Haven, 1981.

18. Miklos Jankovich, *They Rode into Europe*, Harrap, London, 1971.

19. Joseph Needham, *Science and Civilisation in China*, Vol. 5, *Chemistry and Chemical Technology*, Part 7, *Military Technology: The Gunpowder Epic*, Cambridge University Press, Cambridge, 1986.

20. Ibid., pp. 580–1.

21. Iqtidar Alam Khan, *Coming of Gunpowder and the Response of Indian Polity*, Centre for Studies in Social Science, Calcutta, 1981.

22. Le Strange, op. cit. p. 288.

23. Fernand Braudel, *La Méditerranée et Le Monde Méditerranéen à l'époque de Philippe II*, Armand Colin, Paris, 1949, p. 1100.

24. J. V. G. Mills (ed.), *Ma Huan, Ying-yai Sheng-lan, The Overall Survey of the Ocean's Shores*, Hakluyt Society, Cambridge, 1970, pp. 173–8.

25. Joanot Martorell, Marti Joan de Galba, *Tirant Lo Blanc*, Warner Books Edition, New York, 1984, p. 7.

26. Fischel, *Ibn Khaldun and Tamerlane* p. 35.

27. Le Strange, op. cit. pp. 291–2.

28. Le Strange, op. cit. p. 152.

6 The Timurids and the Republic of Letters

1. Beatrice Forbes Manz, *The Rise and Rule of Tamerlane*, Cambridge University Press, Cambridge, 1989, p. 129.

2. Guy Le Strange, *Clavijo, Embassy to Tamerlane 1403–1406*, Routledge, London, 1928, pp. 221, 280, 282.

3. Ibid., pp. 220, 254.

4. Ibid., pp. 201, 356.

5. Joseph Fletcher, 'China and Central Asia', John K. Fairbank (ed.), *The Chinese World Order*, Harvard University Press, Cambridge, Mass., 1968, pp. 206–24, 337–68.

6. A. S. Beveridge, *The Babur-Nama in English*, 2 Vols., Luzac, London, 1922, I, pp. 258, 283, 300.
7. Le Strange, op. cit., p. 268.
8. Thomas W. Lentz and Glenn D. Lowry, *Timur and the Princely Vision, Persian Art and Culture in the Fifteenth Century*, Los Angeles County Museum of Art, Los Angeles, 1989, p. 9.
9. Ibid., p. 14.
10. Ibid., p. 14.
11. Ibid., p. 90.
12. Sikorski, pp. 190–223.
13. Lisa Golombek and Donald Wilbur, *The Timurid Architecture of Iran and Turan*, 2 Vols., Princeton University Press, Princeton, 1988.
14. Lentz and Lowry, op. cit. p. 114.
15. Godfrey Goodwin, *A History of Ottoman Architecture*, Thames and Hudson, London, 1971, p. 137.
16. John Ure, *The Trail of Tamerlane*, Constable, London, 1980, p. 163.
17. N. Elias and E. Denison Ross, *A History of the Moghuls of Central Asia,*. London, 1895.
18. Mildred Cable with Francesca French, *The Gobi Desert*, Hodder and Stoughton, London, 1946, pp. 132–45.
19. Renée Simon (ed.), *Le P. Antoine Gaubil, Correspondence de Pékin*, Droz, Geneva, 1970.
20. Benjamin A. Elman, *From Philosophy to Philology, Intellectual and Social Aspects of Change in Late Imperial China*, Harvard University Press, Cambridge, Mass., 1984.
21. Jean Delumeau, *La Peur en Occident (XIVe –XVIIIe siècle)*, Fayard, Paris, 1979; *Le Péché et la Peur, Rassurer et Protéger. Le sentiment de sécurité dans l'Occident d'autrefois*, Fayard, Paris, 1989.
22. Joseph Needham, *Science and Civilisation in China*, Vol. III, *Mathematics and the Sciences of the Heavens and of the Earth.* Cambridge University Press, Cambridge, 1959, pp. 49–50.
23. Ibid., p. 300 and figs. 120–2.
24. Alexandre Bennigsen *et al.*, *Le Khanat de Crimée dans les Archives du Musée du Palais de Topkapi*, Mouton, Paris, 1978.
25. Denis Sinor, *Inner Asia. A Syllabus*, Indiana University Press, Bloomington, Indiana, 1969, pp. 183–4.
26. Stanford J. Shaw, *Between Old and New. The Ottoman Empire under Sultan Selim III 1789–1807*, Harvard University Press, Cambridge, Mass., 1971; *History of the Ottoman Empire and Modern Turkey*, Vol. I, *Empire of the Gazis: The Rise and Decline of the Ottoman Empire, 1280–1808*, Cambridge University Press, Cambridge, 1976.
27. John Prebble, *The King's Jaunt, George IV in Scotland in 1822*, Fontana-Collins, London, 1989.

7 Uzbeks, Zunghars and the Religious Internationals

1. Jean-Louis Bacqué-Grammont, 'Une Liste Ottomane de Princes et d'Apanages Abul-Khayrides', *Cahiers du Monde Russe et Soviétique*, Vol. XI, July–September 1970, pp. 423–53; Vincent Fourniau, 'Irrigation et

nomadisme en Asie Centrale: La politique d'implantations des Ousbeqs au XVIᵉ siècle', *Central Asian Survey*, Vol. 4,. no. 2, 1985, pp. 1–39.

2. Hamid Algar, 'The Naqshbandi Order: A Preliminary Survey of its History and Significance', *Studia Islamica*, 44, 1975–76, pp. 123–32.

3. Delumeau, *Rassurer et Protégér*, Fayard, Paris, 1989, pp. 242–60.

4. Altan Gokalp, 'Une Minorité Chiite en Anatolic: Les Alevi', *Annales, Économies, Sociétés, Civilisations*, 35, 3–4, May–August 1980, pp. 748–63.

5. Pierre Julien, 'In Quest of the Holiest Place in Central Asia', *Central Asian Survey*, Vol. 4, no. 1, 1985, pp. 115–19.

6. M. Courant, *L'Asie Centrale aux XVIIᵉ et XVIIIᵉ siécles: Empire kalmouck au L'Empire mandehu*, Lyon, 1912.

7. C. R. Bawden, *Shamans, Lamas and Evangelicals*, Routledge and Kegan Paul, London, 1985, p. 43.

8. Anne Chayet, *Les Temples de Jehol et Leurs Modèles Tibétains*, Editions Recherche sur les Civilisations, Paris, 1985, pp. 35–6, 78, 123–5.

9. Alexandre Bennigsen and Marie Broxup, *The Islamic Threat to the Soviet State*, Croom Helm, London, 1983, pp. 15, 55–60.

10. Mark Mancall, *Russia and China: Their Diplomatic Relations to 1728*, Harvard University Press, Cambridge, Mass., 1971.

11. Jacques Legrand, *L'Administration dans La Domination Sino-Manchue en Mongolie Qalqa*, College de France, Paris, 1976.

12. M. E. Alonso (ed.), *China's Inner Asian Frontier*, Historical Text by Joseph Fletcher, Peabody Museum, Cambridge, Mass., 1979.

13. Alex Wayman, *Calming the Mind and Discerning the Real, Buddhist Meditation and the Middle View*, Columbia University Press, New York, 1978.

14. A. Popovic and G. Veinstein (eds), *Les Ordres Mystiques dans L'Islam*, École des Hautes Etudes en Sciences Sociales, Paris, 1986.

15. Marc Gaborieau, 1989, pp. 1185–204.

16. S. A. A. Rizui, *Rawshaniyya Movement*, Abu Nahrein, Leiden, 1967–68.

17. Hamid Algar, op. cit. p. 140.

18. John Robert Barnes, *An Introduction to Religious Foundations in the Ottoman Empire*, Brill, Leiden, 1987, pp. 42–3.

19. Popovic and Veinstein, op. cit. pp. 54–6; Barnes, p. 53.

20. Mahmud Tahir, 'Abunnasir Kursavi, 1776–1812,'· *Central Asian Survey*, Vol. 8, no. 2, 1989, pp. 155–8.

21. Popovic and Veintstein, op. cit., p. 78.

22. Michael Khodarkovsky, 'Uneasy Alliance: Peter the Great and Ayuki Khan', *Central Asian Survey*, Vol. 7, no. 4, 1988, pp. 1–45.

23. Forbes, *Warlords and Muslims in Chinese Central Asia*, Cambridge University Press, Cambridge, 1986, pp. 60–1, 70–3, 252.

24. Sechen Jagchid, 'The Rise and Fall of Buddhism in Inner Mongolia,' A. K. Narain (ed.), *Studies in the History of Buddhism*, B. R. Publishing Corporation, Delhi, pp. 93–109.

25. Chayet, *Les Temples de Jehol et Leurs Modèles Tibétains*, pp. 97, 117.

26. Dominique Bertrand, S. J., *La Politique de S. Ignacc de Loyola*, Cerf, Paris, 1985.

27. Ibid., p. 373.

28. Cornelius Wessels, *The Early Jesuit Travellers in Central Asia 1603–1721*, Nijhoff, The Hague, 1924.

29. C. R. Bawden, *Shamans*, pp. 235–6.

30.   Dom Bede Griffiths, *Return to the Centre*, Collins, London, 1976.
31.   Michael Cooper, S. J., *Rodrigues the Interpreter. An Early Jesuit in Japan and China*, Weatherhill, New York, 1974, p. 325.
32.   Father Joseph de Acosta, *The Natural Moral History of the Indies*, London, 1606, p. 532.
33.   Paul Dumont, 'Disciples of the Light – The Nurju Movement in Turkey', *Central Asian Survey*, Vol. 5, no. 2, 1986, pp. 33–60.

8   The World Market and Early Modern Central Asia

1.   Arminius Vambéry, *Travels and Adventures in Central Asia*, Allen, London, 1864, pp. 214–15; Ludwig W. Adamec, *Historial and Political Gazetteer of Afghanistan*, Vol. 3, *Herat and Northwestern Afghanistan* (Graz: Akademische Druck-u Verlagsanstalt, 1976), p. 174.
2.   C. A. Bayly, *Imperial Meridian. The British Empire and the World 1780–1830*, Longman, London and New York, 1989.
3.   Pierre Chaunu, *Séville et L'Atlantique (1506–1650)*, Partie Interprétative, Tome VIII, one, *Structures*, S.E.V.P.E.N., Paris, 1959; *Les Philippines et Le Pacifiques des Ibériques (XVIe, XVIIe, XVIIIe siècles)*, S.E.V.P.E.N., Paris, 1960.
4.   Pierre Chaunu, *Au cœur religieux de L'Histoire*, Perrin, Paris, 1986.
5.   Timothy Green, *The World of Diamonds*, Weidenfeld and Nicholson, London, 1981; Redcliffe N. Salaman, *The History and Social Influence of the Potato*, Cambridge University Press, Cambridge, 1949.
6.   Lillian M. Li, *China's Silk Trade, Traditional Industry in the Modern World 1842–1937*, Council on East Asian Studies, Harvard University, Cambridge, Mass., 1981.
7.   Richard Gascon, *Grand Commerce et Vie Urbaine au XVIe siècle, Lyon et ses marchands (environ de 1520 – environ de 1580)*, Mouton, Paris, 1971.
8.   Fernand Braudel, *Civilisation Matérielle, Économie et Capitalisme*, Vol. III, *Le Temps du Monde*, Armand Colin, 1979, pp. 118–44.
9.   Ursula Ewald, *The Mexican Salt Industry 1560–1980. A Study in Change*, Gustav Fischer, Stuttgart, 1985, pp. 12–13, 223–4.
10.   Jean Delumeau, *Vie Économique et Sociale de Rome dans la seconde moitié du XVIe siècle*, 2 Vols., Bocard, Paris, 1959, pp. 783–824.
11.   Chaunu, *Les Philippines*, pp. 126–7, 269.
12.   Lien-Sheng Yang, *Money and Credit in China, A Short History*, Harvard University Press, Cambridge, Mass., 1952, p. 48.
13.   E. Le Roy Ladurie (etc.), 'Sur Les Traces de l'argent du Potosi', *Annales, Économics, Sociétiés, Civilisations*, 45:2, March–April 1990, pp. 483–505.
14.   Frédéric Mauro, *Le Portugal et L'Atlantique au XVIIe siècle (1570–1670)*, S.E.V.P.E.N., Paris, 1960; Anthony Reid, *Southeast Asia in the Age of Commerce 1450–1680*, Vol. I, *The Lands below the Wind*, Yale University Press, New Haven, 1988.
15.   Calvin Wells, *Bones, Bodies and Disease*, Thames and Hudson, London, 1964, pp. 121–8.
16.   Louis Dermigny, *La Chine et L'Occident: Le Commerce à Canton au XVIIIe siècle 1719–1833*, 3 Vols., S.E.V.P.E.N., Paris, 1964, pp. 111–12, 427–8.
17.   Delumeau, *Réassurer et Protéger*, pp. 523–39.

18. Daniel Dessert, *Argent, Pouvoir et Société au Grand Siècle*, Fayard, Paris, 1984, pp. 390–2.

19. Roger Penrose, *The Emperor's New Mind: Concerning Computers, Minds and the Laws of Physics*, Vintage, London, 1990.

20. Immanuel Wallerstein, *The Modern World-System, Capitalist Agriculture and the Origins of the European World-Economy in the Sixteenth Century*, Academic Press, New York, 1974; Ilkoy Sunar, 'Anthropologie Politique et Économique: L'Empire Ottoman et sa Transformation', *Annales, Économies, Sociétés, Civilisations*, 35:3–4, May–August 1980, pp. 551–79; Huri Islamoglu-Inan (ed.), *The Ottoman Empire and the World Economy*, Cambridge University Press, Cambridge, 1987.

21. Daniel Panzac, *La Peste dans L'Empire Ottoman 1700–1850*, Peeters, Louvain, 1985.

22. Yen-p'ing Hao, *The Commercial Revolution in Nineteenth Century China*, University of California Press, Berkeley, 1986.

23. Antoine Ignace Anthoine, baron de Saint Joseph, *Essai Historique sur Le Commerce et La Navigation de la Mer Noire*, Agasse, Paris, 1805.

24. Roberta Allbert Dayer, *Finance and Empire: Sir Charles Addis 1861–1945*, Macmillan, London, 1988.

25. Pan Ling, *Old Shanghai, Gangsters in Paradise*, Heinemann, Hong Kong, 1984.

26. William T. Rowe, *Hankow. Commerce and Society in a Chinese City, 1796–1889*, Stanford University Press, Stanford, 1984; Gail Hershatter, *The Workers of Tianjin, 1900–1949*, Stanford University Press, Stanford, 1986.

27. Robert Delort, *Le Commerce des Fourrures; Les Animaux ont une Histoire*, Editions du Seuil, Paris, 1984.

28. A. Bennigsen and Chantal Lemereier-Quelquejay, 'Les marchands de la Cour attotmane et le commerce des fourrures moscovites dans la seconde moitié du XVIᵉ siècle', *Cahiers du Monde Russe et Soviétique*, Vol. XI, July–Steptember 1970, pp. 363–90; Chantal Lermereier-Quelquejay, 'Les Routes Commerciales et Militaires au Caucasus du Nord aux XVIᵉ et XVIIᵉ siècles', *Central Asian Survey*, Vol. 4, no. 3, 1985, pp. 1–19.

29. Mark Mancall, 'The Kiakhta Trade', C. D. Cowan (ed.), *The Economic Development of China and Japan*, Allen and Unwin, London, 1964, pp. 19–48.

30. Georges Florovsky, *Ways of Russian Theology*, part one, Belmont, Mass., 1990.

31. Alexander Burnes, *Travels in Bokhara*, 3 Vols., London, 1836, Vol. I, pp. 309–10.

32. Saguchi Toro, *The Eastern Trade of the Khoqand Khanate*, Toyo Bunko, Tokyo, 1965.

33. Guy Le Strange, *Clavijo, Embassy to Tamerlane 1403–1406*, Routledge, London, 1928, p. 278.

34. John K. Fairbank and Ssu-yu Teng, *Ch'ing Administration. Three Studies*, Harvard University Press, Cambridge, Mass., 1968, pp. 107–206, esp. 155–7.

35. Burnes, *Travels in Bokhara*, Vol. I, p. 277; M. Sanjdorj, *Manchu Chinese Colonial Rule in Northern Mongolia*, St. Martin's Press, New York, 1980, pp. 88–9.

36. Burnes, *Travels in Bokhara*, Vol. II, pp. 453–4.

37.   B. F. Musallam, Eve Levin, *Sex and Society in the World of the Orthodox Slavs*, Cornell University Press, Ithaca, 1989.

9   The Higher Polytechnic and Modern Central Asia

1.   Colin Renfrew, *The Emergence of Civilisation, The Cyclades and the Aegean in the Third Millenium B.C.*, Methuen, London, 1972, pp. 22–3; *Towards an Archaeology of Mind*, Cambridge University Press, Cambridge, 1982.

2.   J. C. D. Clarke, *English Society 1688–1832*, Cambridge University Press, Cambridge, 1985, pp. 64–93.

3.   Kenneth Warren, *Chemical Foundations: The Alkali Industry in Britain to 1926*, Clarendon Press, Oxford, 1980.

4.   J. P. Bardet, etc., *Le Bâtiment, Enquéte d'historie économique 14ᵉ – 19ᵉ siècles*, Mouton, Paris, 1971, especially introductory essay by Pierre Chaunu.

5.   Robert Tichane, *Ching-te-chen*, New York State Institute for Glaze Research, New York, 1983.

6.   Pierre Darmon, *La Longue Traque de la Variole*, Perrin, Paris, 1986, pp. 175–98.

7.   Etienne Juillard, *L'Europe Rhénane*, Armand Colin, Paris, 1968; Joel Mokr, *Industrialization in the Low Countries 1795–1850*, Yale University Press, New Haven, 1976; Alain Dewerpe, *L'Industrie aux Champs*, École Française de Rome, Rome 1985.

8.   Kim Ho-dong, *The Muslim Rebellion and the Kashgar Emirate in Chinese Central Asia, 1864–1877*, U. M. I., Harvard, 1988.

9.   Masami Hamada, 'La Transmission du Movement Nationaliste au Turkestan oriental (Xinjiang)', *Central Asian Survey*, Vol. 9, no. 1, 1990, pp. 29–48.

10.   Lo Hui-min (ed.), *The Correspondence of G. E. Morrison*, Vol. II, 1912–1920, Cambridge University Press, Cambridge, 1978, pp. 468, 470, 545–6.

11.   Andrew Forbes, *Warlords and Muslims in Chinese Central Asia*, Cambridge University Press, Cambridge, 1986, p. 242.

12.   Remy Dor, 'Return to Karagunduz, with the Kirghiz in Turkey', *Central Asian Survey*, Vol. 6, no. 3, 1987, pp. 61–72.

13.   Special Report of the Ottoman Public Debt, Year 26, 1907–1908, pp. 91–2.

14.   Special Report of the Ottoman Public Debt, Year 24, 1905–1906, pp. 25–6.

15.   Lady Gwendolen Cecil, *Life of Robert Marquis of Salisbury*, Vol. II, 1868–1880, Hodder and Stoughton, London, 1921, pp. 374–8; David Gillard, *The Struggle for Asia 1828–1914*, Methuen, London, 1977, pp. 154–7.

16.   The Hon. George N. Curzon, M. P., *Russia in Central Asia*, Longmans, London, 1889, p. 380.

17.   Kwang-Ching Liu, *Anglo-American Steamship Rivalry in China 1862–1874*, Harvard University Press, Cambridge, Mass., 1962.

18.   Ralph William Huenemann, *The Dragon and the Iron Horse. The Economics of Railroads in China 1876–1937*, The Council on East Asian Studies, Harvard University, Cambridge, Mass., 1984.

19. Arthur N. Young, *China's Nation-Building Effort 1927–1937: The Financial and Economic Record*, Hoover, Stanford, 1971; O. J. Todd, *Two Decades in China*, Ch'eng Wen, Taipei, 1971; *First Five-Year Plan for Development of the National Economy of the People's Republic of China in 1953–57*, Foreign Language Press, Peking, 1956.

20. G. Kurgan-Van Hentenryk, *Léopold II et les groupes financiers belges en China*, Palais des Académies, Brussels, 1971, pp. 187–8.

21. *Ta Ch'ing Shih-lu*, Taipei, 1965, Kuang-hsü, Vol. 8, ch. 572: 22, p. 5245.

22. *First Five-Year Plan*, p. 145.

23. Peter Levi, *The Light Garden of the Angel King*, Collins, London 1972, pp. 148–9; Richard S. Newell, 'the Government of Muhammed Moussa Shafiq: The Last Chapter of Afghan Liberalism', *Central Asian Survey*, Vol. I, no. 1, 1982, pp. 53–64.

24. M. Siddieq Noorzay, 'Soviet Economic Interests in Afghanistan', *Problems of Communism*, May–June 1987, pp. 43–54.

25. Olivier Roy, *Islam and Resistance in Afghanistan*, Cambridge University Press, Cambridge, 1986, pp. 182–90.

26. Yuan Qing-li, 'Population Changes in the Xinjiang Uighur Auto-nomous Region (1949–1984)', *Central Asian Survey*, Vol. 9, no. 1, 1990, pp. 49–73.

27. Allen S. Whiting and General Sheng Shih-ts'ai, *Sinkiang: Pawn or Pivot*, Michigan State University Press, East Lansing, Michigan, 1958.

28. Donald H. McMillan, *Chinese Communist Power and Policy in Xinjiang, 1949–1977*, Westview, Boulder, 1979.

29. Nick Danziger, *Danziger's Travels: Beyond Forbidden Frontiers*, Grafton, London, 1987, p. 272.

30. Martha Brill Olcott, *The Kazakhs*, Hoover Institution Press, Stanford, California, 1987; 'Pereystroyka in Kazakhstan', *Problems of Communism*, July–August 1990, pp. 65–77.

31. Boris Z. Rumer, *Soviet Central Asia: 'A Tragic Experiment'*, Unwin Hyman, Boston, 1989; Patricia M. Carley, 'The Price of the Plan, Perception of Cotton and Health in Uzbekistan and Turkmenistan,' *Central Asian Survey*, Vol. 8, no. 4, 1987, pp. 1–38.

10 The Common Consensus and Contemporary Central Asia

1. This is one of the major theories of Wallerstein, *The Modern World System*, Academic Press, New York, 1974.

2. Chow Tse-tsung, *The May Fourth Movement: Intellectual Revolution in Modern China*, Harvard University Press, Cambridge, Mass., 1960.

3. Katherine H. Tachau, *Vision and Certitude in the Age of Occam: Optics, Epistemology and the Foundations of Semantics 1250–1340*, E. J. Brill, Leiden, 1988.

4. Bernard J. F. Lonergan, *Method in Theology*, Darton, Longman and Todd, London, 1972.

5. Roger Penrose, *The Emperor's New Mind*, Vintage, London, 1990, pp. 123–8, 552–7.

6. Bernard J. F. Lonergan, S. J., *Insight, A Study of Human Understanding*, Philosophical Library, New York, 1970, p. XXII.

7. R. F. Harrod, *The Life of John Maynard Keynes*, Macmillan, London, 1951, pp. 193–4.

8. Claude Rivière, *Les Liturgies Politiques*, P. U. F., Paris, 1988.

9. Norman Stone, *Europe Transformed 1878–1919*, Fontana, London, 1983, p. 315.

10. Mary Brown Bullock, *An American Transplant, The Rockefeller Foundation and Peking Union Medical College*, University of California Press, Berkeley, 1980.

11. Steven I. Levine, *Anvil of Victory. The Communist Revolution in Manchuria*, 1945–1948, Columbia Unversity Press, New York, 1987.

12. Raphael Israeli, *Muslims in China, A Study in Cultural Confrontation*, Curzon Press, London, 1980.

13. Paul Dumont, 'Disciples of the light – The Nurju Movements in Turkey', *Central Asian Survey*, Vol. 5, no. 2, 1986, pp. 33–60.

14. Azada-Aysc Rorlich, *The Volga Tatars. A Profile in National Resilience*, Hoover, Stanford, California, 1986.

15. Mahmud Tahir, 'Abunasir Kursavi 1776–1812', *Central Asian Survey*, Vol. 8, no. 2, 1989, pp. 154–8.

16. Olivier Roy, 'The Origins of the Islamist Movement in Afghanistan', *Central Asian Survey*, Vol. 3, no. 2, 1984, pp. 117–27.

17. Masami Hamada, 'La Transmission du Mouvement Nationaliste ou Turkestan oriental (Xinjiang)', *Central Asian Survey*, Vol. 9, no. 1, 1990, pp. 29–48.

18. Andrew Forbes, *Warlords and Muslims in Chinese Central Asia*, Cambridge University Press, Cambridge, 1986, pp. 247–8, 255–8, 298.

19. Forbes, op. cit., p. 235; Masami Hamada, op. cit. p. 43.

20. Christchurch *Star*, February 12 1991.

21. Bernard V. Olivier, 'Korenizatsiia', *Central Asian Survey*, Vol. 9, no. 3, 1990, pp. 77–98.

22. Martha Brill Olcott, '*Pereystroyka* in Kazakhstan', *Problems of Communism*, July–August 1990, pp. 65–77.

23. Alexandre Bennigsen, S. Enders Wimbush, *Muslims of the Soviet Empire*, Indiana University Press, Bloomington, 1986, p. 66.

24. Frederique Diat, 'Olzhas Sulejmenov: *Az I Ja*', *Central Asian Survey*, Vol. 3, no. 1, 1984, pp. 101–26.

25. Bennigsen, Wimbush, op. cit., p. 50.

26. Gregory Gleason, 'Sharaf Rashidov and the Dilemmas of National Leadership', *Central Asian Survey*, Vol. 5, nos. 1–4, 1986, pp. 133–60.

27. Boris Z. Rumer, *Soviet Central Asia: 'A Tragic Experiment'*, Unwin Hyman, Boston, 1989, pp. 151–9.

Bibliography

Acosta, Father Joseph de (1606) *The Natural and Moral History of the Indies* (London).

Adamec, Ludwig W. (ed.) (1975) *Historical and Political Gazetteer of Afghanistan* Vol. 3, *Herat and Northwestern Afghanistan* (Graz: Akademische Druck-u Verlagsanstat).

Aimé Martin, M. L. (ed.) (1853) *Lettres Edifiantes et Curieuses* (Paris).

Alam Khan, Iqtidar (1981) *Coming of Gunpowder and the Response of Indian Polity* (Calcultta: Centre for Studies in Social Science).

Alexandrescu-Dersca, M. M. (1942) *La Campagne de Timur en Anatolie (1402)* (Bucharest).

Algar, Hamid (1976) 'The Naqshbandi Order: A Preliminary Survey of its History and Significance', *Studia Islamica*, 44, pp. 123–32.

Allson, Thomas J. (1987) *Mongolian Imperialism, The Policies of the Grand Qan Mongke in China, Russia and the Islamic Lands 1251–1259* (Berkeley: University of California Press).

Alonso, M. E. (ed.) (1979) *China's Inner Asian Frontier*, Historical Text by Joseph Fletcher (Cambridge, Mass.: Peabody Museum).

Anthoinc, Antoinc Ignace, baron de Saint Joseph (1805) *Essai Historique sur Le Commerce et La Navigation de la Mer Noire* (Paris: Agasse).

Atiya, Aziz S. (1981) *A History of Eastern Christianity* (London: Methuen).

Barber, A. Colborne (1882) *Travels and Researches in Western China* (London: Murray).

Bacon, Elizabeth E. (1966) *Central Asians under Russian Rule* (Ithaca, New York: Cornell University Press).

Bacqué-Grammont (1970) 'Une Liste Ottomane de Princes et d'Apanages Abul-Khayrides', *Cahiers du Monde Russe et Soviétique*, Vol. XI, July–September pp. 423–53.

Balard, Michel (1978) *La Romanie Génoise (XIIᵉ – Debut du XVᵉ siècles)*. 2 Vols., (Rome: École Française de Rome).

Bardet, J. P., etc (1971) *Le Bâtiment, Enquéte d'histoire économique 14ᵉ – 19ᵉ siècles* (Paris: Mouton).

Barnes, John Robert (1987) *An Introduction to Religious Foundations in the Ottoman Empire* (Leiden: Brill).

Barrow, John D. and Frank J. Tipler (1988) *The Anthropic Cosmological Principle* (Oxford: Oxford University Press).

Barthold, V. V. (1928) *Turkestan down to the Mongol Invasion* (London: Probsthaine).

Basham, A. L. (1954) *The Wonder that was India* (New York: Grove).

Bawden, C. R. (1985) *Shamans, Lamas and Evangelicals* (London: Routledge and Kegan Paul).

Bayly, C. A. (1989) *Imperial Meridian. The British Empire and the World 1780–1830* (London and New York: Longman).

Beck, R. (1981), 'Mithraism since Franz Cumont', *Augstieg und Niedergang der Romischen Welt*, II, 16, 4 Berlin, pp. 2002–115.

Beckwith, Christopher J. (1987) *The Tibetan Empire in Central Asia* (Princeton: Princeton University Press).

Bennigsen, A. and Chantal Lemereier-Quelquejay (1970) 'Les marchands de la Cour Ottomane et le commerce des fourrures moscovites dans la seconde moitié du XVIᵉ siècle', *Cahiers du Monde Russe et Soviétique*, Vol. XI, July–September, pp. 363–90.

Bennigsen, A. *et al.* (1978) *Le Khanat de Crimée dans les Achives du Musée du Palais de Topkapi* (Paris: Mouton).

Bennigsen, Alexandre, and Marie Broxup (1983) *The Islamic Threat to the Soviet State* (London: Croom Helm).

Bennigsen, Alexandre and S. Enders Wimbush (1986) *Muslims of the Soviet Empire* (Bloomington: Indiana University Press).

Bensidoun, Sylvain (1979) *Samarcande et la vallée du Zerafshan* (Paris: Anthropos).

Bertrand, Dominique S. J. (1985) *La Politique de S. Ignace de Loyola* (Paris: Cerf).

Beverage, A. S. (1922) *The Babur-Nama in English*, 2 Vols. (London: Luzac).

Biraben, Jean-Noel (1975–6) *Les Hommes et La Peste en Frances et dans les pays européens et mediterranéens*, 2 Vols., (Paris: Mouton).

Botero, Giovanni (1956) *The Reason of State* and *The Greatness of Cities* (London: Routledge and Kegan Paul).

Boyce, Mary (1975) *A History of Zoroastrianism*, Vol. 1, *The Early Period*, (Leiden: Brill).

Boyce, Mary (1982) *A History of Zoroastrianism*, Vol. II, *Under the Achaemenids*, (Leiden: Brill).

Boyle, J. A. (ed.) (1968) *The Cambridge History of Iran*, Vol. 5, *The Saljuq and Mongol Periods*, (Cambridge: Cambridge University Press).

Boyle, John Andrew (tr.) (1971) *The Successors of Genghis Khan, Rashid al-Din Tabib* (New York: Columbia University Press).

Braudel, Fernand (1949) *La Méditerranée et Le Monde Méditerranéen à l'époque de Philippe II* (Paris: Armand Colin).

Braudel, Fernand (1979) *Civilisation Matérielle, Économic et Capitalisms*, Vol. III, *Le Temps du Monde* (Paris: Armand Colin).

Briant, Pierre (1984) *L' Asise Centrale et Les Royaumes Proche-Orientaux du Première Millenaire (e. VIIIᵉ – IVᵉ siècles avant notre ère)* (Paris: Editions Recherche sur les civilisations).

Bulliet, Richard W. (1975) *The Camel and the Wheel* (Cambridge, Mass.: Harvard University Press).

Bullock, Mary Brown (1980) *An American Transplant. The Rockefeller Foundation and the Peking Union Medical College* (Berkeley: University of California Press).

Bureau, Jacques (1985) 'L'Espace Politique Ethiopien', *Annales, Economies, Sociétés, Civilisations*, 40:6; Nov–Dec pp. 1379–93.

Burnes, Alexander (1836) *Travels in Bokhara*, 3 Vols. (London).

Cable, Mildred with Francesca French (1946) *The Gobi Desert* (London: Hodder and Stoughton).

Carley, Patricia M. (1987) 'The Price of the Plan. Perception of Cotton and Health in Uzbekistan and Turkmenistan', *Central Asian Survey*, Vol. 8, no. 4, pp. 1–38.

Carrière, C., M. Courdurié and F. Rebuffat (1968) *Marseille, Ville Mort, La Peste de 1720* (Marseille: Garcon).

Cecil, Lady Gwendolen (1921) *Life of Robert Marquis of Salisbury*, Vol. II 1868–1880 (London: Hodder and Stoughton).

Chamay, Francois-Bernard (1975) *Expedition de Timour-i-lenk (Tamerlane) Contre Toqtamiche en 1391 de J. C.*, St. Petersburg 1834–35, (Amsterdam: Philo Press Reprint).

Chandler, Asa C. and Clark P. Read (1961) *Introduction to Parasitology* (New York: Waley).

Chaunu, Pierre (1959) *Séville et L'Atlantique (1506–1650)*, Partie Interprétive, Tome VIII, one, *Structures* (Paris: S.E.V.P.E.N.).

Chaunu, Pierre (1960) *Les Philippines et Le Pacifiques des Ibériques (XVIe XVIIe XVIIIe siècles)* (Paris: S.E.V.P.E.N.).

Chaunu, Pierre (1986) *Au coeur religieux de L'Histoire* (Paris: Perrin).

Chayet, Anne (1985) *Les Temples de Jehol et Leurs Modèles Tibétains* (Paris: Editions Recherche sur les Civilisations).

Chow Tse-tsung (1960) *The May Fourth Movement: Intellectual Revolution in Modern China* (Cambridge, Mass.: Harvard University Press).

Christchurch *Star*, February 12, 1991.

Clarke, J. C. D., (1985) *English Society 1688–1832* (Cambridge: Cambridge University Press).

Cooper, Michael S. J. (1974) *Rodrigues the Interpreter, An Early Jesuit in Japan and China* (New York: Weatherill).

Courant, M. (1912) *L'Aise Centrale aux XVIIe et XVIIIe siècles: Empire kalmouck ou L'Empire mandchu* (Lyon).

Crone, Patricia (1980) *Slaves on Horses. The Evolution of the Islamic Polity* (Cambridge: Cambridge University Press).

Crone, Patricia and Martin Hinds (1986) *God's Caliph, Religious Authority in the First Centuries of Islam* (Cambridge: Cambridge University Press).

Curzon, The Hon. George N. (1889) *Russia in Central Asia* (London: Longmans).

Danziger, Nick (1987) *Danziger's Travels: Beyond Forbidden Frontiers* (London: Grafton).

Dardess, John W. (1973) *Conquerors and Confucians, Aspects of Political Change in Late Yüan China* (New York: Columbia University Press).

Darmon, Pierre, (1986) *La Longue Traque de la Variole* (Paris: Perrin).

Dayer, Roberta Allbert (1988) *Finance and Empire: Sir Charles Addis 1861–1945* (London: Macmillan).

Delort, Robert (1978) *Le Commerce des Fourrures en Occident à la fin du Moyen Age*, 2 Vols., (Rome: École Française de Rome).

Delort, Robert (1984) *Les Animaux ont une Histoire* (Paris: Editions du Seuil).

Delumeau, Jean (1983) *Vie Économique et Sociale de Rome dans la seconde moitié du XVIe siècles*, 2 Vols. (Paris: Bocard).

Delumeau, Jean (1983) *Le Péché et La Peur. La Culpabilisation en Occident XIIIe – XVIIIe siècles* (Paris: Fayard).

Delumeanu, Jean (1989) *Rassurer et Protéger, Le sentiment de sécurité dans l'Occident d'autrefois* (Paris: Fayard).

Dermigny, Louis (1964) *La Chine et L'Occident: Le Commerce à Canton au XVIIIe siècle 1719–1833*, 3 Vols. (Paris: S.E.V.P.E.N.).

Dessert, Daniel (1986) *Argent, Pouvoir el Société au Grand Siècle* (Paris: Fayard).

Dewerpe, Alain (1985) *L'Industrie aux Champs* (Rome: École Française de Rome).

Diat, Frederique (1984) 'Olzhar Sulejmenov: Az I Ja', *Central Asian Survey*, Vol. 3, no. 1, pp. 101–26.

Dols, Michael W. (1977) *The Black Death in the Middle East* (Princeton NJ: Princeton University Press).

Dor, Remy (1987) 'Return to Karagunduz, with the Kirghiz in Turkey', *Central Asian Survey*, Vol. 6, no. 3, pp. 61–72.

Doresse, Jean (1960) *The Secret Books of the Egyptian Gnostics* (London: Hollis and Carter).

Dumont, Paul (1986) 'Disciples of the Light – The Nurju Movement in Turkey', *Central Asian Survey*, Vol. 5, no. 2, pp. 33–60.

Dunnell, Ruth Wilton (1985) *Tanguts and the Tangut State of Ja Hsia* (Princeton University from, New Jersey).

Dunstan, Helen (1975) 'The Late Ming Epidemics: A Preliminary Survey', *Ch'ing-shih wen-t'i*, Vol. 3, no. 3, November pp. 1–59.

Elias, N. and E. Denison Ross (1895) *A History of the Moghuls of Central Asia* (London).

Elman, Benjamin A. (1984) *From Philosophy to Philology, Intellectual and Social Aspects of Change in Late Imperial China* (Cambridge, Mass.: Harvard University Press).

Engels, Donald W. (1978) *Alexander the Great and the Macedonian Army* (Berkeley: University of California Press).

Evans, Allan (ed.) (1936) *Francesco Balducci Pegolotti, La Practica della Mercatura* (Cambridge, Mass.: Medieval Academy of America).

Ewald, Ursula (1985) *The Mexican Salt Industry 1560–1980. A Study in Change* (Stuttgart: Gustav Fischer).

Fairbank, John K. and Ssu-yu Teng (1960) *Ch'ing Administration, Three Studies* (Cambridge, Mass.: Harvard University Press).

Fennel, John (1983) *The Crisis of Medieval Russia 1200–1304* (London: Longmans).

Firdausi (1965) *The Epic of the Kings, Shah-Nama*, trans. Reuben Levy (London: Routledge and Kegan Paul).

First Five Year Plan for Development of the National Economy of the People's Republic of China in 1953–57 (Peking: Foreign Language Press).

Fischel, Walter J. (1952) *Ibn Khaldun and Tamerlane*, (Berkeley: University of California Press).

Fletcher, Joseph (1968) 'China and Central Asia', John K. Fairbank (ed.), *The Chinese World Order* (Cambridge, Mass.: Harvard University Press).

Fletcher, Joseph (1978) 'Ch'ing Inner Asia c.1880', in John K. Fairbank (ed.), *The Cambridge History of China*, Vol. 10 (Cambridge: Cambridge University Press).

Fletcher, Joseph (1978) 'Blood Tanistry: Authority and Succession in the Ottoman Indian Muslim and Later Chinese Empires', in *The Conference for the Theory of Democracy and Popular Participation* (Bellagio).

Fletcher, Joseph (1986) 'A Bibliography of the Publications of Joseph Fletcher', *Harvard Journal of Asiatic Studies*, Vol. 46, no. 2, June, pp. 7–10.

Florovsky, Georges (1990) *Ways of Russian Theology* (Belmont, Mass.: Part One).

Forbes, Andrew D. W. (1986) *Warlords and Muslims in Chinese Central Asia* (Cambridge: Cambridge University Press).

Fourniau, Vincent (1985) 'Irrigation et nomadisme en Asie Centrale: La politique d'implantations des Ousbegs en XVIᵉ siècle', *Central Asian Survey*, Vol. 4, no. 2, pp. 1–39.

Franks, Herbert, 'The Forest Peoples of Manchuria: Kitans and Jurchen', Denis Sinor (ed.), *The Cambridge History of early Inner Asia* (Cambridge: Cambridge University Press), pp. 400–23.

Fydodorov-Davydov, G. A. (1984) *The Culture of the Golden Horde Cities*, B.A.R. International Series 198 (Oxford: B.A.R.).

Gaborieau, Marc (1989) 'Les Oulémas/Sufis dans L'Inde Moghole: Anthropologic Historique de Religieux Mussulmans', *Annales, Économies, Sociétés, Civilisations*, 44:5, Sept–Oct, pp. 1185–1204.

Gascon, Richard (1971) *Grand Commerce et Vie Urbaine au XVIᵉ siècle, Lyon et ses marchands (environ de 1520 – environ de 1580)* (Paris: Mouton).

Gilard, David (1977) *The Struggle for Asia 1828–1914* (London: Methuen).

Gimburtas, Marija (1988) 'Accounting for a great change', *Times Literary Supplement*, June 24–30, p. 714.

Gleason, Gregory (1986) 'Sharaf Rashidov and the Dilemmas of National Leadership', *Central Asian Survey*, Vol. 5, nos. 3–4, pp. 133–60.

Goblot, Henri (1963) 'Dans L'Ancien Iran, Les Techniques de L'Eau et La Grande Histoire', *Annales, Économies, Sociétés, Civilisations*, 18:3, May–June, pp. 499–520.

Gokalp, Altan (1980) 'Une Minorité chiite en Anatolic: Les Alevis', *Annales, Économics, Sociétés, Civilisations*, 35:3–4, May–August, pp. 748–63.

Golombek, Lisa and Donald Wilbur (1988) *The Timurid Architecture of Iran and Turan*, 2 Vols. (Princeton: Princeton University Press).

Goodwin, Godfrey (1971) *A History of Ottoman Architecture* (London: Thames and Hudson).

Goody, Jack (1987) *The Interface between the Written and the Oral* (Cambridge: Cambridge University Press).

Gorbunova, N. G. (1986) *The Culture of Ancient Ferghana* (Oxford: B.A.R.).

Gordon, R. L. (1972) 'Mithraism and Roman Society: Social factors as the explanation of religious changes in the Roman Empire', *Religion*, Vol. 2, pp. 92–119.

Green, Timothy (1981) *The World of Diamonds* (London: Weidenfeld and Nicolson).

Griffiths, Dom Bede (1976) *Return to the Centre* (London: Collins).

Grmek, Mirko D. (1983) *Les Maladies de L'Aube de la Civilisation Occidentale* (Paris: Payot).

Grube, Ernst J. and Eleanor Sims (eds.) (1980) *Between China and Iran. Colloquies on Art and Archaeology in Asia No. 10* (London: University of London Press).

Gumilev, L. N. (1987) *Searches for an Imaginary Kingdom: The Legend of the Kingdom of Prester John* (Cambridge: Cambridge University Press).

Halpern, Charles J. (1985) *Russia and the Golden Horde. The Mongol Impact on Medieval Russian History* (Bloomington: Indiana University Press).

Hamada, Masami (1990) 'La Transmission du Movement Nationaliste au Thurhestan oriental (Xinjiang)', *Central Asian Survey*, Vol. 9, no. 1, pp. 29–48.

Hao, Yen-p'ing (1986) *The Commercial Revolution in Nineteenth Century China* (Berkeley: University of California Press).

Harrod, R. F. (1951) *The Life of John Maynard Keynes* (London: Macmillan).

Hartman, Charles (1986) *Han Yü and the T'ang Search for Unity* (Princeton: Princeton University Press).

Hershatter, Gail (1986) *The Workers of Tianjin 1990–1949* (Stanford: Stanford University Press).

Hirth, F. and W. W. Rockhill (trs.) (1911) *Chao Ju-kuo. His Work on the Chinese and Arab trade in the twelfth and thirteenth centuries entitled 'Chu-Fan Chih'* (St. Petersburg: Imperial Academy of Sciences).

Holt, F. L. (1988) *Alexander the Great and Bactria* (Leiden: Brill).

Hsiao, Ch'i-ch'ing (1978) *The Military Establishment of the Yüan Dynasty* (Cambridge, Mass.: Harvard University Press).

Huenemann, Ralph William (1984) *The Dragon and the Iron Horse. The Economics of Railroads in China 1876–1937*, The Council on East Asian Studies (Cambridge, Mass.: Harvard University Press).

Huntington, Ellsworth (1917) *Pulse of Asia* (Boston: Houghton Mifflin)

Huntington, Ellsworth (1945) *Mainsprings of Civilisation* (New York: Wiley).

Islamoglu-Inan, Huri (ed.) (1987) *The Ottoman Empire and the World Economy* (Cambridge: Cambridge University Press).

Israeli, Raphael (1980) *Muslims in China. A Study in Cultural Confrontation* (London: Curzon Press).

Jackson, Peter, and Laurence Lockhart (1986) *The Cambridge History of Iran*, Vol. 6, *The Timurid and Safavid Periods* (Cambridge: Cambridge University Press).

Jagchid, Sechin and Paul Hyer (1979) *Mongolia's Culture and Society* (Boulder, Colorado: Westview).

Jagchid, Sechin (1980) 'The Rise and Fall of Buddhism in Inner Mongolia', A. K. Naraln (ed.), *Studies in the History of Buddhism* (Delhi: B.R. Publishing Corporation).

Janetta, Ann Bowman (1987) *Epidemics and Mortality in Early Modern Japan* (Princeton, New Jersey: Princeton University Press).

Jankovich, Miklos (1971) *They Rode into Europe* (London: Harrap).

Jelf, Richard William (ed.) (1848) *The Works of John Jewel, D. D., Bishop of Salisbury*, Vol. VIII (Oxford: Oxford University Press).

Juillard, Ékienne (1968) *L'Europe Rhénance* (Paris: Armand Colin).

Julien, Pierre (1985) 'In Quest of the Holiest Place in Central Asia', *Central Asian Survey*, Vol. 4, no. 1, pp. 115–19.

Juvaini, Ata-malik (1958) *The History of the World Conqueror*, John Andrew Boyle (tr.), 2 Vols. (Cambridge, Mass.: Harvard University Press).

Kahn, Paul (1984) *The Secret History of the Mongols* (San Francisco: North Point).

Keightley, David N. (ed.) (1983) *The Origins of Chinese Civilisation* (Berkeley: University of California Press).

Khodarkovsky, Michael (1988) 'Uneasy Alliance: Peter the Great and Ayuki Khan', *Central Asian Survey*, Vol. 7, no. 4, pp. 1–45.

Kim He-dong (1988) *The Muslim Rebellion and the Kashgar Emirate in Chinese Central Asia. 1866–1877* (Harvard: U. M. I.).

Kohl, Philip L. (1984) *Central Asia: Palaeolithic Beginnings to the Iron Age* (Paris: Éditions Recherche sur les Civilisations).

Kuhrt, Amélie and Susan Sherwin-White (eds.) (1987) *Hellenism in the East* (Berkeley: University of California).

Kurgan-Van Hentenryk, G. (1971) *Léopold II et les groupes financiers belges en Chine* (Brussels: Palais des Académies).

Langlois, John D., (ed.) (1981) *China Under Mongol Rule* (Princeton, New Jersey: Princeton University Press).

Lattimore, Owen (1962) 'La Civilisation, mère de Barberie', *Annales, Économies, Sociétés, Civilisations*, 17:1, Jan–Feb, pp. 95–106.

Legrand, Jacques (1976) *L'Administration dans La Domination Sino-Manchue en Mongolie Qalqa* (Paris: College de France).

Lemercier-Quelquejay, Chantal (1985) 'Les Routes Commerciales et Militaires au Caucasus du Nord aux XVIᵉ et XVIIᵉ siècles', *Central Asian Survey*, Vol. 4, no. 3, pp. 1–19.

Lentz, Thomas W., and Glenn D. Lowry (1989) *Timur and the Princely Vision, Persian Art and Culture in the Fifteenth Century* (Los Angeles: Los Angeles County Museum of Art).

Le Roy Ladurie, Emmanuel (1974) 'L'histoire immobile', *Annales, Économies, Sociétés, Civilisations*, 29:3, May–June, pp. 673–92.

Le Roy Ladurie, Emmanuel etc. (1990) 'Sur Les Traces de l'argent du Potosi', *Annales, Économies, Sociétés, Civilisations*, 45:2, March–April, pp. 483–505.

Le Strange, Guy (1928) *Clavijo, Embassy to Tamerlane 1403–1406* (London: Routledge).

Levi, Peter (1972) *The Light Garden of the Angel King* (London: Collins).

Levin, Eve (1989) *Sex and Society in the World of the Orthodox Slavs* (Ithaca, New York: Cornell University Press).

Levine, Steven I. (1987) *Anvil of Victory. The Communist Revolution in Manchuria, 1945–1948* (New York: Columbia University Press).

Lévi-Strauss, C., (1970) *Tristes Tropiques* (Harmondsworth: Penguin).

Li, Lillian M. (1981) *China's Silk Trade. Traditional Industry in the Modern World 1842–1937* (Cambridge, Mass.: Harvard University Council on East Asian Studies).

Lieu, Samuel N. C. (1985) *Manichaeism in the Later Roman Empire and Medieval China. A Historical Survey* (Manchester: Manchester University Press).

Lieu, Samuel N. C. (1986) 'Captives, Refugees and Exiles, A Study of Cross-Frontier Civilian Movements and Contacts between Rome and Persia from Valerian to Jovian', in Philip Freeman and David Kennedy (eds.), *The Defence of the Roman and Byzantine East* (Oxford: B.A.R.), pp. 475–505.

Liu, Kwang-Ching (1962) *Anglo-American Steamship Rivalry in China 1862–1874* (Cambridge, Mass.: Harvard University Press).

Liu, Ming-wood (1981) 'The P'an-chiao system of the Hua-yen school in Chinese Buddhism', *T'oung-pao*, Vol. LXVII, 1–2, pp. 10–47.

Lo Hui-min (ed.) (1978) *The Correspondence of G. E. Morrison*, Vol. II, 1912–1920 (Cambridge: Cambridge University Press).

Lonergan, Bernard J. F. (1970) *Insight. A Study of Human Understanding* (New York: Philosophical Library).

Lonergan, Bernard J. F. (1972) *Method in Theology* (London: Darton, Longman and Todd).

Mancall, Mark (1971) *Russia and China: Their Diplomatic Relations to 1728* (Cambridge, Mass.: Harvard University Press).

Manz, Beatrice Forbes (1989) *The Rise and Rule of Tamerlane* (Cambridge:

Cambridge University Press).

Martorell, Joanot and Marti Joan de Galba (1984) *Tirant Lo Blanc* (New York: Warner Books Edition).

Matossian, Mary Kibourne (1989) *Poisons of the Past, Moulds, Epidemics, and History* (New Haven: Yale University Press).

Mauro, Frédéric (1960) *Le Portugal et L'Atlantique au XVIIᵉ siècle (1570–1670)* (Paris: S.E.V.P.E.N.).

McMillen, Donald H. (1979) *Chinese Communist Power and Policy in Xinjiang, 1949–1977* (Boulder: Westview).

Mills, J. V. G. (1970) *Ma Huan, Ying-yai sheng-lan. The Overall Survey of the Ocean's Shore* (Cambridge: Hakluyt Society).

Mokr, Joel (1976) *Industrialization in the Low Countries 1795–1850* (New Haven: Yale University Press)

Montgomery of Alamein, Viscount (1972) *A Concise History of Warfare* (London: Collins).

Musallam, B. F. (1983) *Sex and Society in Islam* (Cambridge: Cambridge University Press).

Naby, Eden (1984) 'The Uzbeks in Afghanistan', *Central Asian Survey*, Vol. 3, no. 1, pp. 1–21.

Needham, Joseph (1954) *Science and Civilisation in China* (Cambridge: Cambridge University Press).

Needham, Joseph and Lu Guei-djen (1985) *Trans-Pacific Echoes and Resonances. Listening Once Again* (Singapore and Philadelphia: World Scientific).

Newell, R. S. (1982) 'The Government of Muhammed Moussa Shafiqi. The Last Chapter of Afghan Liberalism', *Central Asian Survey*, Vol. 1, no. 1, pp. 53–64.

Noorzay, M. Siddieq (1987) 'Soviet Economic Interests in Afghanistan', *Problems of Communism*, May–June, pp. 43–54.

Olcott, Martha Brill (1987) *The Kazakhs* (Stanford: Hoover).

Olcott, Martha Brill (1990) 'Pereystroyka in Kazakhstan', *Problems of Communism*, July–August, pp. 65–77.

Olivier, Bernard V. (1990) 'Korenizatsia', *Central Asian Survey*, Vol. 9, no. 3, pp. 77–98.

Olschki, L. (1962) *Marco Polo's Asia* (Berkeley: University of California Press).

Pan Ling (1984) *Old Shanghai, Gangsters in Paradise* (Hong Kong: Heinemann).

Panzac, Daniel (1985) *La Peste dans L'Empire Ottoman 1700–1850* (Louvain: Peeters).

Penrose, Roger (1990) *The Emperor's New Mind: Concerning Computers, Minds and the Law of Physics* (London: Vintage).

Pepys, Samuel (1920) *The Diary of Samuel Pepys* (ed.) Henry P. Wheatley (London: Bell).

Pipes, Daniel (1981) *Slave Soldiers in Islam. The Genesis of a Military System* (New Haven: Yale University Press).

Polo, Marco (1958) *The Travels of Marco Polo*, (trans.) R. E. Latham, (Harmondsworth: Penguin).

Popovic, A. and G. Veinstein (eds.) (1986) *Les Ordres Mystiques dans L'Islam* (Paris: École des Hautes Etudes en Sciences Sociales).

Prebble, John (1989) *The King's Jaunt. George IV in Scotland in 1822* (London: Fontana-Collins).

Pritsak, Omeljan (1981) 'The Khazar Kingdom's Conversion to Judaism', *Studies in Medieval Eurasian History* (London: Variorum).

Rachelwiltz, I. de (1971) *Papal Envoys to the Great Khans* (London: Faber and Faber).

Reid, Anthony (1988) *Southeast Asia in the Age of Commerce 1450–1690*, Vol. 1, *The Lands below the Wind* (New Haven: Yale University Press).

Renfrew, Colin (1982) *Towards an Archaeology of Mind* (Cambridge: Cambridge University Press).

Renfrew, Colin (1987) *Archaeology and Language. The Puzzle of Indo-European Origins* (London: Cape).

Richard, Jean (1977) *La Papauté et Les Missions d' Orient au Moyen Age (XVIIIe – XVe siècles)* (Rome: École Française de Rome).

Rivière, Claude (1988) *Les Liturgies Politiques* (Paris: P.U.F.).

Rizvi, S. A. A. (1968) *Rawshaniyya Movement* (Leiden: Abu Nahrein).

Rorlich, Azada-Ayse (1986) *The Volga Tatars. A Profile in National Resilience* (Stanford, California: Hoover).

Rossabi, Morris (ed.) (1983) *China Among Equals. The Middle Kingdom and its Neighbours, 10th – 14th Centuries* (Berkeley: University of California Press).

Rossabi, Morris (ed.) (1988) *Khubilai Khan. His Life and Times* (Berkeley: University of California Press).

Rotours, R. de and Lin Lu-tche (1981) *Le Règne de l' Empereur Hiuan-Tsong (713–756)* (Paris: Institut des Hautes Études Chinoises).

Rowe, William T. (1984) *Hankow, Commerce and Society in a Chinese City, 1796–1889* (Stanford: Stanford University Press).

Roy, Olivier (1984) 'The Origins of the Islamist Movement in Afghanistan', *Central Asian Review*, Vol. 3, no. 2, 1984, pp. 117–27.

Roy, Olivier (1986) *Islam and Resistance in Afghanistan* (Cambridge: Cambridge University Press).

Ruffié J. and J. C. Sournia (1984) *Les Epidémies dans l'Histoire de l'Homme* (Paris: Flammarion).

Rumer, Boris Z. (1989) *Soviet Central Asia: 'A Tragic Experiment'* (Boston: Unwin Hyman).

Sacki, P. Y. (1951) *The Nestorian Documents and Relics in China* (Tokyo).

Saguchi Toro (1965) *The Eastern Trade of the Khoqand Khanate* (Tokyo: Toyo Bunko).

Salaman, Redcliffe N. (1980) *The History and Social Influence of the Potato* (New York: Cambridge University Press).

Sanjdorj, M. (1980) *Manchu Chinese Colonial Rule in Northern Mongolia* (New York: St. Martin's Press).

Schafer, Edward H. (1963) *The Golden Peaches of Samarkand* (Berkeley: University of California Press).

Schamioglu, Uli (1986) *Tribal Politics and Social Organization in the Golden Horde*, Columbia University, Ph.D. Thesis.

Schurman, Herbert Franz (1956) *Economic Structure of the Yüan Dynasty* (Cambridge, Mass.: Harvard University Press).

Shaw, Stanford J. (1971) *Between Old and New, The Ottoman Empire under Sultan Selim III 1789–1807* (Cambridge, Mass.: Harvard University Press).

Shaw, Stanford J. (1976) *History of the Ottoman Empire and Modern Turkey*, Vol.

I, *Empire of the Gazis: The Rise and Decline of the Ottoman Empire, 1280–1808* (Cambridge: Cambridge University Press).

Sheldrake, Rupert (1983) *A New Science of Life* (London: Paladin).

Sikorski, Radek (1989) *Dust of the Saints* (London: Chatto and Windus).

Simon, J. L. (1981) *The Ultimate Resource* (Princeton: Princeton University Press).

Simon, Renée (1970) *Le P. Antoine Gaubil, Correspondence de Pékin* (Geneva: Droz).

Sinor, Denis (1969) *Inner Asia. A Syllabus* (Bloomington, Indiana: Indiana University Press).

Sinor, Denis (ed.) (1990) *The Cambridge History of Early Inner Asia* (Cambridge: Cambridge University Press).

Smith, John Masson (1970) 'Mongol and Nomadic Taxation', *Harvard Journal of Asiatic Studies*, Vol. 30, pp. 46–85.

Smith, John Masson (1984) 'Ayn Jalut: Mamluk Success or Mongol Failure', *Harvard Journal of Asiatic Studies*, Vol. 44, pp. 307–45.

Special Report of the Ottoman Public Debt, Year 24, 1905–1906.

Special Report of the Ottoman Public Debt, Year 26, 1907–1908.

Stone, Norman (1983) *Europe Transformed 1878–1919* (London: Fontana).

Sunar, Ilkoy (1980) 'Anthropologie Politique et Économique: L'Empire Ottoman et sa Transformation', *Annales, Économies, Sociétés, Civilisations*, 35:3–4, May–August, pp. 551–79.

Tachau, Katherine H. (1988) *Vision and Certitude in the Age of Occam: Optics, Epistemology and the Foundations of Semantics 1250–1340* (Leiden: E. J. Brill).

Ta Ch'ing Shih-lu, Taipei, 1965.

Tahir, Mahmud (1989) 'Abunasir Kursavi, 1776–1812', *Central Asian Survey*, Vol. 8, no. 2, pp. 155–8.

Tao Jing-shen (1976) *The Jurchen in Twelfth Century China, A Study in Sinicization* (Seattle: University of Washington).

Telfer, J. Buchan (ed.) (1970) *The Bondage and Travels of Johann Schiltberger*, Hakluyt Society, First Series 58 (New York: Burl-Franklin).

Tichane, Brendan (1983) *Ching-te-chen* (New York: New York State Institute for Glaze Research).

Todd, O. J. (1971) *Two Decades in China* (Taipei: Ch'eng Wen).

Tsukamoto, Zenryu (1985) *A History of Early Chinese Buddhism from its introduction to the death of Hui-yuan* (Tokyo: Kodansha).

Twigg, Graham (1984) *The Black Death. A Biological Appraisal* (London: Batsford).

Ure, John (1980) *The Trail of Tamerlane* (London: Constable).

Vambéry, Arminius (1868) *Sketches of Central Asia* (London: Allen).

Wallerstein, Immanuel (1974) *The Modern World-System: Capitalist Agriculture and the Origins of the European World-Economy in the Sixteenth Century* (New York: Academic Press).

Warren, Kenneth (1980) *Chemical Foundations: The Alkali Industry in Britain to 1926* (Oxford: Clarendon Press).

Wayman, Alex (1978) *Calming the Mind and Discerning the Real, Buddhist Meditation and the Middle View* (New York: Columbia University Press).

Wells, Calvin (1964) *Bodies, Bones and Disease* (London: Thames and Hudson).

Wessels, Cornelius (1924) *Early Jesuit Travellers in Central Asia 1603–1721* (The Hague: Nijhoff).

Whiting, Allen S. and General Sheng Shih-ts'ai (1958) *Sinkiang: Pawn or Pivot* (East Lansing, Michigan: Michigan State University Press).

Wittfogel, Karl A. and Feng Chia-sheng (1949) *History of Chinese Society: Liao (907–1125)* (Philadelphia: American Philosophical Society).

Wittfogel, Karl A. (1957) *Oriental Despotism: A Comparative Study of Total Power* (New Haven: Yale University Press).

Wittfogel, Karl A. (1978) *China und die Osteurasische Kavallerie Revolution* (Wiesbaden: Horrosowitz).

Wu Lien-teh (1959) *Plague Fighter. The Autobiography of a Modern Chinese Physician* (Cambridge: Heffers).

Yang, Lien-sheng (1952) *Money and Credit in China. A Short History* (Cambridge, Mass.: Harvard University Press).

Young, Arthur N. (1971) *China's Nation-Building Effort 1927–1932. The Financial and Economic Record* (Stanford: Hoover).

Yuan Qing-li (1990) 'Population Changes in the Xinjiang Uighur Autonomous Region (1949–1984)', *Central Asian Survey*, Vol. 9, no. 1, pp. 49–73.

Yule, Sir Henry (1915) *Cathay and the Way Thither*, 4 Vols., Second Series, no. XXXVIII (London: Hakluyt Society).

Zaehner, R. C. (1955) *Zurvan. A Zoroastrian Dilemma* (Oxford: Clarendon Press).

Zurcher, E. (1959) *The Buddhist Conquest of China*, 2 Vols. (Leiden: Brill).

Index